INNOVATE HIGHER EDUCATION TO ENHANCE GRADUATE EMPLOYABILITY

The worldwide marketization of higher education has resulted in a growing pressure on universities' accountability, particularly in terms of more tangible learning outcomes directly related to paying higher tuition fees. Covering globally diverse perspectives, *Innovate Higher Education to Enhance Graduate Employability* uses a range of international case studies to help practitioners and researchers review, reflect on and refresh their ability to bridge the gap between university and industry.

A timely response to the need to improve the quality of higher education in order to build work readiness in students, this book:

- Adds a critical, global dimension to this topical area in higher education as well as society's concerns
- Provides a number of practice-based case studies on how universities can transform their programmes to enhance graduate employability
- Acts as a source of practical suggestions for how to improve students' sufficient employability including their skills, knowledge and attitudes
- Provides insights from theory, practices and policy perspectives.

A crucial read for anyone looking to engage with the global issue of graduate employability, *Innovate Higher Education to Enhance Graduate Employability* covers both theoretical frameworks and practical models through an exploration of how universities around the world are using innovative techniques to enhance employability.

Hong T. M. Bui is an associate professor in Higher Education Management at the School of Management, University of Bath, UK.

Hoa T. M. Nguyen is a senior lecturer in the School of Education, UNSW, Australia.

Doug Cole is deputy director of Employability at Nottingham Trent University, UK.

INNOVATE HIGHER EDUCATION TO ENHANCE GRADUATE EMPLOYABILITY

Rethinking the Possibilities

Edited by Hong T. M. Bui, Hoa T. M. Nguyen and Doug Cole

Routledge
Taylor & Francis Group

LONDON AND NEW YORK

First published 2019
by Routledge
2 Park Square, Milton Park, Abingdon, Oxon, OX14 4RN

and by Routledge
52 Vanderbilt Avenue, New York, NY 10017

Routledge is an imprint of the Taylor & Francis Group, an informa business

British Library Cataloguing-in-Publication Data
A catalogue record for this book is available from the British Library

Library of Congress Cataloging-in-Publication Data
Names: Bui, Hong T. M., editor. | Nguyen, Hoa T. M., editor. |
    Cole, Doug, 1971– editor.
Title: Innovate higher education to enhance graduate employability :
    rethinking the possibilities / edited by Hong T.M. Bui, Hoa T.M.
    Nguyen and Doug Cole.
Description: Abingdon, Oxon ; New York, NY : Routledge, 2019. |
    Includes bibliographical references.
Identifiers: LCCN 2018060193| ISBN 9780367179847 (hbk) |
    ISBN 9780367179861 (pbk) | ISBN 9780429058899 (ebk)
Subjects: LCSH: Education, Higher—Aims and objectives. | College
    graduates—Employment. | Employability.
Classification: LCC LB2322.2 .I55 2019 | DDC 378/.01—dc23
LC record available at https://lccn.loc.gov/2018060193

ISBN: 978-0-367-17984-7 (hbk)
ISBN: 978-0-367-17986-1 (pbk)
ISBN: 978-0-429-05889-9 (ebk)

Typeset in Bembo
by Swales & Willis Ltd, Exeter, Devon, UK

Printed and bound by CPI Group (UK) Ltd, Croydon, CR0 4YY

CONTENTS

CONTRIBUTORS

Dennis Alonzo is a test and scale developer, program evaluator, curriculum designer, and applied statistician at UNSW, Australia. His area of interest revolves around assessment for learning, particularly in supporting teachers to make highly contextualized, consistent, fair and trustworthy assessment decisions to effectively support student learning. He has been involved in national and international research in a broad range of topics including student IT experiences, blended and online learning, standards-based assessment and learning analytics to help inform curriculum design, professional development and policy. He has received various scholarships from the Philippines and Australian governments and a public diplomacy scholarship from the Ministry of Foreign Affairs of Korea. He was the Dean of Education at the University of Southeastern Philippines before joining UNSW.

Daniela Petrova Bariakova is a PhD candidate at Southampton Business School, UK. Her research focuses on how organizational learning and its tools – systems thinking and design thinking – can be used for social innovation in the higher education context. Her current research centres on organizational learning, social innovation and higher education. Daniela has an MSc in Management from Bournemouth University, UK, and has undertaken a nine-month internship in the Social and Labor Committee in the Bulgarian government. Daniela worked with Dr. Hong Bui on her master's thesis, which was titled "Systems Thinking: How It Is influenced By the Big Five Personality Traits and Organizational culture" and which was a whole theory based on strong quantitative methods.

Maksim Belitski is an Associate Professor in Entrepreneurship and Innovation at Henley Business School and a Research Fellow at the Institute for Development Strategies, Indiana University, US. Before joining Henley, he worked in the University of Bolzano, Italy, the University of Bratislava, Slovakia, Vilnius

University, Lithuania, Loughborough University, UK and Brunel University West London, UK. He holds a PhD in Social Sciences from the University of Leicester and University of Milan. He teaches Innovation and Market Entry, Financing for Entrepreneurship, the MBA in Entrepreneurship and couching start-ups and SMEs in the Thames Valley region. He is Editor, *Small Business Economics Journal*, Editor, *Journal of Management Development* and Associate Editor, *Electronic Commerce Research and Applications Journal*. Maksim has worked with local UK businesses across sectors, with an emphasis on IT, finance, creative sectors and local borough councils to enhance university-private-public collaborations.

Chevonne Brady, MBChB (Hons), BMSc (Hons), MRCS, is a Core Surgical Trainee currently in training with University College London and Imperial College, UK, working towards a career in plastic surgery. Prior to this, she was a surgical trainee at the Cleveland Clinic in Ohio, US, one of the world's leading healthcare organizations. As well as being a surgical trainee, she is currently pursuing a Master of Medical Education with the University of Dundee, UK. Her main research interests include medical education and the integration of non-traditional skills into the undergraduate curriculum, as well as plastic and reconstructive surgery with a focus on burns patients and their management.

Hong T. M. Bui is an Associate Professor in Higher Education Management at the School of Management, University of Bath, UK. She earned her PhD at the Norwich Business School, University of East Anglia, UK, in 2010. Her research covers a wide range of areas of organizational behaviour and human resource development, including learning organization, innovation and leadership. Her research has been mainly conducted in the context of public sector and higher education, though some are in private sectors. She has published more than 60 articles in leading, high-impact international journals, books and international conferences including *Public Administration Review, Management Learning, Group and Organization Management, Journal of Business Ethics, International Journal of Human Resource Management,* and so on. She can be reached at H.T.Bui@bath.ac.uk.

Jane Chang is a Principal Research Fellow at Buckingham University. Prior to that, she was a Senior Lecturer at Westminster Business School. Jane has developed entrepreneurial training programmes in Malaysia and the UK in the area of new venture creation and corporate entrepreneurship. She has initiated six entrepreneurial ventures in the area of education and the integrated food industry. A scholar in cognitive entrepreneurship and a specialist in entrepreneurship education, Jane has published widely in reputable international journals, presented at various conferences and served as a reviewer for a number of scholarly journals and conferences.

Doug Cole is a Senior Fellow of the Higher Education Academy and an Honorary Fellow of the Institute for Enterprise and Entrepreneurs, UK, with over 14 years' experience in the sports industry and 11 years in higher education. Doug is currently

Deputy Director of Employability at Nottingham Trent University, the largest team of its kind in the UK. Prior to this, Doug spent three years with the Higher Education Academy focused on the areas of learning and teaching, employability and student success. In 2012, Doug developed the concept of a national framework for embedding employability to support institutions in developing graduates with the qualities and characteristics that are vital for success, not only in securing employment, but more broadly in life, too. In 2013, Doug co-authored the Higher Education Academy publication, *Defining & Developing Your Approach to Employability: A Framework for Higher Education Institutions,* with Maureen Tibby.

Jose Arturo Garza-Reyes is a Professor of Operations Management and Head of the Centre for Supply Chain Improvement at the College of Business, Law and Social Sciences, University of Derby, UK. He is actively involved in industrial projects where he combines his knowledge, expertise and industrial experience in operations management to help organizations achieve excellence in their internal functions and supply chains. He has also led and managed international research projects funded by the British Academy, British Council and Mexico's National Council of Science and Technology (CONACYT). As a leading academic, he has published over 100 articles in leading scientific journals and international conferences, and four books in the areas of operations management and innovation, manufacturing performance measurement and quality management systems. Areas of expertise and interest include general aspects of operations and manufacturing management, business excellence, quality improvement and performance measurement. He is a Chartered Engineer (CEng), a certified Six Sigma Green Belt and has over eight years of industrial experience working as Production Manager, Production Engineer and Operations Manager for several international and local companies in both the UK and Mexico. He is also a fellow member of the Higher Education Academy (FHEA) and a member of the Institution of Engineering Technology (MIET).

Jill Jameson is Professor of Education and Director, Centre for Leadership and Enterprise, Faculty of Education and Health, University of Greenwich, UK. Jill is also a Visiting Fellow and Associate of Lucy Cavendish College, Cambridge, and an Associate Member of the Cambridge Educational Dialogues Research Group in the Faculty of Education, University of Cambridge, UK. She was Chair of the Society for Research into Higher Education (2012–17), and Convenor for the Post-Compulsory and Lifelong Learning SIG, British Educational Research Association (BERA). She has published widely in education and is Editor of a forthcoming book on *Global Leadership in Higher Education: Critical Thinking* (Routledge) as part of the OxCHEPS Series on *International Studies on Higher Education* at New College, University of Oxford.

Vikas Kumar is a Professor in Operations and Supply Chain Management at Bristol Business School, University of the West of England, UK. He holds a PhD degree in Management Studies from Exeter Business School, UK, and has a Bachelor of Technology (first class distinction) degree in Metallurgy and Material Science Engineering from NIFFT, India. He has published more than 160 articles in leading, high-impact international journals and international conferences including the *International Journal of Production Research, International Journal of Production Economics, Expert System with Applications, Computers & Industrial Engineering, and Production Planning & Control.* He serves on the editorial board of six international journals including the *International Journal of Services, Economics and Management, International Journal of Manufacturing Systems and the International Journal of Lean Enterprise Research.* Dr. Vikas Kumar also serves on the scientific committees of several international conferences, and he has held visiting positions at a number of universities across the globe including Telecom Ecole de Paris, France, National Chiao Tung University, Taiwan, Khon Kaen University, Thailand and the Indian Institute of Management, Ranchi, India. His current research interests include sustainable supply chain management, short food supply chains, process modelling, lean and agile systems and service operations management.

Roger McDermott is a Senior Lecturer and University Teaching Fellow in the School of Computing Science and Digital Media of the Robert Gordon University, UK. His main areas of teaching are in mathematics, basic programming capabilities, the development of problem-solving skills and data security. He is also a pedagogical researcher with interests in topics such as the psychology of learning, the development of professional competencies and competence models and the nature of academic quality in higher education.

Hoa T. M. Nguyen is a Senior Lecturer in Teacher Professional Learning in the School of Education, UNSW, Australia. She specializes in teacher development and mentoring. She has experience teaching and training pre-service and in-service teachers in Asia and Australia. Her research was highly recognized by several awards, most recently a Research Recognition Award for Early Career Researcher by the Australian Teacher Education Association. She currently holds an honorary position at the University of Sydney. Hoa has published one sole-authored book, one edited book, 14 book chapters and 23 articles. She has been publishing in well-regarded peer-reviewed journals, including Q1 and Q2 and international prestigious publishers. Her recent book *Models of Mentoring in Language Teacher Education* (Springer) has recently been nominated for the 2018 Dean Award for Best Monograph.

Justin O'Brien teaches marketing, strategy, management and entrepreneurship in the School of Business and Management at Royal Holloway University of London, UK. His scholarship interests centre on experiential learning and in particular case study writing and teaching, borne of an extensive commercial career in the aviation industry. His British Airway Executive Global MBA is from Lancaster University, UK.

Ly Thi Pham is as an independent researcher in higher education studies, who has experiences in both public and private sectors in tertiary education. In 2008, she was a Fulbright scholar at the Pratt Institute, New York, US, and has spoken at several national and international conferences. Dr. Ly's fields of expertise are educational policies, university governance and international education. She serves as Editor for three monthly newsletters in international education in Vietnam, as well as a reviewer for *Studies in Higher Education* (Australia). She was the Dean, Research Program at International Education Institute, Vietnam National University, Ho Chi Minh City and Director of the Center for Higher Education Evaluation and Research, Nguyen Tat Thanh University. Ly Pham is the founder of Ly Pham Consulting, LLC. She is currently appointed by the Prime Minister as a Member of Vietnam National Committee for Education and Human Resource Development (2016–2020). Most of her writing can be accessed at her own website: www.lypham.net.

Thanh Pham has been working in higher education for more than ten years. Her main research areas are intercultural education, globalization and internationalization. She has been conducting substantial research on internationalization of the curriculum and higher education in Vietnam and other Asian countries in response to globalization. Pham's contributions to the research field of international education have been recognized through various awards. Pham has presented her research at conferences in Australia, Vietnam, Singapore and Germany. Pham has produced 70 publications (published or in press) in a wide range of outlets including books, edited research books, book chapters, refereed articles, magazines and conference papers. Pham's current research focuses on employability of international students. She is conducting research on the studying and working experiences of Australian and Japanese returnees, the demands of the labour markets and requirements of employers in Asia and Australia.

Val Quimno is an information systems researcher, engineer and consultant particularly focused on technologies implemented in developing countries. His research interests include understanding the local contextual factors affecting the adoption of information systems in low-resourced settings. He has been involved in several ICT development projects that have significant impact in communities using contemporary information technologies. He has received various scholarships including the Australian Development Scholarship, Temasek Foundation Scholarship and Australia Awards. He has been nominated to the Australian Alumni Excellence Award in 2017 under the Innovation Excellence category for his work related to education technology. He is currently an Associate Professor at the University of Southeastern Philippines and is involved in a number of technology-based research projects.

Mark Rahimi is a quantitative social sciences researcher and Postdoctoral Fellow in the Faculty of Arts and Education, Deakin University, Australia. He has extensive experience in quantitative and mixed methods research in education. His research interest is devoted to inbound and outbound mobility of graduates and graduate employability in an international context. He can be contacted at m.rahimi@deakin.edu.au

Christine Rivers is Co-Director of the Centre for Management Learning (CML) at Surrey Business School, UK, and Programme Director for the first credit-bearing Post Graduate Certificate in Management Education. Before taking on the role as Co-Director CML, Christine held a number of leadership roles in the school: Director for Undergraduate Studies, Post Graduate Studies and MBA Programmes. Outside Surrey, Christine collaborates with various institutions and designs curriculum and teaching development programmes specifically for management education. Recent projects include collaboration with the University of Cambridge, University of East Anglia, Chartered Association of Business Schools, Majan College, Oman and MCI Innsbruck, Austria, to name a few. In addition, Christine is SIG Chair for Knowledge and Learning, British Academy of Management and Senior Fellow of the Higher Education Academy, and reviewer for the *Journal Academy of Management, Learning and Education*. Her research interests include curriculum design for blended learning journeys, teacher training and coaching in management education. Christine's full profile can be found at www.surrey.ac.uk/sbs/people/christine_rivers/ and can be followed via Twitter @CBRivers.

Ainurul Rosli is a Reader in Enterprise and Entrepreneurship at Brunel University London, UK. She worked for several years with the R&D arm of a telecommunication company in Malaysia as well as a consultant for London-based firms. She has co-founded several entrepreneurial ventures and has been involved in designing and running entrepreneurial programmes in higher education and public sectors. Her research interests focus on interfirm collaboration, knowledge co-creation, entrepreneurial community and impactful entrepreneurial action which drives forward business and societal transformation.

Eisuke Saito currently works as a Lecturer for the Faculty of Education, Monash University (Australia). Before joining Monash University, Eisuke served for the National Institute of Education, Singapore and was a consultant for international educational development in developing Asian countries. Eisuke researches in school reform, teacher professional development, education policy and pedagogical reform.

Glen Stafford is Director, Internationalisation Strategy at the University of Adelaide, Australia, and was previously Executive Officer of the university's Confucius Institute. He completed his BA (Asian Studies) (Hons) and PhD in Asian Studies at the University of Adelaide. His research interests include internationalization of higher education and international student mobility.

Ly Thi Tran is an Associate Professor in the School of Education, Deakin University, Australia and an Australian Research Council Future Fellow. Her work focuses on internationalization of education, international student mobility and the New Colombo Plan. Ly has produced over 150 publications including seven books and edited books with Routledge, Springer and Palgrave. Ly's book, *Teaching International Students in Vocational Education: New Pedagogical Approaches*, won the International Education Association of Australia (IEAA) Excellence Award for Best Practice/Innovation in International Education.

Thi Tuyet Tran (DEd) is a mobile researcher. She has worked in three countries, Australia, Vietnam and Germany, and has developed an interest in interdisciplinary research. Her interests range from labour economics and human resource management to various areas in education research such as graduate employability, work-integrated learning, university-industry collaboration, language education and cultural study. She is currently based at RMIT University, Australia and is working towards a project investigating workplace integration of professional skilled migrants in the Australian labour market.

Arvind Upadhyay is a Principal Lecturer in Logistics and Supply Chain Management at Brighton Business School, University of Brighton, UK. He holds a PhD in Logistics and Supply Chain Management from the University of Bergamo, Italy in collaboration with SDA Bocconi Italy and MIT-Zaragoza Logistics Centre, Spain. As a doctoral researcher, he spent one year at the Cambridge Judge Business School and King's College, University of Cambridge and at the Cranfield School of Management, UK. He is a Senior Fellow of the Higher Education Academy (HEA), UK. His MSC degree in Strategic Project Management European was on a European Commission's Erasmus Mundus Scholarship from Heriot-Watt University, Edinburgh, UK in collaboration with the MIP Business School of Politecnico di Milano, Italy and Umea University, Sweden. He also holds a first degree in Electrical Engineering and a Master of Business Administration (MBA). He has published his research work in books, book chapters, case studies and academic journals and is a regular presenter at conferences throughout the world. He is on the editorial and review committee board of various journals and is also a member of the Chartered Institute of Procurement and Supply (CIPS), British Academy of Management (BAM), Production and Operations Management Society (POMS) and the European Operations Management Association (EurOMA).

Thao Thi Phuong Vu is an award-winning Educational Designer at Monash University, Australia and a PhD candidate at the Melbourne Centre for the Study of Higher Education, Melbourne Graduate School of Education, University of Melbourne. Her research interests include learning and teaching in higher education and internationalization of education, with recent co-authored publications on international student mobility and the New Colombo Plan.

Mark Zarb (FHEA, MBCS) is a course leader and foundation year coordinator within the School of Computing Science and Digital Media at the Robert Gordon

University in Aberdeen, UK. His main research area is typically computing education, looking at ways to improve the student experience throughout their time in higher education from application to graduation. He teaches on a variety of modules within the School, focusing on programming, physical computing, software engineering and entrepreneurship. He can be contacted at m.zarb@rgu.ac.uk.

1

HIGHER EDUCATION, INNOVATION, AND EMPLOYABILITY

Hong T. M. Bui and Hoa T. M. Nguyen

Higher education

Higher education in the world has experienced tremendous growth with increasingly marketized and privatized services in order to meet society's pressing demand for education (Mok, 2016). Governments in many countries have considered education an effective strategy to enhance international partnerships, public diplomacy, and economic growth. The 'education as trade' perspective comes with increased competition and pressures higher education institutions (HEIs) to transform and innovate to achieve excellence so they can attract and retain high-quality students (Hewitt-Dundas & Roper, 2018) and produce quality graduates to meet the growing demands of the work force (Boden & Nedeva, 2010; Mason et al., 2009; Yorke, 2006).

Higher education, with its significant expansion and complexity, also faces the challenge to keep up with societal changes such as internationalization and information technology progress. Lašáková et al. (2017), in their case study of ten European universities, concluded that the barriers to innovation in higher education are also barriers to social development, including "lack of transparency, corruption, nepotism, economic instability, rigid control, distrust and lack of collaboration" (p. 70). At the institutional level, the challenges are various – the impractical curriculum, the outdated curriculum, lack of investment in technology, poorly qualified staff, the lack of connection between current teaching and learning practices and the demands of the labour market, employers' expectations, and students' needs to name a few (Jackson, 2013; Lašáková et al., 2017).

The slowness in adopting emerging technology also hinders universities' ability to compete in the current challenging market. High-quality teaching, research, and modern technology are crucial for universities to become globally recognized to attract both domestic and international students. A lack of funding and resources is a barrier to technological progress and updated facilities of higher education and creates staff inefficiencies and a lack of social opportunities for students (Drape et al., 2016). In other words, resources are not keeping pace with the rapid and large enrolment of fee-paying students in HEIs.

With the substantial increase in costs associated with universities, students and society expect more and more of their results, being the enhanced probability of vocational success (Vedder, 2017) or, in other words, students' employability. Generally, employers and policy-makers expect higher education to increase students' marketable skills and/or employable skills (e.g. Asonitou, 2015; Boden & Nedeva, 2010). Graduate employability, in fact, has become one of the most important factors in university rankings worldwide and a key means to attract students. Nevertheless, student employability is being hindered by impractical curricula, among other things, creating a graduate skills gap (Chan & Lin, 2016; Tran, 2018).

However, it is unfair to blame the gaps in skill formation of graduates on HEIs alone. A body of research shows the lack of linkage between institutions and industry. HEIs generally are at the crossroads of traditional liberal arts education and industry preparation. The tension between business and academia remains strong due to conflicting interests, resulting in a dissatisfaction on both sides of the partnership (Derouet & Villani, 2015).

The massification of higher education, furthermore, has resulted in unemployment, insecure work, and the slow growth of salary level of graduates (Mok & Jiang, 2018). Recent studies have consistently shown that the competitiveness of the job market due to a large number of graduates has caused a lot of difficulty for graduates to find jobs that match their knowledge and skill sets (Mok, 2016). This has resulted in over-qualification, where new graduates have to take low salary positions that do not require high skill levels, which is demotivating. Some researchers argue that the enrolments in HEIs now are higher than the number of good, high-paying jobs, known as 'over-investment' in higher education (Vedder, 2017). This has the potential to alienate both students and the public. The increasing demands from the neoliberal government, employers, and students themselves have positioned graduate employability as an evolving driver of change in higher education worldwide (Cox & King, 2006; Sin & Neave, 2016). This echoes the need for an innovative transformation of higher education. The term innovation has been widely discussed in education as a new trend in implementing radical changes to address a number of concerns.

Innovation in higher education

Innovation is also crucial for HEIs to empower their roles and innovation capabilities (Hamid et al., 2015). "The role of the university goes far beyond the 'engine of innovation' perspective. Universities contribute much more than simply pumping out commercial technology or generating startup companies" (Florida et al., 2006, p. 35). Tierney and Lanford (2016) highlighted four challenges confronting higher education when thinking about innovation. These are the emergence of the knowledge-intensive economy, the need to train a creative and innovative workforce, global trends in higher education (massification vs. world-class aspirations), and decreased funding and resources for higher education. Christensen and Eyring (2011, p. xxii) argued that universities are at "great risk of competitive disruption and potentially poised for an innovation-fuelled renaissance".

Lueddeke (1999) developed a framework called the adaptive-generative development model that guides change and innovation in higher education. The model comprises six interrelated elements, including needs analysis, research and development, strategy formation and development, resource support, implementation and dissemination, and evaluation. The model has been applied in teaching, learning, and curriculum innovation (e.g. Furco & Moely, 2012; Harvey & Kamvounias, 2008; Larkin & Richardson, 2013). There are three functions in higher education innovation systems, namely, education, research, and engagement (Brennan et al., 2014). However, within the scope of this book, we focus on innovation in the function of education in its relationship with graduate employability. We may possibly explore innovation in research and engagement in future books.

Regarding innovation in higher education, scholars have mainly discussed pedagogical innovation and technology-enhanced innovation. For example, Chhokar (2010) presented a case in India which sought to innovate its curriculum for sustainable development by embedding philosophy, policy, and practice in higher education. Christensen and Eyring (2011) showed that universities have reengineered themselves by embracing online learning technology. Online learning is seen to be a classic example of a disruptive technology (Christensen & Eyring, 2011), introducing a unique and exciting era in higher education in which the use of multimedia and interactive simulations or games in online learning are increasing (Kim & Bonk, 2006). Salmon (2005) developed a strategic framework that blends e-learning and pedagogical innovation. This innovation can personalize individual learning needs. Salmon (2005, p. 215) concluded that "focusing on e-learning is a key way of providing for multidisciplinary and interdisciplinary research agendas in the applications of core and peripheral learning technologies and the associated innovative pedagogy". Fidalgo-Blanco et al. (2014) developed a conceptual framework which combines epistemological and ontological knowledge spirals to transform individuals' educational innovation experiences into organizational knowledge. Lytras et al. (2018) stated that innovative use of ICT tools in higher education can engage students in the learning process, empower them, and enhance their employability. In contrast, Martín et al. (2015) looked at innovation in higher education from a behavioural perspective. Their study showed that previous innovation behaviours as freshmen, current levels of autonomy, and cognitive demands are key factors that determine students' innovation in higher education.

Graduate employability

Graduate employability has attracted substantial attention from wider society because of higher fees and stronger competition in the higher education sector

(Tomlinson, 2007). Employability is a complex, and somewhat vague, concept that is difficult to articulate and define (Andrews & Higson, 2008; Clark, 2017). What constitutes graduate employability is controversial and varies. However, most definitions encompass a certain set of work-ready skills for employment. For example, Yorke and Knight (2006) defined employability as a set of achievements including skills, knowledge, and personal attributes that make people more employable and successful in their career, and benefit the workforce and wider society. These concepts of employability have been developed based on the assumption that there is a big gap between what has been taught at university and what is required for the work force.

As a result, universities and scholars have worked hard to enhance graduate employability. Andrews and Higson (2008) argued that to be employable, graduates need both 'soft' skills, such as communication skills and team working skills, and 'hard' business knowledge, such as qualifications and the ability to apply theoretical and conceptual knowledge to real-life business situations. Alongside soft skills and hard business knowledge, Bridgstock (2009) suggested that graduate employability could be enhanced through developing career development skills. Holmes (2001) highlighted the role of social practices and graduate identity, which are significant for understanding human behaviour in certain social arenas (e.g. certain workplace environments). This leads to suggestions for curriculum improvement intended to help students gain entry into and be successful in graduate employment. Pool and Sewell (2007) developed a practical model of graduate employability called CareerEDGE, in which career development, work and life experience, degree (subject knowledge, understanding, and skills), generic skills, and emotional intelligence are key to employability. However, the issue of employability moves beyond the enhancement of these skills in higher education to the supply and demand of the labour market. Such argument is well embedded in Clarke's (2017) definition of graduate employability, which encompasses four main interrelated components: human capital, social capital, individual behaviours, and individual attributes. This opens a new agenda in reforms in higher education which focus on the interplay among different factors and equip graduates with more employment opportunities.

The link between higher education innovation and graduate employability

This book is the first attempt to show the link between innovation in higher education and graduate employability in particular. It is designed to serve students, researchers, and practitioners in higher education who are interested in innovation and student employability. It covers internationally diverse perspectives of innovations in higher education which ultimately enhance graduate employability. Each chapter has been developed from current research or/and research-based practice to showcase the best practices in higher education to enhance graduate employability in varied contexts. This book has been organized in order to present a wide range of innovation in higher education in diverse contexts. There are three main sections in this book highlighted in the following overview.

The largest section is about *conceptualization* related to employability. In *Chapter 2*, Hong T. M. Bui from the University of Bath (UK) proposes building multidisciplinary programmes that engage industry to enhance graduate employability. She argues that most of the collaboration between universities and industry is based on single disciplines, which provide students a narrow view of the world. This needs to be changed by developing multidisciplinary programmes at universities.

Chapter 3 provides a review of theoretical foundations of entrepreneurship education and recommends a toolbox for knowledge commercialization and engagement with entrepreneurial communities. Maksim Belitski from the University of Reading (UK) argue that if universities commit to entrepreneurial education, it will result in greater engagement with local entrepreneurial communities, co-curriculum educational development, new venture creation, and academic spin-offs.

In *Chapter 4*, Jill Jameson from the University of Greenwich (UK) suggests that it is critical for universities to develop trust and leadership skills for students to avoid future economic and value crises. These skills can enhance their employability for the ethical business world.

In *Chapter 5*, Daniela Bariakova from the University of Southampton (UK) conducts a systematic review on social innovation in higher education systems within the European Economic Area (EEA). The findings show a deficit of empirical studies on social innovation in higher education. She argues that EEA's higher education needs to pay more attention to social innovation, which consequently will improve graduate employment.

Chapter 6 is a review study by Arvind Upadhyay (University of Brighton, UK), Vikas Kumar (University of West England, UK), and Jose Arturo Garza-Reyes (University of Derby, UK) on facilitating doctoral students' transition to the workplace through doctoral research positions and the role played by their PhD supervisors. They highlight the role of universities in assisting successful transition of doctoral students to the workplace.

In *Chapter 7*, Val Quimno (University of Southeastern Philippines) and Dennis Alonzo (UNSW, Australia) review and evaluate research trends, focuses, and regional priorities in leading innovation centres in HEIs in the context of developing countries. As a result, they develop a framework for establishing and leading innovation centres that ensure graduate employability by enhancing student leadership and entrepreneurial skills.

The second section of the book contains *practices and case studies* on what universities have done to enhance graduate employability. *Chapter 8* presents findings from a tested framework called Teaching Inside Out (TIO), which enables students to work in a volatile, uncertain, complex, and ambiguous environment (VUCA). Christine Rivers and Justin O'Brien from the University of Surrey (UK) provide guidance on how to implement TIO at module, programme, and curriculum level.

Chapter 9 by Ly Tran (Deakin University, Australia), Glen Stafford (University of Adelaide, Australia), Thao Thi Phuong Vu (Monash University, Australia), and

Mark Rahimi (Deakin University, Australia) shows evidence of enhanced student employability. This is the outcome of the Australian government's New Colombo Plan (NCP) in 2014. This programme engaged students in international experience in Asian countries and regions, such as China, Hong Kong, Malaysia, Indonesia, Japan, Thailand, and India. It has helped develop students' international outlook, experiential learning, networking, and cross-cultural understandings.

In *Chapter 10*, Thanh Pham and Eisuke Saito from Monash University (Australia) show evidence that the Australian government, accreditation bodies, universities, academics, and industries have pushed mutual collaborations to develop attributes that are believed to help graduates with employability. Their findings show that graduate attributes selected by universities and academics largely match the employability skills required by employers, but the quality is not as high as employers expect.

In line with the Scottish government's ambition to become a world-leading entrepreneurial and innovative nation, *Chapter 11* presents a case study of an entrepreneurship module taught to final-year undergraduate computing students. Mark Zarb (Robert Gordon University, UK), Chevonne Brady (University of Dundee, UK), and Roger McDermott (Robert Gordon University, UK) discuss the design and implementation of such a module and its impact on students' employability.

The third section of the book is about *policy implications* for employability. In *Chapter 12*, Jane Chang (Buckingham University, UK) and Ainurul Rosli (Brunel University, UK) explore entrepreneurship education and the employability agenda in Malaysia, with its missionary, top-down approach towards supporting entrepreneurship education. They propose a synergistic learning platform to practise entrepreneurship to help integrate university-level curriculum with national programmes to support the employability agenda.

Chapter 13 presents a case study of Vietnamese policies on the employability of university graduates by Ly Pham (Ly Pham Consulting, LLC). She discusses the impacts of these policies on admission, curriculum design, teaching methodologies, outcome assessment, and learning environment, all of which affect graduate employability in Vietnam.

Chapter 14 looks at a broader landscape of higher education worldwide to show the differences between developed and developing contexts. Thi Tuyet Tran (RMIT University, Australia) suggests that universities should not only help their students to develop their human capital, but also draw student awareness to the outside societal and labour market conditions and find the way to enhance their human capital, social capital, and cultural capital.

References

Andrews, A., & Higson, H. (2008). Graduate employability, 'soft skills' versus 'hard' business knowledge: A European study. *Higher Education in Europe, 33*(4), 411–422.

Asonitou, S. (2015). Employability skills in higher education and the case of Greece. *Procedia – Social and Behavioral Sciences, 175*(2015), 283–290.

Boden, R., & Nedeva, M. (2010). Employing discourse: Universities and graduate 'employability'. *Journal of Education Policy, 25*(1), 37–54.

Brennan, J., Broek, S., Durazzi, N., Kamphuis, B., Ranga, M., & Ryan, S. (2014). Study on innovation in higher education: Final report. *European Commission Directorate for Education and Training Study on Innovation in Higher Education*, Publications Office of the European Union, Luxembourg.

Bridgstock R. (2009). The graduate attributes we've overlooked: Enhancing graduate employability through career management skills. *Higher Education Research & Development, 28*(1), 31–44.

Chan, S. J., & Lin, J. W. (2016). Aiming for better employment: A holistic analysis from admission to labour market. *Journal of Higher Education Policy and Management, 38*(3), 282–296.

Chhokar, K. B. (2010). Higher education and curriculum innovation for sustainable development in India. *International Journal of Sustainability in Higher Education, 11*(2), 141–152.

Christensen, C. M., & Eyring, H. J. (2011). *The innovative university: Changing the DNA of higher education from the inside out.* San Francisco, CA: Jossey-Bass.

Clarke, M. (2008). Plodders, pragmatists, visionaries and opportunists: career patterns and employability. *Career Development International, 14*(1), 8–28.

Clarke, M. (2017). Rethinking graduate employability: The role of capital, individual attributes and context. *Studies in Higher Education, 43*(11), 1923–1937.

Cox, S., & King, D. (2006). Skill sets: An approach to embed employability in course design. *Education and Training, 48*(4), 262–274.

Derouet, J. L., & Villani, M. (2015). ESSEC Business School case study report. For EU Lifelong Learning Programme, project no. 539628-LLP-1-2013-1-NL-ERASMUS-EIGF. Governance and adaptation to innovative modes of higher education provision (GAIHE). Unpublished GAIHE project report.

Drape, T. A., Rudd, R., Lopez, M., & Radford, D. (2016). Challenges and solutions to higher education institutions in Africa. *International Journal of Education, 8*(1), 43–58.

Fidalgo-Blanco, Á., Sein-Echaluce, M. L., & García-Peñalvo, F. J. (2014). Knowledge spirals in higher education teaching innovation. *International Journal of Knowledge Management, 10*(4), 16–37.

Florida, R., Gates, G., Knudsen, B., & Stolarick, K. (2006). The university and the creative economy. Retrieved from http://creativeclass.com/rfcgdb/articles/University_andthe_Creative_Economy.pdf (accessed on 22/11/2018).

Furco, A., & Moely, B. E. (2012). Using learning communities to build faculty support for pedagogical innovation: A multi-campus study. *The Journal of Higher Education, 83*(1), 128–153.

Hamid, M. R. A., Abdullah, M., Mustafa, Z., Abidin, N. B. b. Z., & Ahmad, H. (2015). Conceptual framework of innovation excellence model for higher education institutions. *Procedia – Social and Behavioral Sciences, 174*(2015), 2846–2848.

Harvey, A., & Kamvounias, P. (2008). Bridging the implementation gap: A teacher-as-learner approach to teaching and learning policy. *Higher Education Research & Development, 27*(1), 31–41.

Hewitt-Dundas, N., & Roper, S. (2018). Innovation in UK higher education: A panel data analysis of undergraduate degree programmes. *Research Policy, 47*(1), 121–138.

Holmes, L. (2001). Reconsidering graduate employability: The 'graduate identity' approach. *Quality in Higher Education, 7*(2), 111–119.

Jackson, D. (2013). Business graduate employability – where are we going wrong? *Higher Education Research & Development, 32*(5), 776–790.

Kim, K.-J., & Bonk, C. J. (2006). The future of online teaching and learning in higher education. *Educause Quarterly, 4*, 22–30.

Larkin, H., & Richardson, B. (2013). Creating high challenge/high support academic environments through constructive alignment: Student outcomes. *Teaching in Higher Education, 18*(2), 192–204.

Lašáková, A., Bajzíková, L'., & Dedze, I. (2017). Barriers and drivers of innovation in higher education: Case study-based evidence across ten European universities. *International Journal of Educational Development, 55*(2017), 69–79.

Lueddeke, G. R. (1999). Toward a constructivist framework for guiding change and innovation in higher education. *The Journal of Higher Education, 70*(3), 235–260.

Lytras, M. D., Papadopoulou, P., Marouli, C., & Misseyanni, A. (2018). Higher education out-of-the-box: Technology-driven learning innovation in higher education. *Engaged Scholarship and Civic Responsibility in Higher Education*, doi:10.4018/978-1-5225-3649-9.ch004

Martín, P., Potočnik, K., & Fras, A. B. (2015). Determinants of students' innovation in higher education. *Studies in Higher Education, 42*(7), 1229–1243.

Mason, G., Williams, G., & Cranmer, S. (2009). Employability skills initiatives in higher education: What effects do they have on graduate labour market outcomes? *Education Economics, 17*(1), 1–30.

Mok, K. H. (2016). Massification of higher education, graduate employment and social mobility in the Greater China Region. *British Journal of Sociology of Education, 37*(1), 51–71.

Mok, K. H., & Jiang, J. (2018). Massification of higher education and challenges for graduate employment and social mobility: East Asian experiences and sociological reflections. *International Journal of Educational Development, 63*(2018), 44–51.

Pool, L. D., & Sewell, P. (2007). The key to employability: Developing a practical model of graduate employability. *Education + Training, 49*(4), 277–289.

Salmon, G. (2005). Flying not flapping: A strategic framework for e-learning and pedagogical innovation in higher education institutions. *ALT-J, Research in Learning Technology, 13*(3), 201–218.

Sin, C., & Neave, G. (2016). Employability deconstructed: Perceptions of Bologna stakeholders. *Studies in Higher Education, 41*(8), 1447–1462.

Tierney, W. G., & Lanford, M. (2016). Conceptualizing innovation in higher education. In M. B. Paulsen (ed.), *Higher education: Handbook of theory and research*, pp. 1–40. Switzerland: Springer International Publishing.

Tomlinson, M. (2007). Graduate employability and student attitudes and orientations to the labour market. *Journal of Education and Work, 20*(4), 285–304.

Tran, L. H. N. (2018). Game of blames: Higher education stakeholders' perceptions of causes of Vietnamese graduates' skills gap. *International Journal of Educational Development, 62*(2018), 303–312.

Vedder, R. (2017). Seven challenges facing higher education. Retrieved from www.forbes.com/sites/ccap/2017/08/29/seven-challenges-facing-higher-education/#79810e2e3180

Yorke, M. (2006). *Employability in higher education: What it is – what it is not* (Vol. 1). York, England: Higher Education Academy.

Yorke, M., & Knight, P. T. (2006). *Embedding employability into the curriculum*. York, England: Higher Education Academy.

2

BUILDING MULTIDISCIPLINARY PROGRAMMES THAT ENGAGE INDUSTRY

A critical task for higher education to enhance graduate employability

Hong T. M. Bui

The collaboration between universities and industry has been perceived as a vehicle to enhance innovation through knowledge exchange (Ambos et al., 2008; Freitas et al., 2013). University-industry collaboration has mainly been understood as the interaction between university and industry aiming to encourage knowledge and technology exchange (Bekker & Freitas, 2008; D'Este & Patel, 2007). This topic has been well researched, particularly with recent systematic reviews by Al-Tabbaa and Ankrah (2016) and Perkmann et al. (2013). Al-Tabbaa and Ankrah (2016) identify five key aspects, namely, motivation, formation, organisation, operation, and outcomes, which together are integrated into an overarching process framework of university-industry collaboration.

However, the broad literature does not seem to pay enough attention to an important influence of this collaboration on graduate employability. Visionary partnerships between industry and universities not only accelerate innovation and help deliver solutions to pressing social challenges, but also improve student employability. In order to achieve that, universities, in particular research universities, need to redefine their mission to one that produces a highly skilled workforce for a globally competitive economy (Edmondson et al., 2012).

Employability is defined as "a set of achievements – skills, understanding and personal attributes – that make individuals more employable and successful in their chosen occupations, which in turn benefits themselves, the workforce, the community, and the economy" (Yorke & Knight, 2006, p. 8). Graduate employability has globally become a critical area for higher education due to the social pressure and global competition in this sector (Rae, 2007; Tomlinson, 2007). Therefore, this chapter suggests that universities should build multidisciplinary programmes that engage industry-based work via the university-industry collaboration. The following parts discuss the reasons and approaches to achieve that task.

Discrepancies in graduate skills and employability

Universities largely embrace a model developed over 100 years ago, which derived from teaching and public service research (Edmondson et al., 2012). The way that many universities divide into schools and faculties, and many other single disciplinary universities around the world, show every single discipline's silos. Consequently, this results in the low employability rate of university graduates and means that such industries often complain that graduates do not have the sufficient skills and/or knowledge to adapt to new work environments (Nair et al., 2009). Specific transferable skills such as problem-solving, leadership, teamwork, empathy, and social/emotional intelligence are still being left out of the curricula in most higher education institutions (Van Velsor & Wright, 2012). This contributes to widening the skill gap. This skill gap phenomenon seems to apply to the whole global context. For example, it is estimated that by 2020, the United States will have a shortage of approximately 1.5 million college graduates because workers do not have the skills to transition to and from their new jobs (Dobbs et al., 2012). On the other hand, it is predicted that India will be short of more than 160 million skilled workers in various industries by the same time (Lakshmi, 2013). The reasons for this, said Greg Butler, Senior Director Worldwide Education Strategy at Microsoft, are that "young people were not being equipped with the skills needed to be successful in employment. You only have to look at unemployment and mismatch of skills and jobs" (cited in Edmondson et al., 2012, p. 14). This skill gap will inevitably create economic consequences.

In addition, there is a mismatch of skills between graduates and the industry (Gergen & Rego, 2014). Following an international survey conducted with graduates, educators, and employers from nine countries, Mourshed et al. (2014) recognised the significant difference between the world of education and employment. State universities had an inflated confidence regarding the relevance of what they were teaching, while fewer than half of their surveyed students and employers believed that graduates were adequately prepared for entry-level positions. "Something is clearly wrong when only 11% of business leaders, compared to 96% of chief academic officers, believe that graduates have the requisite skills for the workforce" (Weise, 2014, p. 1). Thus, the increasing skills gap and severe competition for global talent has driven open-minded businesses to develop partnerships with reputable universities to develop new skills for a next-generation workforce (Edmondson et al., 2012).

To attract industries, universities must embrace multidisciplinary programmes

In a large study of EU and ASEAN technology-based firms, Yap and his colleagues (2000) showed those firms' dissatisfaction with their working relationships with universities were due to lack of trust and confidence with universities. For example, universities lack the skills necessary to cooperate with industry; they lose sight of industry's needs and are unaware of industry's constraints (Yap et al., 2000). Society's problems do not exist in silos. Climate change, for example, is a systemic problem involving scientific, economic, social, and environmental issues. Pursuing solutions to complex, systems-level problems requires cross-disciplinary expertise. This contrasts with the service provided by many universities. In addition, the recent encouragement of many governments (including the UK) to further develop internships and apprenticeships, together with the demand for higher levels of graduate employability, are forcing more and more universities to develop partnerships with different industries. This, again, is likely to create an increasing competition among universities to develop partnerships with the most innovative and socially responsible companies.

According to Blessinger and Carfora (2015), an increasing number of interdisciplinary, multidisciplinary, and even transdisciplinary programmes have recently been developed in higher education as academics seek new knowledge that lies at the intersection of traditional disciplinary boundaries. However, this view about academics' research and development is biased. The other side is about students' employability and social benefits from higher education including business and industry. Therefore, to attract industries, universities are embracing multidisciplinary programmes, not only to create new knowledge, but also to attract and encourage such industries to provide hands-on experience for their staff and students and attract more funding for this sector (Edmondson et al., 2012).

An exemplary instance is the case of the multidisciplinary programme, International Design Business Management (IDBM), by the Helsinki School of Economics, Aalto University, the University of Art and Design, and the Helsinki University of Technology, which works to complement majors in engineering, design, and business among other subjects (www.idbm.fi). The programme is balanced between business, engineering, and design learning. IDBM has challenged the notion that universities' traditional role is to pass on existing knowledge and provide absolute answers (Karjalainen et al., 2011). IDBM multidisciplinary teams tackle industry problems and produce innovative solutions over the course of a one-year programme and receive around €20,000 from each company. Thus, this multidisciplinary programme has not only created income, but also significantly enhanced Aalto University's links with hundreds of companies and provided training for thousands of students via various projects that have led to the development of real-world innovative services and products, creating major value for its industry partners.

Another example of success is the Energy Bioscience Institute (EBI), a groundbreaking strategic research partnership between BP, the University of California, Berkeley, the Lawrence Berkeley National Laboratory, and the University of Illinois at Urbana-Champaign to develop sustainable next-generation biofuels and reduce the impact of climate change (http://energybiosciencesinstitute.org/). BP took proposals from university teams around the world to ensure they covered all the capabilities needed for the new institute, but the UC Berkeley consortium was the most enthusiastic about taking a multidisciplinary approach, leading to the EBI receiving a $500 million grant from BP. The EBI has enabled academics from various disciplines to become recognised leaders in a new cross-disciplinary field and to start winning more external grants due to EBI's increased competitiveness.

These examples are clear evidence to show universities' attraction to innovative companies through their provision of multidisciplinary programmes and research teams.

Skills that industry-engaged multidisciplinary programmes provide to students

Companies can offer students real-world, open-ended problems to learn from and solve that the company may not be able to address itself. They are also the places where students can digest their academic knowledge faster, and their skill development is better assisted (Jackson, 2015). While working for companies, students can benefit from on-the-job training, coaching, and mentoring which foster their ability to solve problems, think critically, communicate, work effectively with others, develop a better understanding of what constitutes professional and efficient practice in their chosen field, and enhance their understanding of social, corporate, and personal responsibility and how technology and data are used within their discipline (Jackson, 2015).

A successful example of skills development for university students is the partnership called Assessment and Teaching of 21st Century Skills (ATC21S) between Microsoft, Cisco, Intel, and the University of Melbourne (http://atc21s.org). The partnership was set up to transform education for the 21st century by focusing on the critical skill sets for a global knowledge economy. The partnership identified two core, discrete skill sets, namely, *collaborative problem-solving* and *digital literacy*, and managed a highly complex global academic research effort across 60 research institutions to successfully develop a new set of tools (computer-based collaboration and problem-solving) to assess skills that will form the basis of the new curricula. Robin Horn, the education sector manager for the World Bank, stated that "measuring skills such as critical thinking, problem-solving, collaboration and teamwork, ICT competencies, and information literacy, in a rigorous and pragmatic way, has been totally out of reach until now . . . It is a harbinger of a wholly new approach to standards and assessment for the 21st century" (Edmondson et al., 2012, p. 14).

The previous example of IDBM is an effort to create individuals who can think outside their own profession because breakthrough innovations are often done in inter- and multidisciplinary teams (Edmondson et al., 2012). Engagement with industry in using cross-disciplinary teams is a ground-breaking approach to transforming teaching and learning (Karjalainen et al., 2011; Zimbardi & Myatt, 2014). Such programmes develop students with innovative mind-sets through collaborative, cross-disciplinary problem-solving (Edmondson et al., 2012). In addition, industry-engaged learning has improved a range of employability skills including *team work, problem-solving, communication, information literacy*, and *professionalism* (Coll et al., 2009; Freudenberg et al., 2011). Experience in industry-relevant research programmes makes students more attractive and employable to companies and is very useful for their own start-ups because they have opportunities to learn from and solve real-world problems.

Key learning methods for industry-engaged multidisciplinary programmes

To deliver industry-engaged multidisciplinary programmes, educators must be very innovative in their thinking, teaching, and learning methods. This chapter presents some key thinking and learning methods that will assist industry-engaged multidisciplinary programmes.

Problem-based learning

Problem-based learning (PBL) is "an instructional (and curricular) learner-centred approach that empowers leaders to conduct research, integrate theory and practice, and apply knowledge and skills to develop viable solutions to a defined problem" (Savery, 2015, p. 5). PBL has since evolved from innovative health sciences (Boud & Feletti, 1997). In PBL, students work in small collaborative groups and learn what they need to know in order to solve a problem. Meanwhile, the teacher acts as a facilitator to guide student learning through the learning cycle (Hmelo-Silver, 2004).

PBL has been seen as a critical tool for education in general and higher education in particular. Many universities and programmes have used PBL to integrate research and curriculum development. An example is the PBL Lab, established in 1993 in the Department of Civil and Environmental Engineering at Stanford University. Its mission is

> to educate the next generation workforce by engaging graduate and under-graduate students, faculty, and industry practitioners in multi-disciplinary, collaborative, geographically distributed PBL activities. PBL is a process of teaching and learning that focuses on problem-based, project centred activities that produce a product for a client. PBL will be based on re-engineering processes that bring people from multiple disciplines together.
>
> *(PBL Lab, n.d.)*

The PBL Lab has become a global, project-based class where students develop green architecture. The scope of the lab includes researching how high-end technology can be used in virtual work spaces.

Systems thinking

Systems thinking is defined as a "discipline for seeing wholes and a framework for seeing interrelationships, rather than things; and for seeing patterns of change rather than static snapshots" (Senge, 1990, p. 68). The main attribute of systems thinking is to holistically examine a complicated issue which is influenced by the interaction of its elements and the changes that may happen internally or externally (Senge & Sterman, 1992). It operates on five disciplines: openness, purposefulness, multidimensionality, emergent property, and counterintuitive behaviour (Gharajedaghi, 2011). Openness refers to the system boundary in which people have less control over the system, more influence on the transactional environment, and appreciate the contextual environment. This discipline implies that no problem or solution is valid free of context, and best practices are in fact not as good as people often think. Purposefulness refers to the dimensions of choice. When people make a decision, they often have to choose and balance between rational, emotional, and cultural factors based on their own context. Multidimensionality refers to the fact that people live in multiple dimensions; they have to find balance in order to optimise the best of limited resources. Emergent property refers to the properties of the parts and the whole. It is not about the sum of the actions but about the quality of the interactions. In other words, the all-star team is not necessarily the best team; the best one is the result of high-quality interactions that share the same vision and goals. Counterintuitive behaviour refers to the fact that relationships are not always linear; they can be upside-down, U-turn, or in spiral shapes. Behaviour can become better before it becomes worse (Senge, 2006).

Systems thinking can gain an in-depth understanding of the problems as it examines all the factors that may cause these problems, as well as their interrelationships (Cezarino & Beltran, 2009; Richardson, 2014). It also helps people and organisations deal effectively with any complexities and uncertainties (Adam & de Savigny, 2012; O'Connor, 2008; Senge et al., 2010). Students (and even academics) must be academically equipped to have a general understanding of systems thinking and how systems work before exposing them to the industry. This will teach and support students to deal better with complex issues and collaborate with people from other disciplines/perspectives more effectively.

Design thinking

Recently, Roberts et al. (2016) defined design thinking as "a systematic innovation process that prioritises deep empathy for end-user desires, needs and challenges to fully understand a problem, in hopes of developing more comprehensive and effective solutions" (p. 12). According to Hassi and Laakso (2011), design thinking is a popular but vague concept, and there appears to be two different streams in design thinking: one in design and the other in management. De Mozota (2011) developed a set of skills to apply design thinking to a transition economy in which risk-taking, experimentation, teamwork, narrative building, holistic thinking, and open-mindedness that transcend the existing barriers of industrial silos are considered the most important skills. To make it more relevant and forward-looking to university-industry collaboration, a table of design thinking skills has been developed from de Mozota's (2011) table of designer skills

TABLE 2.1 Design thinking skills developed from de Mozota (2011)

Knowledge	Attitude Values	Applied Skills	Understanding Skills
Design process	Risk-taking	Practical design skills	Observation
	Managing uncertainty	Prototyping	Integrative thinking
		Drawing ability	
Material	Originality	Lateral thinking	Researching
Market	Anticipating future trends	Commercial skills	Prioritising
			Structuring problems
	Forward-thinking		
Technology	Proactive in developing relationships	Computer skills	Analysing
			Logical thinking
User awareness	Open-minded	Communication skills	Scenario building
		Emotional intelligence	Narrative
			Attention to detail
Culture	Understanding multidisciplinary context	Teamwork	Social intelligence
Aesthetic awareness	Focusing on usability	Creative techniques	Intuitive thinking and action
			Design for manufacture
Human factors	Consumer and stakeholder needs	Self-awareness	Human empathy
		Personal mastery	
Manufacturing process	Learning from errors	Optimisation	Synthesising
	Learning from others	Project management	Holistic thinking

(see Table 2.1). It shows that in order to fully equip future graduates with design thinking, both universities and industries must collaborate closely for the benefits of all partners: industry, universities, and knowledge workers.

Both design thinking and systems thinking are disciplines that belong to holistic thinking (Cross, 2011; Jackson, 2006). Many scholars state that design thinking is one of the components of systems thinking as systems thinking includes more than just design thinking (Senge, 2006; Kimbell, 2011; Gharajedaghi, 2011), while others argue that systems thinking is a part of design thinking (e.g., de Mozota, 2011). Regardless of one's view of the above, they all agree that systems thinking and design thinking are crucial for innovation (Johansson & Woodila, 2011; Senge et al., 2010).

How to develop industry-engaged multidisciplinary programmes in higher education

Multidisciplinary programmes have been well developed in medical education (e.g., McAlister et al., 2004; Meguid et al., 2016). Medical education research shows that most multidisciplinary programmes/strategies can improve the outcomes of medical treatments and reduce mortality and all-cause hospitalisation. However, multidisciplinary programmes in other areas are less developed. In Blessinger and Carfora's (2015) book, most contributors, with the exception of Bata and Whitney (2015) and Marquis and Tam (2015), consider multidisciplinary programmes a means to enhance teaching and learning in class and to engage students in taking responsibility for connecting their learning through exploration and inquiry, and in defining solutions to the real-world issues.

The live experience in university-industry collaboration will help to attract and retain global student talent (Vauterin et al., 2013). In order to develop such multidisciplinary programmes, universities need to have the right people.

> The key issue is having people who cross boundaries – you need multidisciplinary individuals who are mentors. The university has to be open to giving people, who usually would not be chosen, leading positions. You need bridge-builders. That's the bottom line. This kind of collaboration doesn't happen by itself. People make this kind of change happen. You have to be constantly on the lookout for people and create incentives for them to grow.
>
> *(Edmondson et al., 2012, p. 19)*

Conclusion

The relationship between universities and industry is never an easy one to build for mutual benefits. This chapter has focused on what universities should develop in order to not only work well with industry, but also develop their students. I conclude that multidisciplinary programmes that engage industry will be a good springboard for improving graduate employability in the context of an uncertain and complex world. Although there is no recipe for universities/higher education to develop such programmes, design thinking, systems thinking, and PBL tend to be the foundation in their curriculum development.

References

Adam, T., & de Savigny, D. (2012). Systems thinking for strengthening health systems in LMICs: Need for a paradigm shift. *Health Policy and Planning*, 27, iv1–iv3.

Al-Tabbaa, O., & Ankrah, S. (2016). Social capital to facilitate 'engineered' university–industry collaboration for technology transfer: A dynamic perspective. *Technological Forecasting and Social Change*, 104, 1–15.

Ambos, T. C., Makel, K., Birkinshaw, J., & D'Este, P. (2008). When does university research get commercialized? Creating ambidexterity in research institutions. *Journal of Management Studies*, 45, 1424–1447.

Bata, M., & Whitney, A. (2015). Using inquiry-based learning outside of the classroom: How opportunities for affective practice can animate course-based learning. In P. Blessinger & J. M. Carfora (Eds.), *Inquiry-based learning for multidisciplinary programs: A conceptual and practical resource for educators*. Bingley: Emerald.

Bekker, R., & Freitas, I. M. B. (2008). Analysing knowledge transfer channels between universities and industry: To what degree do sectors also matter? *Research Policy*, 37(10), 1837–1853.

Blessinger, P., & Carfora, J. M. (Eds.) (2015). *Inquiry-based learning for multidisciplinary programs: A conceptual and practical resource for educators*. Bingley: Emerald.

Boud, D. J., & Feletti, G. I. (1997). *The challenge of problem-based learning* (2nd ed.). London: Kogan Page.

Cezarino, L. O., & Beltran, A. C. (2009) Diagnosis of organizational soft problems in a Peruvian financial institution by systemic thinking. *Systemic Practice and Action Research*, 22, 101–110.

Coll, R., Eames, R., Paku, L., Lay, M., Hodges, D., Bhat, R., . . . & Martin, A. (2009). An exploration of the pedagogies employed to integrate knowledge in work-integrated learning. *Journal of Co-operative Education and Internship*, 43(1), 14–35.

Cross, J. (2011). *Informal learning: Rediscovering the natural pathways that inspire innovation and performance*. San Francisco: John Wiley & Sons.

de Mozota, B. B. (2011). Strategic view of design in business. *IDBM Papers Vol. 1*, pp. 40–49. Helsinki: Aalto University.

D'Este, P., & Patel, P. (2007). University–industry linkages in the UK: What are the factors underlying the variety of interactions with industry? *Research Policy*, 36, 1295–1313.

Dobbs, R., Madgavkar, A., Barton, D., Labaye, E., Manyika, J., Roxburgh, C., & Madhav, S. (2012). The world at work: Jobs, pay, and skills for 3.5 billion people. Retrieved from www.mckinsey.com/insights/employment_and_growth/the_world_at_work

Edmondson, G., Valigra, L., Kenward, M., Hudson, R., & Belfield, H. (2012). Making industry-university partnership work: Lessons from successful collaborations. [online]. *Science Business Innovation Board*. Retrieved from http://sciencebusiness.net/Assets/94fe6d15-5432-4cf9-a656-633248e63541.pdf

Freitas, I. M. B., Marques, R. A., & de Paula e Silva, E. M. (2013). University–industry collaboration and innovation in emergent and mature industries in new industrialized countries. *Research Policy*, 42(2), 443–453.

Freudenberg, B., Brimble, M., & Cameron, C. (2011). WIL and generic skill development: The development of business students' generic skills through work-integrated learning. *Asia Pacific Journal of Cooperative Education*, 12(2), 79–93.

Gergen, C., & Rego, L. (2014, February 19). Educating a new generation of entrepreneurial leaders. *Stanford Social Innovation Review*. Retrieved from www.ssireview.org/blog/entry/educating_a_new_generation_of_entrepreneurial_leaders

Gharajedaghi, J. (2011). *System thinking: Managing chaos and complexity*. Burlington: Elsevier.

Hassi, L., & Laakso, M. (2011). Making sense of design thinking. *IDBM Papers* Vol. 1, pp. 50–63. Hensinki: Aalto University.

Hmelo-Silver, C. E. (2004). Problem-based learning: What and how do students learn? *Educational Psychology Review*, 16(3), 235–266.

Jackson, D. (2015). Employability skill development in work-integrated learning: Barriers and best practice, *Studies in Higher Education*, 40(2), 350–367.

Jackson, M. C. (2006). Creative holism: A critical systems approach to complex problem situations. *Systems Research and Behavioral Science*, 23(5), 647–657.

Johansson, U., & Woodila, J. (2011). Creating a synergistic dialogue among design thinking, strategy, and innovation. *IDBM Papers* Vol. 1, pp. 64–73. Hensinki: Aalto University.

Karjalainen, T.-M., Koria, M., & Salimäki, M. (Eds.) (2011). *IDBM Papers* Vol. 1. Helsinki, IDBM Programme: Aalto University.

Kimbell, L. (2011). Rethinking design thinking: Part I, design and culture. *The Journal of the Design Studies Forum*, 3(3), 285–306.

Lakshmi, R. (2013, March 18). In India, students' aspirations are misaligned with job market. *The Washington Post*. Retrieved from www.washingtonpost.com/world/asia_pacific/indian-skills-dont-match-available-jobs/2013/03/18/ad38a99a-8bfc-11e2-af15-99809eaba6cb_story.html

Marquis, B., & Tam, V. (2015). Developing an interdisciplinary course on global justice: An inquiry-informed, cross campus, collaborative approach. In P. Blessinger & J. M. Carfora (Eds.), *Inquiry-based learning for multidisciplinary programs: A conceptual and practical resource for educators*. Bingley: Emerald.

McAlister, F. A., Stewart, S., Ferrua, S., & McMurray, J. J. V. (2004). Multidisciplinary strategies for the management of heart failure patients at high risk for admission: A systematic review of randomized trials. *Journal of the American Colleague of Cardiology*, 44(4), 810–819.

Meguid, C., Schulick, R. D., Schefter, T. E., Lieu, C. H., Boniface, M., Williams, N., . . . & Edil, B. H. (2016). The multidisciplinary approach to GI cancer results in change of diagnosis and management of patients. Multidisciplinary care impacts diagnosis and management of patients. *Annals of Surgical Oncology*, 23(12), 3986–3990.

Mourshed, M., Patel, J., & Suder, K. (2014). Education to employment: Getting Europe's youth into work. *McKinsey Center for Government*, Washington, DC. Retrieved from www.mckinsey.com/insights/social_sector/converting_education_to_employment_in_europe

Nair, C. S., Patil, A., & Mertova, P. (2009). Re-engineering graduate skills: A case study. *European Journal of Engineering Education*, 34(2), 131–139.

O'Connor, G. C. (2008) Major innovation as a dynamic capability: A systems approach. *Journal of Product Innovation Management*, 25(4), 313–330.

PBL Lab (n.d.). *Home*. Retrieved from http://pbl.stanford.edu/

Perkmann, M., Tartari, V., McKelvey, M., Autio, E., Brostrom, A., D'Este, P., . . . & Sobrero, M. (2013). Academic engagement and commercialisation: A review of the literature on university–industry relations, *Research Policy*, 42(2), 423–442.

Rae, D. (2007). Connecting enterprise and graduate employability: Challenges to the higher education culture and curriculum? *Education + Training*, 49(8/9), 605–619.

Richardson, N. (2014). Frank Stowell and Christine Welch: The manager's guide to systems practice. *Systemic Practice and Action Research*, 27, 307–308.

Roberts, J. P., Fisher, T. R., Trowbridge, M. J., & Bent, C. (2016). A design thinking framework for healthcare management and innovation. *Healthcare*, 4(1), 11–14.

Savery, J. R. (2015). Overview of problem-based learning: Definitions and distinctions. In A. Walker, H. Leary, C. E. Hmelo-Silver, & P. A. Ertmer (Eds.), *Essential readings in problem-based learning*. Indiana: Purdue University Press.

Senge, P. M. (2006). *The fifth discipline: The art and science of the learning organization*. New York: Currency Doubleday.

Senge, P. M., Smith, B., Kruschwitz, N., Laur, J., & Schley, S. (2010). *The necessary revolution: How individuals and organizations are working together to create a sustainable world*. London: Nicholas Brealey Publishing.

Senge, P. M., & Sterman J. D. (1992). Systems thinking and organizational learning: Acting locally and thinking globally in the organization of the future. *European Journal of Operational Research*, 59(1), 137–150.

Tomlinson, M. (2007). Graduate employability and student attitudes and orientations to the labour market. *Journal of Education and Work*, 20(4), 285–304.

Van Velsor, E., & Wright, J. (2012). Expanding the leadership equation: Developing next-generation leaders: A white paper. Centre for Creative Leadership.

Vauterin, J. J., Michelsen, K.-E., & Linnanen, L. (2013). Attracting and retaining student talent from around the world: The lived experience in university-industry collaboration. *Industry & Higher Education*, 27(3), 163–178.

Weise, M. (2014, October 17). The real revolution in online education isn't MOOCs. *Harvard Business Review*. Retrieved from https://hbr.org/2014/10/the-real-revolution-in-online-education-isnt-moocs/

Yap, C. M., Chou, S. K., Thybussek, I., Gocht, W., & Pozzolo, V. (2000). Comparative practices of EU and ASEAN forms in technology-based interactions with universities. *Industry & Higher Education*, February, 10–16.

Yorke, M., & Knight, P. T. (2006). *Embedding employability into the curriculum*. York: Higher Education Academy.

Zimbardi, K., & Myatt, P. (2014). Embedding undergraduate research experiences within the curriculum: A cross-disciplinary study of the key characteristics guiding implementation. *Studies in Higher Education*, 39(2), 233–250.

3

ENTREPRENEURSHIP ECOSYSTEMS IN HIGHER EDUCATION

Maksim Belitski

Introduction

The entrepreneurship discipline in Europe has expanded from the study of entrepreneurs and the economics of entrepreneurship to a much broader subject, incorporating the promotion of entrepreneurial behavioural patterns for both individuals and institutions. There has been a strong focus in education policy and academia on the creation of entrepreneurship ecosystems in higher education (Fetters et al., 2010). This is to further support academic spin-offs, improve institutional settings in the process of spin-off creation (Caiazz et al., 2014; Belitski and Heron, 2017) and graduate employability, as well as drive innovation and the direct commercialization of research knowledge (Wright et al., 2006).

This is raising new challenges for entrepreneurship educators and scientists demanding a stronger link between teaching, research and commercialization of knowledge (Guerro et al., 2015). Stronger entrepreneurial universities will lead to stronger communities of entrepreneurs in regions supporting the entrepreneurship ecosystems broadly (Isenberg, 2010; Autio et al., 2014; Audretsch and Belitski, 2016).

The idea of entrepreneurship ecosystems in higher education is emerging as a popular topic around the world as entrepreneurship is perceived as a solution for poverty alleviation, economic growth and prosperity (Acs et al., 2013; Kelley et al., 2011). Entrepreneurship ecosystems in higher education embrace diverse stakeholders and the interactions between them – universities, providers of finance and SMEs community, service providers, faculty, students, scientists and entrepreneurs – that help to support economic development and innovation locally (Tether and Tajar, 2008). This is directly associated with the role that universities need to become more "entrepreneurial" and therefor play a greater role in local entrepreneurial communities and create a conducive entrepreneurial environment for scientists, students and faculty to take on opportunity and knowledge.

Despite the growing interest demonstrated in recent years to commercialization of entrepreneurial ideas in universities and entrepreneurial education, there is no perfect agreement on the role that universities play in regional economic development and commercialization of knowledge. There is also no agreement on conditions that enable creation of instruments and mechanisms internally at the university to support entrepreneurial activity and knowledge diffusion (Pirnay et al., 2003; Clarysse and Moray, 2004; Algieri et al., 2013).

The emergence of the empirical and theoretical foundation of entrepreneurial education is very recent (Fetters et al., 2010), with universities being seen as the hub of regional economic development around the world (Audretsch et al., 2012), providing infrastructure, resources and networks to develop entrepreneurial communities locally and nationally. This chapter argues that entrepreneurial education can evolve as the hub of regional economic development and entrepreneurialism, facilitating stronger and faster commercialization of knowledge. I also provide a roadmap of action to follow in order to expand entrepreneurial education in higher education with a greater degree of knowledge and innovation-based market entry.

I propose a framework for creation of entrepreneurship education in higher education that will require many different approaches to teaching, research and business outreach, some of which have not yet been discovered or yet need to be created. The toolbox does not depend on the location or size of a school or university but goes beyond identifying entrepreneurial opportunities and research discoveries, applying, engaging, creating and discussing entrepreneurship education with all stakeholders and leaders (Fernald et al., 2005). Most importantly, the approach requires contribution to three dimensions of the ecosystem stakeholders: culture, resources and formal and informal infrastructure. I introduce this toolbox in light of other current increases in demand for entrepreneurial education across departments in university and knowledge commercialization.

Entrepreneurial ecosystem in higher education

The concept of the "entrepreneurial university" has set an ambitious agenda for universities who want to engage proactively with their immediate business environment and their national economies. Scientific knowledge has been acknowledged as a necessary condition for academic spin-offs and new firm start-ups, which have stimulated innovation within universities since 2000 (Audretsch et al., 2012). The so-called "triple helix" model proposed by Etzkowitz and Leydesdorff (2000) posits the university at the centre of university-industry-government relationships and describes the prominent role universities can play for innovation and economic development in a Knowledge Society. MIT, the global exemplar, has created 30,200 businesses, employing 4.6 million and generating nearly US$2 trillion in annual revenues (Matheson, 2015). Cambridge, the leading entrepreneurial higher education institution in the UK, has seen 1,400 spin-offs, employing 40,000. For example, in the UK, both the National Centre for Entrepreneurship in Education (NCEE) and the Institute for Small Business and Entrepreneurship (ISBE) have provided a range of case studies and research papers on the subject, and the *Times Higher Education* has championed the entrepreneurial university through its annual awards for several years.

Although the number of entrepreneurship ecosystems in higher education has been growing, students and scientists remain the major channel of knowledge transfer in the field to businesses, with much of this knowledge transfer happening in a local proximity to and within entrepreneurial communities linked to the university (Acosta et al., 2011; Bonaccorsi et al., 2013). In remote regions, and regional towns in particular, universities have been identified as an important spill-over of knowledge and innovation (Pinto et al., 2012). A variety of university specializations with the scientists and students involved influences the emergence of knowledge spillovers within industrial clusters, with applied technological knowledge fostering the creation of new firms as start-ups, spin-offs and scale-ups. An academic spin-off (Fini et al., 2011) is intended as a new, high-tech venture promoted and launched by an academic researcher that aims to exploit the results of previous research projects on academic spin-offs and provide insights into creating an entrepreneurial ecosystem supporting the creation of academic spin-offs in regions.

Entrepreneurial ecosystems in higher education thus aim to have at least one academic researcher in the shareholding of a new venture. This enables increased performance, engagement with local entrepreneurial communities and better market understanding. Spin-off and new venture participants in the ecosystem may be students, professors and interns, who are able to monetize their knowledge through university spin-offs or by joining the incumbent forms, increasing competitiveness and supporting innovation in regions (Audretsch, 2012).

Commercialization of university knowledge does not happen automatically. For example, several US counties with large, prize-winning universities demonstrate low entrepreneurship activity (Chinni and Gimpel, 2011), despite the high levels of human capital, creativity and knowledge discovery. This is because their entrepreneurship ecosystems lack the support of entrepreneurial personality and ambition. The university's immediate business environment may not be able to help, should entrepreneurship education be weak or underdeveloped.

A university may be located in one of the most entrepreneurial regions in Europe, as is the University of Reading in Reading, or University of Sussex in Brighton being located in the middle of the largest cluster of digital businesses outside London, but lacking the resource allocation and absorptive capacity to engage with entrepreneurial community and support spin-offs. Although many specialized businesses become tenants of universities in the universities' enterprise centres or business parks, they do not always collaborate with the universities and scientists, and knowledge remains uncommercialized (Acs et al., 2013; Audretsch and Belitski, 2013).

The concept of knowledge spill-overs is crucial in better understanding the role of uncommercialized knowledge. Knowledge spill-overs may arise because of the imperfect appropriability of ideas and knowledge (Audretsch et al., 2006). The benefits of new knowledge accrue to the academics and universities while also "spilling over" to other firms within the same region or country, or across regions and countries. Uncommercialized knowledge within the university becomes a source of opportunities for external academics and firms. This enriches the pool of ideas for the knowledge providers and the knowledge recipients, upon which subsequent innovations can be based.

Entrepreneurial education: the UK case study

This section will draw readers' attention to the growing importance of employability and research commercialization on the one hand, and entrepreneurial education on the other, as evidenced since 2000 (Fini et al., 2009; Audretsch et al., 2012). Many universities in developed and developing countries have embarked on reinforcing entrepreneurialism and employability as a key metric, with the entrepreneurial skills of job creation receiving greater visibility. The system of higher education funding in the UK, for example, has undergone major reforms and changes in the last few years (BIS, 2014). In the UK, a key consequence of higher student fees is increased scrutiny from student stakeholders, with graduate employability becoming a key factor influencing subject and university choice (Universities UK, 2010). As foreshadowed in the recently published green paper "Fulfilling our Potential", the UK government intends to further reinforce employability as a key metric (BIS, 2015).

In addition to the development of employability and entrepreneurial skills in students, stronger entrepreneurial ecosystems need resources allocated for research funding (Brown and Mason, 2017). This has also seen significant changes in the UK, most notably through the increased importance of "impact" through research councils, such as the former Higher Education Funding Council for England and the European Union (Chemistry World, 2015). Success in research translation, and specifically in the commercial success of university research, is of ever greater importance. There is increasing evidence to show that the world's best institutions at creating impactful innovation are also the leading institutions where academics attract private funding and create spin-offs (Caiazza and Audretsch, 2013; Caiazza et al., 2014; Ewalt, 2015; Times Higher Education, 2016).

Investment in research translation initiatives and in regional economic development in the UK welcome the initial steps in creating entrepreneurial universities and universities' entrepreneurial ecosystems, but these investments need to be incorporated into a broader vision for entrepreneurship at the micro level within centres for entrepreneurship, technology transfer offices (TTOs) and university management. The objective of an entrepreneurial university is to explicitly integrate the growing knowledge exchange and research translation initiatives to improve and expand entrepreneurship education and spin-offs exploiting regional advantages.

The role of technology transfer offices and entrepreneurship centres

Along with TTOs, Centres for Entrepreneurship, also known as Centres for Entrepreneurial Excellence, have expanded their teaching, research, co-curricular and outreach activities quickly and successfully, while entrepreneurship education has become well established and popular. Centres for Entrepreneurship help promote entrepreneurial ideas and engage the business community with students in entrepreneurship modules and co-curricular activities. They will remain a central component of the university-based entrepreneurial ecosystems, focused both on the entrepreneurship co-curriculum activities with the community across and beyond campus and across the university departments directly connected to commercialization of their academic research. Centres for entrepreneurship will promote knowledge exchange between entrepreneurs, scientists and students through a host of events, engage with TTOs on commercialization and business model creation for spin-offs coming from across the university (Lockett et al., 2003) and, finally, provide access to new funding opportunities for students and scientists locally through crowdfunding and angel investors' resources. In the ground-breaking paper of Caiazza and Audretsch (2013), a lack of funding and developmental support is described as the main challenge, while spin-offs that are created outside of high-tech clusters tend to remain small and do not become world leaders. In their study, they introduce a general framework for classifying spin-offs according to three main dimensions – internal, relational and external – and draw on the various theoretical perspectives to explicitly distinguish conditions conducive to spin-off growth within a geographical space. It has been also mentioned that in highly competitive environments, it is not the location that matters but the creation of the entrepreneurial mind-set when students, tutors and scientists may experiment with knowledge, enjoying greater support of TTOs and centres for entrepreneurship to further commercialize and test it.

Offering entrepreneurial best practices for higher education

Entrepreneurship in higher education is seen to be a strategic blend of consulting, education, coaching and research, with complementary knowledge created within ecosystems and further monetized. This performance enhancement could be achieved by learning from the famous business schools, such as Bocconi in Milan, MIT and Harvard in Boston, Berkley in San Francisco, George Washington University in Washington DC and Indiana University in Bloomington to name a few, by building on the significant foundation that has already been laid by those schools.

Following their best practices, I propose to not only embrace entrepreneurship on the surface, but also create a highly attractive campus experience for all stakeholders of entrepreneurship ecosystems through the following offerings making a university more entrepreneurial.

Expanding the footprint of entrepreneurial education across the university

It should be mandatory that every single undergraduate programme at the university have an entrepreneurship stream made available. This could be achieved through increasing access to the existing university-wide general modules in entre-preneurship or by creating more subject-specific modules to be included as core within established programmes (e.g. Entrepreneurial Management for Chemical Engineering, Entrepreneurial Management for Creative Artists, Enterprise Education for Biosciences). This would not necessarily have the need to reallocate resources from across the university to business schools, but may be introduced through theory-practice mixed learning in the respective departments. I believe this may implicitly introduce students to entrepreneurship education and skills, and enhance graduate employability across the university, but avoid students with non-business backgrounds feeling obliged to study and practice entrepreneurship.

Action learning and scientists' engagement in entrepreneurial modules

I propose that the teaching experience of entrepreneurship begins to move from being overwhelmingly lecture based to increasingly practice based with the greater engagement of scientists, where students pursue projects jointly with scientists on campus or in incumbent forms or in spin-offs contributing to spin-off legacy. Evidence of the advantage of active learning is in the "Entrepreneurship Theory and Action" approach positioned at Babson College in Boston where students fol-low four major principles of learning: Action trumps everything, start with your means, build partnerships and do not be the best – be the only. Since 1982, this method has helped thousands of entrepreneurial educators and scientists to look differently at the role of entrepreneurial education and to engage in action rather than theorization of knowledge (Neck and Greene, 2011; Neck et al., 2014). There is overwhelming evidence supporting the superiority of practice-based pedagogies over lecture-based ones. This would not only significantly improve the campus-based experience of students but also engage them with scientists to advance and promote scientific discoveries in the universities to further knowledge commer-cialization. This would, first, contribute to entrepreneurship ecosystems and make it easier for academic spin-offs to enter the market while passing the validation test with the help of students, saving precious time for market validation experi-ments, and second, allow entrepreneurship ecosystems to further improve graduate employability of students once they were involved in an applied commercialization of knowledge (Times Higher Education, 2015a).

Providing infrastructure for engagement with entrepreneurial community

Opening centres for entrepreneurship networks and courses to the local entrepre-neurship community will make the knowledge exchange and research translation initiatives from the university available to business. This would improve research commercialization outcomes and improve matches between students, scientists and business. These activities reflect the extent to which entrepreneurship is supported by the university and school leader (Fernald et al., 2005) and requires significant allocation of resources to incentivize faculty and staff to engage students and faculty with the entrepreneurial community.

Investment in creating facilities *for* engagement with the entrepreneurial community, for example, is booming in UK universities, with a recent example of an investment being made by the University of East Anglia, which invested £15 million into new entrepreneurial facilities, including teaching rooms with adaptable furniture and writable walls that can flip between "lecture mode" and "workshop mode", a 300-seat lecture theatre, a careers office specifically for students who want to start their own businesses, office space for entrepreneurs and a collaborative lab for university staff and local enterprises to brainstorm ideas (Times Higher Education, 2015b).

Providing facilities for engagement with students and alumni

The traditional campus is a place that is busy during term time and deserted otherwise, a place students visit for three years and then return to once a year for reunions, if at all. This tradition is perishing in European and UK universities, while still remaining strong in the US top colleges.

An entrepreneurial university requires space for ongoing engagement with both businesses and students; it is a place alumni return to and where innovations, businesses and spin-offs are not only created, but can also grow. Entrepreneurship education changing its mode of delivery to a more practice-based approach enables various forms of entrepreneurial activity, for example, the establishment of start-ups, scale-ups and academic spin-offs as well as first- and second-stage growth businesses, while the final objective is growing spin-offs on campus, which therefore requires improvements in the amenities and educational facilities available to students, scientists and businesses.

In particular, along with building the number of incubator buildings on and around campus, investment should be put into both development of formal infrastructure (facilities, amenities, trees, office equipment, water and electricity supply) and human capital and entrepreneurial environment, for example the "Entrepreneurship Tuesdays" in the Engineering Department at Cambridge University organized by the Centre for Entrepreneurship of Judge Business School.

Financing students' start-ups and spin-offs

Financing for entrepreneurship activity could be raised from various sources, including internal university entrepreneurship and product commercialization resources, sponsorships from key university stakeholders such as investors, venture capitalists, and donors from university alumni. Universities usually hold free spaces and facilities available to rent to business with two objectives: first, because the incubator and other buildings generate a rental income from business, and second, to create an entrepreneurial ecosystem in education.

Conclusion

I started by looking at various different frameworks for the entrepreneurship eco-system (Isenberg, 2010; Mason and Brown, 2017; Autio et al., 2014) and identified the university as a hub of entrepreneurial education with centres for entrepreneur-ship and excellence supporting interactions among all stakeholders (Audretsch et al., 2012; Belitski and Heron, 2017). I have provided a review of other stud-ies and suggested best practices of entrepreneurial education development in business schools in Europe and the US. This study demonstrates that a synthesis of the tools and mechanisms available to stakeholders within the entrepreneur-ship ecosystem in higher education is important to further develop and facilitate entrepreneurial thinking and action. I have highlighted important dimensions of entrepreneurship education such as stakeholders who perform entrepreneurship at schools and in regions, resources available, formal and informal infrastructure (such as networks, co-curriculum activity and financing entrepreneurship) and, most importantly, culture of entrepreneurial education in schools, which take a long time to nurture.

I posit on the importance of including all stakeholders in the discussion on all dimensions of the entrepreneurship education ecosystem in a university, and in particular business communities, which can be large and small but crucial for the dynamics and exchange of knowledge and collaboration with a university. I advo-cate for the three-level model of entrepreneurial university, where the individual level (academics, students) is embedded into the organizational level (university) and then accordingly embedded into a regional entrepreneurship ecosystem and national regulation. The alignment of all three elements of the entrepreneurial ecosystem in education will cut transaction costs, and most importantly engage all interested stakeholders in the knowledge commercialization process. Universities need regional entrepreneurship ecosystems to support them, while regional entre-preneurship ecosystems need prosperous and entrepreneurial universities.

The major resources to support the entrepreneurship education that need to be involved include various types of capital (e.g. social and networks, financial, human), facilities, infrastructure, mentors, culture, time and technology. First, the challenges within the process of changing the entrepreneurial ecosystem in business schools are that it may take a long time, require new courses and new ways to fundraise it, and must overcome "red tape", risk and uncertainty. Second, business schools have different visions and definitions of the ecosystem and entrepreneurial education at their institutions. Educators and scientists personally act on how entrepreneur-ship education is embedded in schools; however, this is merely a starting point. Factors that affect universities' ability to generate spin-offs and graduate start-ups while commercializing knowledge need to be identified. Third, it must be decided how the ecosystem will support start-ups and spin-off activities within schools and across universities, and a roadmap of actions and allocating resources developed, usu-ally involving a mix of internal and private funding for entrepreneurial activities. Wherever we start, entrepreneurship education ecosystems have to be viewed in a context of a specific school, university and entrepreneurial ecosystem, and defined within a specific business environment.

Entrepreneurship education may require several additional dimensions that support entrepreneurial development in order to apply it in teaching, research and knowledge commercialization through spin-offs and new ventures. Educators and entrepreneurs need to reconsider the methods for teaching entrepreneurship theory and entrepreneurial culture (Neck and Greene, 2011; Belitski and Keith, 2017), and knowledge of entrepreneurship needs to be delivered in a way which can be taught while remaining motivational and inspiring (Neck et al., 2014). The influence of entrepreneurial culture and stakeholders on the ecosystem should come through the sharing of knowledge, collection of resources, entrepreneurial insights and experience, introducing a change in schools, small and larger scale experimentation with start-ups and spin-offs, freedom and private interest of students and scientists to pursue ideas, and market entry. Subsequent literature will focus on changing the ecosystem and the way students and scientists deal with the knowledge they create and use to start businesses. More research is required on the creation of a number of support structures, such as TTOs and teaching students the basics of effectuation logic (Chinni and Gimpel, 2011), ecosystem affordable loss (as we know, action trumps everything) and creating unique academic and entrepreneurial offers to the business community.

References

Acosta, M., Coronado, D., & Flores, E. (2011). University spillovers and new business location in high-technology sectors: Spanish evidence. *Small Business Economics, 36*(3), 365–376.

Acs, Z. J., Audretsch, D. B., & Lehmann, E. E. (2013). The knowledge spillover theory of entrepreneurship. *Small Business Economics, 41*(4), 757–774.

Algieri, B., Aquino, A., & Succurro, M. (2013). Technology transfer offices and academic spin-off creation: The case of Italy. *The Journal of Technology Transfer, 38*(4), 382–400.

Audretsch, D. B., Keilbach, M. C., & Lehmann, E. E. (2006). *Entrepreneurship and economic growth*. New York, NY: Oxford University Press.

Audretsch, D. B., Hülsbeck, M., & Lehmann, E. E. (2012). Regional competitiveness, university spillovers, and entrepreneurial activity. *Small Business Economics, 39*(3), 587–601.

Audretsch, D. B., & Belitski, M. (2013). The missing pillar: The creativity theory of knowledge spillover entrepreneurship. *Small Business Economics, 41*(4), 819–836.

Autio, E., Kenney, M., Mustar, P., Siegel, D., & Wright, M. (2014). Entrepreneurial innovation ecosystems and context. *Research Policy, 43*(7), 1097–1108.

Belitski, M., & Heron, K. (2017). Expanding entrepreneurship education ecosystems. *Journal of Management Development, 36*(2), 163–177.

BIS. (2014). Funding per student in higher education. Retrieved from www.gov.uk/government/uploads/system/uploads/attachment_data/file/318628/BIS_performance_indicators_Funding_per_student_in_HE.pdf

BIS. (2015, November). Fulfilling our potential: Teaching excellence, social mobility and student choice. Retrieved from www.gov.uk/government/uploads/system/uploads/attachment_data/file/474227/BIS-15-623-fulfilling-our-potential-teaching-excellence-social-mobility-and-student-choice.pdf

Bonaccorsi, A., Colombo, M. G., Guerini, M., & Rossi-Lamastra, C. (2013). University specialization and new firm creation across industries. *Small Business Economics, 41*(4), 837–863.

Brown, R., & Mason, C. (2017). Looking inside the spiky bits: A critical review and conceptualisation of entrepreneurial ecosystems. *Small Business Economics, 49*(1), 11–30.

Caiazza, R., & Audretsch, D. (2013). A general framework for classifying spin-offs. *International Review of Entrepreneurship, 11*(1).

Caiazza, R., Audretsch, D., Volpe, T., & Debra Singer, J. (2014). Policy and institutions facilitating entrepreneurial spin-offs: USA, Asia and Europe. *Journal of Entrepreneurship and Public Policy, 3*(2), 186–196.

Chemistry World. (2015). Falling Horizon success rates worry research community. Retrieved from www.rsc.org/chemistryworld/2015/10/horizon-2020-eu-funding-success-rate-drops

Chinni, D., & Gimpel, J. (2011). *Our patchwork nation: The surprising truth about the 'real' America.* New York, NY: Gotham Books.

Clarysse, B., & Moray, N. (2004). A process study of entrepreneurial team formation: The case of a research-based spin-off. *Journal of Business Venturing, 19*(1), 55–79.

Etzkowitz, H., & Leydesdorff, L. (2000). The dynamics of innovation: From national systems and "Mode 2" to a triple helix of university–industry–government relations. *Research policy, 29*(2), 109–123.

Ewalt, D. (2015). The world's most innovative universities. Retrieved from www.reuters.com/article/idUSL1N11K16Q20150915

Fernald, L., Solomon, G., & El Tarabishy, A. (2005). A new paradigm: Entrepreneurial leadership. *Southern Business Review, 30*(2), 1–10.

Fetters, M., Greene, P., Rice, M., & Butler, J. (2010). *The development of university-based entrepreneurship ecosystems: Global practices.* Northampton, MA: Edward Elgar Publishing.

Fini, R., Grimaldi, R., Santoni, S., & Sobrero, M. (2011). Complements or substitutes? The role of universities and local context in supporting the creation of academic spin-offs. *Research Policy, 40*(8), 1113–1127.

Guerrero, M., Cunningham, J. A., & Urbano, D. (2015). Economic impact of entrepreneurial universities' activities: An exploratory study of the United Kingdom. *Research Policy, 44*(3), 748–764.

Isenberg, D. J. (2010). How to start an entrepreneurial revolution. *Harvard Business Review, 88*, 41–49.

Kelley, D., Bosman, N., & Amoros, J. (2011). *Global entrepreneurship monitor: 2010 global report.* Wellesley, MA: Babson College.

Lockett, A., Wright, M., & Franklin, S. (2003). Technology transfer and universities' spinout strategies. *Small Business Economics, 20*(2), 185–200.

Matheson, R. (2015). *New report outlines MIT's global entrepreneurial impact.* MIT News. Retrieved from http://news.mit.edu/2015/report-entrepreneurial-impact-1209

Neck, H. M., & Greene, P. G. (2011). Entrepreneurship education: Known worlds and new frontiers. *Journal of Small Business Management, 49*(1), 55–70.

Neck, H. M., Greene, P. G., & Brush, C. G. (2014). *Teaching entrepreneurship: A practice-based approach.* Cheltenham, England: Edward Elgar Publishing.

Pinto, H., Fernandez-Esquinas, M., & Uyarra, E. (2012). Universities and knowledge-intensive business services (KIBS) as sources of knowledge for innovative firms in peripheral regions. *Regional Studies*, 1–19.

Pirnay, F., Surlemont, B., & Nlemvo, F. (2003). Toward a typology of university spin-offs. *Small Business Economics, 21*(4), 355–369.

Tether, B. S., & Tajar, A. (2008). Beyond industry–university links: Sourcing knowledge for innovation from consultants, private research organisations and the public science-base. *Research Policy, 37*(6–7), 1079–1095.

Times Higher Education. (2015a). *Let students build tech products, UK sector told.* Retrieved from www.timeshighereducation.com/news/let-students-build-tech-products-uk-sector-told

Times Higher Education. (2015b). *UEA launches green space for entrepreneurial students and businesses to collide.* Retrieved from www.timeshighereducation.com/news/uea-launches-green-space-entrepreneurial-students-and-businesses-collide

Times Higher Education. (2016). *The world's top universities for attracting industry funding.* Retrieved from www.timeshighereducation.com/world-university-rankings/funding-for-innovation-ranking-2016

Universities UK. (2010). *Changes in student choices and graduate employment. Report.* Retrieved from www.universitiesuk.ac.uk/policy-and-analysis/reports/Pages/changes-in-student-choices-and-graduate-employment.aspx

Wright, M., Clarysse, B., Lockett, A., & Binks, M. (2006). Venture capital and university spin-outs. *Research Policy, 35*(4), 481–501.

4

DEVELOPING INNOVATIVE STUDENT LEADERSHIP FOR ENHANCED GRADUATE EMPLOYABILITY

Jill Jameson

Background and significance

The Edelman 2017 and 2018 Trust Barometers indicate that a crisis of trust has been developing for some years across 20/28 countries, affecting almost all sectors of government, business and public life across the world, barring a few countries showing tendencies in the opposite direction (Edelman, 2017, 2018). In a UK higher education, business and political context, it is increasingly clear that trust in formal UK authority figures, including senior managers in higher education, politicians, business managers, policy makers, media agencies and business leaders across various industries, has been declining in the 21st century. Critical media and research commentary reporting on scandals, injustices and inequalities relating to elite pay, the gender wage gap, sexual abuse, ethnic minority discrimination and cultural alienation reveal increasing cynicism amongst both educated sub-groups and members of the wider public regarding poor and irresponsible performance by top hierarchical figures across many sectors (Higgs, 2003; Solomon, 2007; Prowle and Harradine, 2014; Normore and Brooks, 2017; Edelman, 2017, 2018). Consequently, numerous related problems have occurred indicating unrest, anxiety, employment-related stress and ill health in the workforce of organizations (Olafsen, Niemiec, Halvari, Dec and Williams, 2016), including in higher education (Melo, Sarrico and Radnor, 2010; Carter, Danford, Howcroft, Richardson, Smith and Taylor, 2013; Cribb and Gewirtz, 2013; Rowlands and Rees, 2015). In these situations, there is an increasing need for students to develop their own proactively resilient leadership skills and potential capacities to build trust in work teams to handle difficult situations for enhanced employability.

This chapter on the development of trust and resilient student leadership in higher education to enable innovation for graduate employability is situated within a UK higher education, business and political context. This is against a policy background of major changes looming on the horizon resulting from the UK national political referendum decision to leave Europe, labelled in the popular acronym 'Brexit' (British Exit from the European Union). The UK is facing major, unprecedented change across all sectors of industry and public life in future decades as a result of these macro-scale political and economic developments, whatever their result (Dhingra, Ottaviano, Sampson and Reenen, 2016).

Graduates are already facing increasing difficulties gaining employment in the fiercely competitive UK jobs market. Analysis from a recent working paper by the Institute for Fiscal Studies on English higher education graduate earnings (Britton, Dearden, Shephard and Vignoles, 2016) indicates that graduates from lower income households who obtained degrees from some universities (in specific contexts relating to 23 higher education institutions overall for men and nine for women) might now be better off by avoiding university study at all. This large-scale research demonstrated that, if such graduates have failed to gain graduate-level employment, their lifelong earnings power is likely now to be less than if they had gone straight into employment after school or college rather than progressing to university, only to accumulate large debts from tuition fee loans that they are then unable to pay back (ibid.). However, there is also earlier research that supports a counterposition to this, carried out by Walker and Zhu (2013) and widely reported (BBC, 2017), demonstrating that on average, graduates are rewarded by higher lifetime pay over non-graduates (£250,000 for women; £170,000 for men). Furthermore, 2016 Graduate Labour Market Statistics (GLMS) analyzed by the Department for Education from the Office for National Statistics (ONS) Labour Force Survey (LFS) data reveal that, on average, working age graduates (aged 16–64) earned £9,500 more than non-graduates in 2016, with postgraduates earning on average £6,000 more than graduates (BBC, 2017; Department for Education, 2017). An analysis from the Russell Group of universities also reveals that, after the deduction of fees and studying costs, this graduate earnings advantage over the career lifetime is higher for graduates from top universities, at £177,000, compared with non-graduates. It is even higher for master's and doctoral postgraduate students (Bennett, 2017).

Nevertheless, given that there is an increasing 'global auction' in the competition for young talent in a highly skilled graduate jobs market (Brown, Lauder and Ashton, 2010) and, in combination, a growing crisis of trust and cynicism regarding the effectiveness and integrity of top managers in positional authority (Edelman, 2018), the need for students to take control of their own futures by developing resilient leadership skills and fostering trust themselves becomes clear. The impetus and rationale for students to develop their own 'voice', with integrity and power, has possibly never been more evident.

Managerialism in higher education: new opportunities for student leadership

A considerable literature exists relating to both overt and implied concepts of positional leadership that are generally assumed to be included in critical studies of managerialism and new public management in higher education in England (Clarke and Newman, 1997; Deem, 1998; Deem and Brehony, 2005; Lea, 2011; McNay, 2005). Combined with popular critical commentary on various scandals, injustices and inequalities relating to elite pay, gender, ethnic and cultural problems, this prior literature reveals increasing cynicism amongst both educated sub-groups and the wider public regarding poor performance by top hierarchical figures across many sectors.

In higher education institutions in England, in particular, there has long been a focus on normative models of the positional hierarchical leadership and management that dominates the apex of stratified, prestige-based universities and colleges (Deem, Hillyard and Reed, 2007). Generally, within day-to-day institutional practices in such organizations, there has been a lack of distinction between 'management' and 'leadership', with little recognition of the fact that managers may not be effective leaders, and vice versa. This problem has been exacerbated by a general lack of advanced training and development in academic leadership skills. Authoritative management figures at the top of institutional hierarchies have long been regarded by default as 'the leaders', who hold authority, power and control.

The business-focused discourse relating to leadership and management has also been subject to cynical critical interrogation from academics in subordinate hierarchical positions, such as lecturers and tutors, who are perceived by management, more accurately in post-1992 institutions, though less so in older universities, as 'followers' (Billot, West, Khong, Skorobohacz, Roxå, Murray and Gayle, 2013). Students occupy a somewhat ambivalent position in this reductively simplified, traditional, fixed, hierarchical, pyramidic view. On the one hand, a common area of focus in higher education is to regard students as the first priority of universities and colleges. In this student-centred view, which in a marketized system places emphasis on the student as a key 'client' of the university, enhancing the 'student experience', particularly to ensure positive, measurable key performance indicator (KPI) institutional feedback in student surveys, is an important priority on which the performance of the higher education institution is judged. Students are therefore placed at or towards the top of a pyramidical, institutional hierarchy of market-based performance priorities to achieve good reputational metrics, and therefore their 'voice' is important.

On the other hand, however, despite the rhetoric of this – mainly, though hopefully not exclusively – pragmatic emphasis on the 'student experience', students are also, in the classroom, potentially dependent on and thereby positioned below the relatively powerless academic lecturers and tutors functioning at the bottom of multi-layered institutional bureaucratic hierarchies. In addition to being powerful as 'clients' or 'customers' in their own right, therefore, students are also, by definition, being taught by course instructors at the lowest bureaucratic level. In a fixed model of traditional hierarchy, students could therefore be seen as '[student] followers of [academic lecturer] followers of [management] leaders'; that is, 'followers of followers', with little voice or power. This potential for open-ended ambiguity within the student role therefore may position them simultaneously as either/or/both powerful and powerless in particular universities, dependent on current popular trends and politics, individual situational circumstances and local contexts.

Strong and Williams (2014) discuss the idea of 'students as followers', given that students are at least nominally required to follow the instructional influence of their teachers as course leaders, to some extent, if only to achieve the course aims. Carsten, Uhl-Bien, West, Paterna and McGregor (2010) observe that, in bureaucratic organizations, followers are much more likely to be passive rather than active, and thereby to have little voice or power as critical thinkers and self-directed learners. It is therefore possible that, if students do not use their role as 'clients' to have a voice, and are also passive at the course level, they may have little influence within some powerfully bureaucratic institutions of academia, despite the influential rhetoric of 'student enhancement', unless they develop their own authentic voice of student criticality (Johnston, Ford, Mitchell and Myles, 2011).

In effect, any reductive model of student passivity and dependency, and, in fact, the very term 'followership' itself, has been radically challenged in past decades. The relational space between leaders and followers has been, in some situations, creatively re-envisaged as an interdependent partnership (Bligh, 2011). Increasingly, traditional views of institutional hierarchies have been to some extent overturned by several new developments over past decades. Firstly, the lucrative business leadership and management industry has, since around the 1960s, gradually but persistently challenged normative models of leadership based on fixed concepts of 'power and control' of the few over the many. Older 'great man' or 'heroic' concepts of leadership have tended to be roundly critiqued in these fields of study, falling away from prominence, as the literature, theory and practice of leadership and management have massively expanded (Bass and Bass, 2009). Several developmental phases in leadership theory have emerged, moving through 'situational', 'transformational' and 'post-heroic' theories of leadership to arrive at nuanced understandings informed by more selfless individual and group models of 'servant leadership', 'quiet leadership', 'distributed', 'collaborative' and 'shared' leadership. A democratizing process of leadership development has emphasized the innovative potential of entrepreneurial and action-focused characteristics relating in particular to newer, transformational horizons for employability informed by differential models of collective leadership (Bolden, Petrov and Gosling, 2008) and collegiality (Tapper and Palfreyman, 2002; Elton, 2008; Bolden et al., 2012; Bacon, 2014). This gradual overturning and refreshing of traditional ideas of leadership and management makes space for the new, including especially the roles of younger student leaders and newer graduates, to emerge.

Secondly, relating to the massification and marketization of universities (McNay, 2005; Brown and Carasso, 2013), the practical requirements of top higher education managers to organize, manage and control large-mass higher education institutions (Lea, 2011) have meant that "the managerial template . . . has become the normative model for the organization of the university". A "discourse of quantification" based on "performativity indexing and accountability" has gradually assumed increasing power, with the metrics of performance dominating strategic management understandings (Lea, 2011: 816, 835). Within that context, given the quantifiable power of students and their families as consumers of higher education, students have discovered a new voice in the marketplace of universities and colleges in terms of their mass influence in providing feedback, making complaints, holding top management to account and demanding change, particularly in relation to employment outcomes. While this role may or may not develop into a productive relationship for and with institutions, it nevertheless provides new opportunities for students to have some say in the running of higher education institutions as 'change agents' (Warwick, 2016). This has for many decades now, since the student activism of 1968, the 1970s and 1980s and beyond (Jacoby, 2017), provided new openings for students, as erstwhile 'followers of followers', to turn the tables on existing institutional authorities and become new leaders in their own way themselves.

Thirdly, the emergence of university graduate development courses, internships and 'graduate attributes' taught programmes to meet the performative graduate destinations measurement requirements of institutions has provided new spaces for students to take part in leadership development to further their skills and add new credentials to their own graduate portfolios (Eich, 2008). Graduate development programmes run by particular universities or groups of providers at various stages of higher education study are focused on preparing new graduates for work, sometimes in combination with work placement, mentoring and internship schemes. In the best circumstances, such courses, as well as internships and work placements, enable students to develop their career management capabilities, international experience, cross-cultural diplomacy and problem-solving skills, confidence, knowledge and intrapreneurial understanding as entrepreneurs and leaders in formation.

Fourthly, a generalized global crisis in trust in the integrity of positional authorities in many industries as regards perceived deficits in management capability, ethical behaviour and sustainability (Normore and Brooks, 2017; Edelman, 2018) have opened up a gap for a new kind of innovative, values-based, selfless ecologically aware leadership, in which young graduates can position and find themselves. Values of humility, integrity, collaboration and post-humanist awareness of the need for both human and environmental sustainability in caring for the planet and acting against climate change are strongly emerging. These trends are informed and enriched by generational differences, as younger generations challenge some norms and behaviours that have led to mistakes in the past (Warwick, 2016; Normore and Brooks, 2017). This approach has widened, diversified and enriched hitherto frequently restrictive employability discourses.

Finally, technological innovation in the form of social media innovations, blockchain technology and developments in automation and robotics provide new opportunities for graduate student leaders to shape future social, political and economic systems in building for future generations and new industrial and entrepreneurial development (Coplin, 2013).

However, to capitalize on these opportunities, students, as graduates in the making themselves, need to recognize and understand their own role as resilient leaders now. This is most notably regarding awareness of the need for and methods of building systemic and interpersonal leadership and trust as future leaders of workplaces and in shared team situations. This chapter provides a proposed theoretical model for the development of trust and student leadership skills as part of the 'soft skills' that employers are recognizing are increasingly necessary for graduate employability. Finally, in acknowledging its limitations in providing a theoretical model, the chapter proposes practical recommendations for instantiating these developments, with accompanying suggestions for future research.

Methodology

Recent relevant literature was identified to inform the writing of this chapter from a wide-ranging search using Scopus, ScienceDirect, Google Scholar and the university-wide electronic database catalogues for academic research literature at the University of Cambridge and the University of Greenwich. Search terms included 'student AND leadership', 'graduate attributes', 'employability', 'innovation', 'higher education', 'leadership AND management' and 'university AND trust AND leadership' in a range of combinations. In addition, social psychological literature on the universally recognized traits of 'competence' and 'warmth' was consulted. Building on the prior literature identified and analyzed across the fields of leadership, management and trust in higher education, graduate attributes and social psychology with relevance for student graduate employability, this chapter was written to provide a proposed theoretical model for the development of student leadership and trust-building skills. The model was newly designed for the current chapter from the literature consulted, drawn also from the author's 40 years' experience as a professional teacher, leader and researcher in post-compulsory and higher education. In recognizing its limitations in putting forward an integrated theoretical model informed by literature in a range of fields and from prior experience of work with students in higher education, the chapter provides practical recommendations for implementation of these developments, putting forward proposals for future empirical research.

Integrated student leadership and trust model

The literature and professional practice relating to the development of student graduate attributes has gradually recognized the need for a wider range of interdisciplinary and interpersonal skills than those instrumentalist core 'hard skills', such as specialist disciplinary expertise and content knowledge, that are directly related to employability credentials to demonstrate competence in a particular occupational field. Normand and Anderson (2017) cite Osmani, Weerakkody, Hindi, Al-Esmail, Eldabi, Kapoor and Irani (2015: 373) in observing that employers value 'soft skills' more than 'academic reputation' relating to specialist disciplinary knowledge.

Gradually, in recognition of this trend, a range of generic 'softer skills' have been embraced in higher education graduate programmes for the development of students' future employability. Amongst these 'soft skills', it has been recognized, there is an increasing need to develop students' leadership skills and innovative capacities to handle difficult situations for enhanced employability. There are, however, different terms in use to describe the emphasis of these programmes. Hill, Walkington and France (2016) are amongst those who use the term 'graduate attributes' with particular reference to the work of Spronken-Smith, Bond, McLean, Frielick, Smith, Jenkins and Marshall (2015) in a New Zealand context and Qualifications Framework, aiming to use this term to encompass more than what they identify as the narrower definition of 'employability':

> Graduate attributes are broader and more encompassing than "employability," helping to develop academic, citizenship and career competencies. They are an orientating framework of educational outcomes that a university community agrees its graduates should develop as a result of completing their studies successfully. Some common graduate attributes have gained favour in universities, and these include the following: critical thinking skills, such as intellectual curiosity, analytical reasoning, problem-solving and reflective judgement; effective communication; leadership and teamwork skills; research and inquiry skills; information literacy; digital literacy; personal attributes such as self-awareness, self-confidence, personal autonomy/self-reliance, flexibility and creativity; and personal values such as ethical, moral and social responsibility, integrity, and cross-cultural awareness.
>
> *(Hill et al., 2016: 156)*

However, other experts in the field, including Dacre, Pool and Sewell (2007), the HEA Learning and Employability series (HEA, 2006) and HEA Framework for Employability (HEA, 2013) as well as Knight and Yorke (2004), have developed models of employability in the UK which are wider and richer than the more limited interpretation of 'employability' implied by Hill et al. (2016), developing research-informed employability models that are arguably even more comprehensive than the 'graduate attributes'. Despite this difference in terminology in variable contexts, though, it seems clear that, ideally, the notion of 'employability' encompasses a broader and more comprehensive mixture of attitudes, behaviours, values and skills than those relating only to a narrow view of 'getting a job'. Variable use of definitions in different disciplinary fields and university contexts can lead to some confusion and misunderstanding of the terminology used in this field. There is a need, therefore, to be precise and specific in defining what is meant when using these various terms in order that the numerous stakeholders involved in such definitions, such as employers, can relate to these models effectively.

Given the global crisis of diminishing trust in positional authorities, it is helpful for students to recognize the transformational potential of their own roles as innovative leaders and future graduate employees. This is most notably as regards students' own awareness of the need for and methods of building trust in the workplace. As future leaders of existing and new organizations who will both manage and be part of shared working team situations, newly qualified graduates will have the power to shape new industries and workplace spaces around the value and meaning that they provide (Coplin, 2013).

In proposing a theoretical model for the development of trust and leadership values, behaviours, attitudes and skills for graduate employability, the question of the value and meaning of the workplace itself needs to be considered in a creative way. Possibly amongst the most important employability dimensions for new graduates to consider is the way in which they will be judged by others, including employers and clients, in dynamic working environments.

Two universal traits against which human judgements are routinely and instantly made, as demonstrated in social psychological research carried out with many thousands of people across numerous countries and workplaces (Cuddy, Glick and Beninger, 2011) are the dimensions of *(1) 'competence'*, which in this chapter is broadly equated with graduate 'hard skills' in terms of subject expertise, disciplinary knowledge, scientific/technical or other relevant employability task-based skill, industriousness and intelligence in performing the job role; and *(2) 'warmth' or 'trustworthiness'*, which in this chapter is equated with graduate 'soft skills' in term of socio-emotional competency, people skills, as well as ethical, open and benevolent behaviours, values and characteristics that are capable of generating a sense of 'other-related' trustworthiness. The short-hand terms (1) 'competence' = 'hard skills' and 'warmth' = 'soft skills' used hereinafter are therefore a summary of these wider dimensions, mapped against the two universal traits identified.

In preparing students for future workplaces during graduate employability programmes in higher education, student leadership courses aimed at fostering trust in the workplace would benefit from incorporating dimensions of both high competence in 'hard skills' and high warmth in terms of 'soft skills'.

A functional combination of the best qualities across both traits focuses on qualities such as subject expertise, high scientific/technical/other specialist skills and intelligence, combined with traits such as reliability, diligence and honesty, leading overall to effective, trustworthy student leadership (see Figure 4.1). These two dimensions are demonstrably highly significant in decisions made by employers and by employees across the general workforce as regards unthinking non-verbal subjective stereotyping of others. Cuddy et al. (2011: 93) therefore argue that it is crucially important for leaders to manage the ways in which others perceive them in accordance with these two dimensions. Arguably, also, impression management is not enough in itself, as high performance across both of these universal dimensions is needed in an in-depth, fully functioning sense as part of a lifelong development of all-round comprehensive 'employability' for life. This requires the capacity to remain innovative, knowledgeable, flexible, creative and responsive to both the people and the tasks required for career-long high-quality work across all professions.

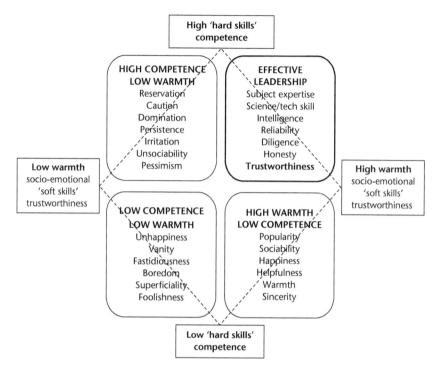

FIGURE 4.1 Integrated 'hard–soft' balanced skills model: graduate leadership and trust

If, by contrast, newly qualified graduates who are high in 'hard skills' competence are perceived as lacking in the dimensions of socio-emotional 'soft skills', they are likely to be regarded as less trustworthy. If they are insufficiently recognized by others for capability in the dimension of 'warmth', this implies that they may be judged in a non-verbal stereotypical way as being too reserved, cautious, overly dominant, inappropriately persistent, or as showing signs of irritation, a lack of sociability or pessimism.

At the other extreme, those new graduates who are high in warmth as regards people-related 'soft skills' such as popularity, sociability, happiness, helpfulness, warmth and sincerity, but who do not also visibly demonstrate high 'hard skills' competence, may find themselves perceived as good socially but incompetent as regards disciplinary knowledge, organizational competence, technical capability and related work skills. Worst of all are those who do not demonstrate either high 'hard skills' or high 'soft skills', as new graduates who are perceived as low in both traits may be those demonstrating behaviours that are seen by employers and other employees to be lazy, unreliable, unhappy, vain, fastidious, boring, superficial or just plain foolish.

A combination of graduate employability training and development programmes that aims to assist students develop high achievement in both 'competence' (hard skills) and 'warmth' (soft skills) therefore seems the ideal approach to encourage students to develop effective leadership that will serve them well in the future.

Discussion and implications

Given the results of the Edelman 2017 and 2018 Trust Barometers, which demonstrate that across global workplaces at a macro level, trust is in decline across 20/28 countries in almost all industries, there is a strong need to prepare future graduates to demonstrate effective leadership and trustworthiness for future flexible work situations. High achievement across the universal social psychological dimensions of 'competence-warmth', or 'task and people' traits will therefore be increasingly necessary. Students will require both 'hard' and 'soft' behaviours, values, capabilities and skills in employment contexts, and may need to learn how to cope with ambiguous, complex situations in which they are quickly judged by other employees and by clients in relatively superficial ways. To avoid unhelpful negative stereotyping from snap judgements made about them in either of these two universal dimensions, there is therefore a need to understand the importance of managing their leadership and general workplace behaviours in a mindful way. Graduate programmes which aim to foster both occupational task-focused competence and people-focused leadership, resilience and trust skills are likely therefore to enable the best form of preparedness to face increasingly cynical and potentially stressful workplace situations.

This needs to include courses that focus on the development of a balance of innovative leadership skills that embrace the capacity to handle ambiguous, challenging and difficult situations. It is helpful for students to know that they need to foster a balanced range of behaviours, values, capabilities and skills across these two universal dimensions. For example, some traits that might be regarded as positive in social situations (enthusiasm, popularity, happiness) may, if not demonstrated in tandem with high competency skills, lead others to judge them as too superficial or frivolous in the workplace. Similarly, students who demonstrate behavioural characteristics that are too focused on high competence in 'hard skills' at the cost of high socio-emotional 'soft skills' warmth (for example, those using approaches that are overly dominant, critical and competitive or persistently lacking in sociability), may be perceived as too cold and unpopular to succeed at work. The integrated model of balanced 'hard-soft skills' is therefore likely to lead to greater success in employability and to well-balanced achievements at work in a range of contexts.

Limitations and future research

This chapter recognizes its limitations in putting forward a theoretical model, providing suggestions for the integration of a balanced 'hard-soft' graduate employability skills model. Since this brings together a range of concepts from different fields of literature and practice, it is recommended that empirical research should be carried out in higher education workplaces providing graduate employability programmes to test the extent to which the 'hard-soft' dimensions specified are appropriate or need further refinement.

Graduate employability training courses incorporating the use of the above leadership model in higher education 'employability preparation' teaching contexts are also recommended in combination with mentoring from experts and feedback from employers and others across the dimensions specified. Longer term self-development programmes incorporating goal-setting, daily self-correcting schedules, critical self-reflection and personal growth for graduates to develop their own values, strengths and capabilities may enrich the longer term growth of more mindful behaviours. In this way, newly graduating student leaders may come to adopt the combined 'hard-soft' leadership approaches of 'high competence' and 'high warmth' for themselves in an ongoing lifelong understanding of the ongoing dynamic need for refreshing change in nurturing workplace employment.

References

Bacon, E. (2014) *Neo-collegiality: Restoring academic engagement in the managerial university*. London: The Leadership Foundation for Higher Education.

Bass, B. M., & Bass, R. (2009) *The Bass handbook of leadership: Theory, research, and managerial applications*. Fourth Edition. New York: Simon & Schuster.

BBC (2017) *Reality check: How much more do graduates get paid?* BBC newspaper article: Reality Check Report. Available online: www.bbc.co.uk/news/uk-politics-40965479. Accessed 28 March 2018.

Bennett, R. (2017) *Top university degree adds £177,000 to graduates' lifetime pay*. Article by the Education Editor, The Times Newspaper, Nov 2, 2017. Available online: www.thetimes.co.uk/article/top-university-degree-adds-177-000-to-graduates-lifetime-pay-bm69xrdqk. Accessed 28 March 2018.

Billot, J., West, D., Khong, L., Skorobohacz, C., Roxå, T., Murray, S., & Gayle, B. (2013) Followership in higher education: Academic teachers and their formal leaders. *Teaching and Learning Inquiry: The ISSOTL Journal, 1*(2), 91–103.

Bligh, M. (2011) Followership and follower-centred approaches. In A. Bryman, D. Collinson, K. Grint, B. Jackson, & M. Uhl-Bien (Eds.), *The Sage handbook of leadership* (pp. 425–436). Los Angeles: Sage Publications.

Bolden, R., Gosling, J., O'Brien, A., Peters, K., Ryan, M. K., Haslam, S. A., & Winklemann, K. (2012) *Academic leadership: Changing conceptions, identities and experiences in UK higher education*. LFHE Research Report. London: Leadership Foundation for Higher Education.

Bolden, R., Petrov, G., & Gosling, J. (2008) *Developing collective leadership in higher education*. London: Leadership Foundation for Higher Education.

Britton, J., Dearden, L., Shephard, N., & Vignoles, A. (2016) *How English domiciled graduate earnings vary with gender, institution attended, subject and socio-economic background*. Working Paper W16/06. London: Institute for Fiscal Studies.

Brown, P., Lauder, H., & Ashton, D. (2010) *The global auction: The broken promises of education, jobs and incomes*. Oxford: Oxford University Press.

Brown, R., & Carasso, H. (2013) *Everything for sale?: The marketisation of UK higher education*. London: Routledge.

Carsten, M. K., Uhl-Bien, M., West, B. J., Paterna, J. L., & McGregor, R. (2010) Exploring social constructions of followership: A qualitative study. *The Leadership Quarterly, 21*, 543–562.

Carter, B., Danford, A., Howcroft, D., Richardson, H., Smith, A., & Taylor, P. (2013) 'Stressed out of my box': Employee experience of lean working and occupational ill-health in clerical work in the UK public sector. *Work, Employment and Society,* 27(5), 747–767.

Clarke, J., & Newman, J. (1997) *The managerial state: Power, politics and ideology in the remaking of social welfare.* London: Sage.

Coplin, D. (2013) *Business reimagined: Why work isn't working and what you can do about it.* Petersfield, Hampshire: Harriman House Limited.

Cribb, A., & Gewirtz, S. (2013) The hollowed-out university? A critical analysis of changing institutional and academic norms in UK higher education. *Discourse: Studies in the Cultural Politics of Education, 34*(3), 338–350.

Cuddy, A. J., Glick, P., & Beninger, A. (2011) The dynamics of warmth and competence judgments, and their outcomes in organizations. *Research in Organizational Behavior, 31,* 73–98.

Dacre Pool, L., & Sewell, P. (2007) The key to employability: Developing a practical model of graduate employability. *Education and Training, 49*(4), 277–289.

Deem, R. (1998) New managerialism in higher education: The management of performances and cultures in universities. *International Studies in the Sociology of Education, 8*(1), 47–70. doi:10.1080/0962021980020014

Deem, R., & Brehony, K. J. (2005) Management as ideology: The case of 'new managerialism' in higher education. *Oxford Review of Education, 31*(2), 217–235. doi:10.1080/03054 980500117827

Deem, R., Hillyard, S., & Reed, M. (2007) *Knowledge, higher education, and the new managerialism: The changing management of UK universities.* Oxford: Oxford University Press.

Department for Education (2017) *Graduate Labour Market Statistics 2016.* London: Crown Copyright.

Dhingra, S., Ottaviano, G. I., Sampson, T., & Reenen, J. V. (2016) *The consequences of Brexit for UK trade and living standards.* CEP LSE Brexit Analysis Paper 02: Centre for Economic Performance, The London School of Economics and Political Science. Available online: http://eprints.lse.ac.uk/66144/1/__lse.ac.uk_storage_LIBRARY_Secondary_ libfile_shared_repository_Content_LSE%20BrexitVote%20blog_brexit02.pdf. Accessed 19 March 2018.

Edelman (2017) *Edelman Trust Barometer global report.* London: Edelman. Available online: www.edelman.com/trust-barometer. Accessed 9 March 2018.

Edelman (2018) *Edelman Trust Barometer global report.* London: Edelman. Available online: www.edelman.com/trust-barometer. Accessed 9 March 2018.

Eich, D. (2008) A grounded theory of high-quality leadership programs: Perspectives from student leadership development programs in higher education. *Journal of Leadership & Organizational Studies, 15*(2), 176–187.

Elton, L. (2008) Collegiality and complexity: Humboldt's relevance to British universities today. *Higher Education Quarterly, 62,* 224–236. doi:0.1111/j.1468-2273.2008.00388.x

HEA: Higher Education Academy (2006) *Learning and employability series 1 and 2.*

HEA: Higher Education Academy (2013) *Defining and developing your approach to employability.*

Higgs, D. (Ed.) (2003) *Review of the role and effectiveness of non-executive directors.* London: Department of Trade and Industry.

Hill, J., Walkington, H., & France, D. (2016) Graduate attributes: Implications for higher education practice and policy, *Journal of Geography in Higher Education, 40*(2), 155–163.

Jacoby, B. (2017) The new student activism: Supporting students as agents of social change. *Journal of College and Character, 18*(1), 1–8.

Johnston, B., Ford, P., Mitchell, R., & Myles, F. (2011) *Developing student criticality in higher education: Undergraduate learning in the arts and social sciences.* London: Continuum/ Bloomsbury Publishing.

Knight, P., & Yorke, M. (2004) *Learning, curriculum and employability in higher education.* London: Routledge Falmer.

Lea, D. R. (2011) The managerial university and the decline of modern thought. *Educational Philosophy and Theory, 43*(8), 816–837. doi:10.1111/j.1469-5812.2009.00565.x

McNay, I. (2005) Managing institutions in a mass HE system. In I. McNay (Ed.), *Beyond mass higher education: Building on experience* (pp. 3–12). Maidenhead, UK: SRHE/Open University Press.

Melo A., Sarrico, C., & Radnor, Z. (2010) The influence of performance management systems on key actors in universities: The case of an English university. *Public Management Review, 12*(2), 233–254.

Normand, C., & Anderson, L. (Eds.) (2017) *Graduate attributes in higher education: Attitudes on attributes from across the disciplines.* Abingdon, Oxon: Routledge.

Normore, A. H., & Brooks, J. S. (Eds.) (2017) *The dark side of leadership: Identifying and overcoming unethical practice in organizations.* Bingley, UK: Emerald Group Publishing.

Olafsen, A. H., Niemiec, C. P., Halvari, H., Dec, E. L., & Williams, G. C. (2016) On the dark side of work: A longitudinal analysis using self-determination theory, *European Journal of Work and Organizational Psychology, 26*(2), 275–285.

Osmani, M., Weerakkody, V., Hindi, N. M., Al-Esmail, R., Eldabi, T., Kapoor, K., & Irani, Z. (2015) Identifying the trends and impact of graduate attributes on employability: A literature review, *Tertiary Education and Management, 21*(4), 367–379.

Prowle, M., & Harradine, D. (2014) Austerity and financial governance: A UK case study of the National Health Service. *International Journal of Public Sector Management, 27*(3), 212–224.

Rowlands K. E., & Rees C. J. (2015) *Organisational change and workplace stress in teaching and learning settings: Case study evidence from a public sector university in the UK.* In F. Dievernich, K. Tokarski, & J. Gong (Eds.), *Change management and the human factor.* Cham: Springer.

Solomon, J. (2007) *Corporate governance and accountability.* Chichester, UK: John Wiley & Son.

Spronken-Smith, R., Bond, C., McLean, A., Frielick, S., Smith, N., Jenkins, M., & Marshall, S. (2015) Evaluating engagement with graduate outcomes across higher education institutions in Aotearoa/New Zealand. *Higher Education Research & Development, 34*(5), 1014–1030

Strong, R., & Williams, J. (2014) Understanding students as followers: Discovering the influence of followership style on self-directed learning. *Journal of Agricultural Education, 55*(2), 201–213.

Tapper, T., & Palfreyman, D. (2002) Understanding collegiality: The changing Oxbridge model. *Tertiary Education & Management, 8*(1), 47–63. Retrieved from https://doi.org/10.1023/A:1017967104176

Walker, I., & Zhu, Y. (2013) *The impact of university degrees on the lifecycle of earnings: some further analysis.* London: Department for Business, Innovation and Skills (BIS) Research Paper Number 112.

Warwick, P. (2016) An integrated leadership model for leading education for sustainability in higher education and the vital role of students as change agents. *Management in Education, 30*(3), 105–111.

5

A SYSTEMATIC REVIEW OF SOCIAL INNOVATION IN HIGHER EDUCATION SYSTEMS AS A DRIVER OF STUDENT EMPLOYABILITY

The case of EE countries

Daniela Petrova Bariakova

Introduction and rationale

The current global dynamic environment has shaken the economies of many countries around the globe, which has inspired scholars to develop research that supports states, sectors and organizations to survive and cope with growing uncertainty. However, these rapid changes are having a serious effect on the higher education sector (Boden and Nedeva, 2010), which has been the subject of great transformation and pressure as higher education institutions must respond to the new economic era shaped by the 2007–2008 financial crisis and the subsequent global recession (Rae, 2010). The new era has highly impacted the higher education sector as it has led to profound economic, social, cultural and educational consequences (Rae, 2010). Universities are now expected to service industry rather being 'intellectually enlightened' (Huq and Gilbert, 2013; Reeve and Gallacher, 2005; Yorke, 2006). This explains why innovation and the employability agenda have thrived in the domain of higher education (Jones, 2010). Rae (2007) also contributes to the discussion of the importance of the link between innovation, enterprise and student employability.

Developing countries are in a less advanced position when it comes to unemployment because of the lack of activities associated with innovation, such as collaboration, research and training (Ishengoma and Vaaland, 2016). Findings from literature show that developed countries within the EU that embed social innovation have much higher student employability (Maxwell, Irwin and Bennett, 2015). Taking UK higher education as an example of a developed country, and the University of Northampton in particular, which is rated number one when it comes to social innovation, we see that 96% of full-time students were employed six months after graduation (HESA, 2015). This situation can be explained by the embedding of social innovation into every aspect of the student experience.

As already discussed, the increasing number of higher education institutions (HEIs) has resulted in a massively increased number of graduates. This outlines a high demand for innovation in higher education (IHE) to increase student employability. In fact, social innovation is a recently emerging field that has been the subject of growing interest among both scholars and policy makers since 2002 (Adams and Hess, 2010; Shaw and Bruin, 2013). Yet somehow, its concept and definition is unclear despite the efforts of scholars and theorists (Cajaiba-Santana, 2014). The reason for this lack of clear definition or concept of social innovation is rooted in a deficiency of empirical research examining it (Windrum et al., 2016), as well as the fact that the field has mostly been developed by reviewing multiple case studies, which has resulted in the mis-measurement of social innovation.

This systematic review aims to understand the literature on social IHE in European Economic (EE) countries context, as the literature indicates a close link between social innovation embedded in universities and student employability rates. In addition, this review focuses mainly but not exclusively on theoretical developments and empirical studies in social innovation and higher education, as the research of the literature shows a deficit of empirical studies when these fields are combined. Specifically, the objectives of this chapter are to:

- systematically and critically review the different theoretical streams of social innovation in the context of higher education;
- identify the major themes and key studies in higher education systems of social innovation in EE countries, by using synthesis analysis.

Research questions

- What are the main themes in relation to social innovation in the higher education systems in EE countries that have been examined so far?
- How has the literature on social innovation in higher education evolved in the past decades?

Methodology

Despite the significant amount of non-empirical academic work that has been conducted in the general area related to social innovation and higher education, since the 1980s, little attempt has been made to translate these findings systematically into a comprehensive review of current knowledge. The complexity of social innovation requires a systematic review, which illustrates all aspects of the existing literature and empirical evidence. This study aimed to fill this gap by improving our understanding of social IHE when examined in the EE countries context. What differentiates systematic reviews from other types of literature review methods is an orderly and transparent research synthesis (Davies, Daniel and Farmer, 2000; Tranfield et al., 2002).

Although systematic review is a very common research method used in the medical fields, it has a somewhat new and unsettled history in the social sciences

(Rashman, Withers and Hartley, 2009; Tranfield et al., 2002). In this particular case, not all elements of the orthodox methodology of systematic review in the management field are adopted. This chapter adopts Rashman, Withers and Hartley's (2009) methodological strategy and proposes a qualitative rather than quantitative approach, as it aims to provide a deeper explanation. This chapter emphasizes the context in which social innovation is examined so it builds on the meta-ethnography method and lines-of-argument (LOA) synthesis, which involves 'building up a picture or the whole (e.g., system, organization, culture etc.) from studies of its parts' (Barnett-Page and Thomas, 2009: 5). The methodology used in this chapter consists of two stages:

- Providing a transparent, scientific and replicable literature review (Tranfield, Denyer and Smart, 2003);
- Mapping and framing the enquiry, as well as presenting the results.

This systematic review used data extraction sheets, which are commonly used in systematic reviews in furtherance of making the material sources and their evaluation and assessment transparent. This exact method was used to identify key themes in the higher education sector which can directly or indirectly influence innovation within the sector. Furthermore, this approach also allows the researcher to identify the studies in which social innovation and innovation in general have been examined or explored in the context of higher education. Studies were included which observe higher education systems in both Western and Eastern European countries due to the limited academic research which examines innovation in the higher education sector in the context of EE countries, and because all European countries experience common as well as specific-to-the-context issues regarding IHE, so categorization of the problematic issues in this aspect was necessary. Three types of academic work related to the topic were included in this systematic review: studies that examine the context of higher education, studies that examine social innovation or IHE, and some articles that explore the concept, principles and definitions of social innovation.

The systematic review procedure adopted in this study is summarized in Figure 5.1. The purpose of this review procedure and strategy was to discard as much bias as possible and be extensive by conducting a database search, cross-referencing and employing inclusion criteria at each stage. As can be seen from Figure 5.1, the first stage involved the review of 15 scoping papers in the field of social innovation and innovations in the higher education context. This first stage of investigation was key to drawing attention to the following stages. At this point and later, and in common with other reviews on social innovation (e.g., Adams and Hess, 2010), this study discovered that studies examining social innovation or IHE in the context of EE countries from a system perspective were sparse. This required the extension of literature to include articles examining contemporary issues of the higher education system, not only the countries of Eastern Europe or articles exploring only the phenomenon of social innovation. The articles in this systematic review were included for a number of reasons, such as providing a good review of the existing literature or were well supported by empirical data. Some studies which were deemed too 'industry' or 'country' specific were still included in case they provided either a good introduction or a review of the existing literature.

The database search was the next stage of the employed methodology. Two databases were used – Thomson Reuters's Web of Science and Elsevier's Scopus – with a search period of 1999 to 2017, with an exception for significant academic works pre 1999. In general, about 90% of the included studies were from the past five years, with many articles published in 2016 and 2017. This period was chosen because in 1999, the Bologna declaration was signed by education ministers from 29 European counties. Since then, there have been significant transformations in the education system across Europe which have not yet ended as a result of the alignment of the Bologna Framework (Slantcheva-Durst, 2010). This systematic review searched peer-reviewed articles written in English only. The database

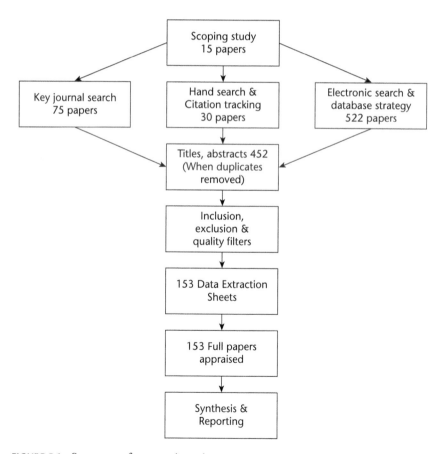

FIGURE 5.1   Summary of systematic review process

searches, key journal searches and citation tracking identified 452 initial references. Standards for inclusion, which are mentioned above, helped the researcher to exclude the irrelevant works after reading the 452 titles. After narrowing the searches based on their title relevance, the abstracts of the related papers were examined for further selection.

At this stage, 136 papers were taken further in the process, having been considered to have met the fundamental criteria of relevance and quality on the basis of the abstract search. Data extraction sheets of those 136 papers were prepared on a standard Excel document illustrating the inclusion criteria and key details of the selected papers (i.e. author, title year, method, journal, inclusion arguments and orientation of the paper such as individual, organizational and system). Therefore, this chapter presents an analysis of the review of literature on social innovation and IHE, and outlines the main issues of higher education which might impact innovation, as otherwise, the approach will be fragmented.

Social innovation

The reason for the lack of clear definition or concept of social innovation is rooted in the deficiency of the empirical research examining it (Windrum et al., 2016), as well as the fact that the field has mostly been developed by reviewing multiple case studies, which has resulted in the mis-measurement of social innovation. Theorists claim that research efforts are still necessary in this field (Shaw and Bruin, 2013; Windrum et al., 2016), which is supported by Adams and Hess (2010), who are convinced that there is a mismatch between practice and theory. Research data shows that practice is much more advanced than theory in terms of the development and understanding of the social innovation phenomenon. Theoretical research on social innovation has been an object of criticism for being 'fragmented' and 'non-cumulative' (Cajaiba-Santana, 2014; Dawson and Daniel, 2010; Pol and Ville, 2009). Researching social innovation is crucial because it is one of the main drivers of sustainability and long-term success required for organizations to operate in a highly competitive environment (Bruni and Verona, 2009). In this regard, Brown and Eisenhardt (1997) take the view that organizations with a bigger capacity to innovate are better and faster at adapting to environmental challenges compared to those that are less able to innovate. However, these adjustments create new challenges for management and policy practice (van der Have and Rubalcaba, 2016).

Literature on social innovation offers numerous definitions of the term, which are influenced by two main streams: sociological and business. The main difference between the two streams is that the sociological conceptualizations of social innovation are more concentrated on 'social practices', while the business and economic conceptualizations are orientated more towards the 'outcome' related to 'ideas', 'services' and 'new systemic transformations and changes' (van der Have and Rubalcaba, 2016).

Ims and Zsolnai (2014) offer a definition of social innovation with a sociological orientation: 'Social innovations involve proposing original solutions to old societal problems and issues, which are more efficient, effective and sustainable than the existing ones'. An example of a business-orientated definition is provided by Peredo and McLean (2006) who define social innovation as 'believed to be related to the phenomena of social entrepreneurship and enterprise'. Last, Parra-Requena, Ruiz-Ortega and Garcia-Villaverde (2013) provide a mixed definition with both economic and social orientation: 'The design and implementation process as well as a process of disseminating new social practices and policies to promote change in the social organization of people to promote economic ends'.

Innovation in higher education

When social innovation is observed in the context of higher education, it has been explored within the limitations of two mainstream bodies in the literature (Hasanefendic et al., 2017), one seeing IHE as a process of institutional adaptation to environmental challenges (Chatterton and Goddard, 2000) and the other seeing IHE as depending on the internal characteristics of HEIs (Kezar and Eckel, 2002). The role of these two literature bodies is to grasp both external (system) and internal (institutional, i.e. culture, identity and structure) features of universities that affect their ability to innovate and face environmental pressures. The first body of literature also describes that multiple governance adjustments and professional identities of organizational actors exist synchronously (Dee and Leišytė, 2016) to create novel and improved practices for innovation in order to face environmental challenges. These practices can be found in many levels and forms such as institutional structures and highe education curricula (Davis and Jacobsen, 2014; McClure, 2015). For instance, Merton et al. (2009) found that the norms and values of institutions affect the success of change and transformation. This is also argued by Fumasoli, Pinheiro and Stensaker (2015), who explain that institutional structures consist of authority, communication, rights and obligations, which impact the successful implementation of innovation at an institutional level, as the identity of HEIs is directly related to their strategy-creating capabilities. The second literature body also examines the role of university culture for innovation success (Kezar and Eckel, 2002).

When it comes to national social innovation, innovative capacity is strictly dependant on the institutions within the state (Van Waarden, 2001). Moreover, the quality of interactions and collaboration among institutions with a different role and contribution to the process of innovation in fact enhances innovative capacity. However, this depends on the context they operate in, as institutions can be more or less influenced by policies, regulations and norms (Van Waarden, 2001). The examination of the literature identified a positive relationship between investment in education and socio-economic development, as HEIs can be drivers of both growth and development for countries (Hasanefendic et al., 2017) because of their natural ability to innovate (Crosling, Nair and Vaithilingam, 2015). Higher education innovation is perceived as an outcome of changes in both economic and regional contexts in which HEIs are operating (Pinheiro, Geschwind and Aarrevaara, 2014; Pinheiro, Geschwind and Aarrevaara, 2016), as well as emerging from changes in public policies affecting HEIs (e.g. Richmond, 2015).

Results

Capturing the complexity of the phenomena of social innovation involves three main levels: system, institutional and individual (Jepperson and Meyer, 2011). Therefore, this systematic review synthesized the findings and classified the academic works conducted in the sphere of social IHE in accordance with these three levels. This chapter identifies both the empirical and non-empirical studies conducted in each of the categories, which are presented in Graph 5.1.

As can be seen from Graph 5.1, there is a vast deficit of empirical studies that examine IHE with a focus on the system. Only two studies were identified, both qualitative (Slantcheva-Durst, 2013; Wu, Chen and Chen, 2012), which do not provide the large enough scope needed for such research. In contrast to the number of empirical research papers with a system orientation, the number of non-empirical research papers with this orientation is relatively big and has increased in the last five years. This is not the case with the academic studies that focus on organization as the number of empirical articles and non-empirical articles is almost equal (eight and nine). Seven of eight studies are qualitative, except for the study of Saad, Guermat and Brodie (2015), which is quantitative. The work of Lašáková, Bajzíková and Dedze (2017) examines organizations from both Western and Eastern European contexts, which makes their work quite valuable. Yet there are limitations and disadvantages of their study, which will be discussed in the next section. When it comes to the last category of studies that focus on individuals, it can be stated that the research is sufficient.

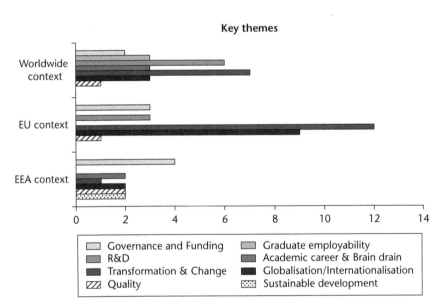

GRAPH 5.1 Focus and category of academic works examining innovation in the context of higher education

Although the number of empirical studies (five) is average, it can be still considered sufficient as it involves studies employing the three main types of research methodology: qualitative (Finch et al., 2016), quantitative (Kunnari and Ilomäki, 2016) and a mix of both (Al-Hussein and Elbeltagi, 2016). Overall, Graph 5.2 shows that most of the studies in each category were published recently. The number of

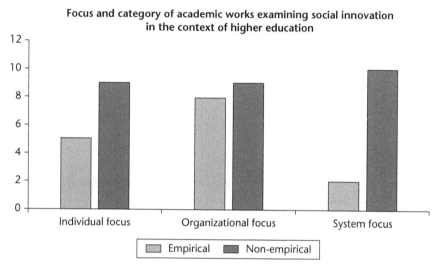

GRAPH 5.2   Summary of the focus and type of academic works examining social innovation in the context of higher education (n=43)

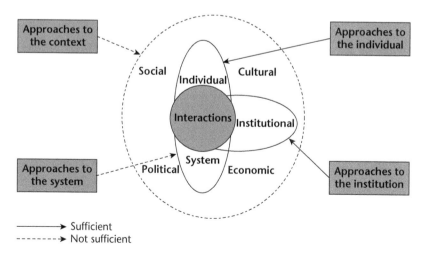

FIGURE 5.2   Summary of the research coverage in the literature examining social innovation in higher education

studies focusing on social innovation has increased in the last five years, which shows that the interest among researchers to examine IHE has been growing gradually over those five years.

Graph 5.2 summarizes the findings of the data analysis and synthesis of this systematic review. As can be seen from Figure 5.2, the research approach to the context in respect to social innovation is also included, as the role of the context in the examination of social innovation is crucial (Shaw and Bruin, 2013; Hasanefendic et al., 2017). There are studies researching social innovation from an individual (i.e. Hasanefendic et al., 2017; Saad, Guermat and Brodie, 2015) and institutional (i.e. Baumann et al., 2016; Davis and Jacobsen, 2014; McClure, 2015) perspectives. However, there is insufficient research examining social innovation from a system perspective.

Discussion and implications

Despite the growing interest among scholars and researchers in social innovation, there is a deficiency of empirical research examining it. Windrum et al. (2016), whose study on social innovation theories was also based on reviewing multiple case studies, claim that social innovation suffers from mis-measurement, as the research conducted on the phenomenon is mainly secondary. Social innovation has a young and unsettled history, which highlights the importance of both inter and multidisciplinary approaches (van der Have and Rubalcaba, 2016), as well as different contexts to be examined (Shaw and Bruin, 2013). The literature on social innovation in the context of higher education examined by this systematic review shows that there is a deficit of empirical studies, especially from a system perspective. Most of the empirical studies are qualitative (i.e. Baumann et al., 2016; Davis and Jacobson, 2014; Finch et al., 2016; Lašáková et al., 2017; McClure, 2015; Slantcheva-Durst, 2014; Wu, Chen and Chen, 2012), which offer the advantage of going beyond description and proposing insight on the context and process of social innovation for expanding the breadth of knowledge about contemporary significant phenomena like social innovation (Short, Moss, and Lumpkin, 2009). Yet quantitative research is critical, as it helps the researcher to achieve not only the depth but also the breadth of knowledge (Shaw and Bruin, 2013). This study identified a limited number of quantitative studies (i.e. Kunnari and Ilomäki, 2016; Saad et al., 2015). Last, Short et al. (2009) claim that there is a need for social innovation to be tested through a variety of research methods, including large-scale quantitative studies and longitudinal, case-based research.

This chapter also faced limitations, which resulted from the limited number of academic studies that focus on IHE and those which examine higher education systems in an Eastern European context. This is not surprising, as social IHE has been under studied, so efforts must be made in future. Future empirical research must be conducted to identify the barriers and drivers of innovation in an Eastern European context with a system orientation.

References

Adams, D., & Hess, M. (2010). Social innovation and why it has policy significance. *The Economic and Labour Relations Review, 21*(2), 17.

Al-Husseini, S., & Elbeltagi, I. (2016). Transformational leadership and innovation: A comparison study between Iraq's public and private higher education. *Studies in Higher Education, 41*(1), 159–181.

Barnett-Page, E., & Thomas, J. (2009). Methods for the synthesis of qualitative research: A critical review. *BMC medical research methodology, 9*(1), 59.

Baumann, T., Mantay, K., Swanger, A., Saganski, G., & Stepke, S. (2016). Education and innovation management: A contradiction? How to manage educational projects if innovation is crucial for success and innovation management is mostly unknown. *Procedia-Social and Behavioral Sciences, 226*, 243–251.

Boden, R., & Nedeva, M. (2010). Employing discourse: Universities and graduate 'employ-ability'. *Journal of Education Policy, 25*(1), 37–54.

Brown, S. L., & Eisenhardt, K. M. (1997). The art of continuous change: Linking complex-ity theory and time-paced evolution in relentlessly shifting organizations. *Administrative science quarterly*, 1–34.

Bruni, D. S., & Verona, G. (2009). Dynamic marketing capabilities in science-based firms: An exploratory investigation of the pharmaceutical industry. *British Journal of Management, 20*, S101-S117.

Cajaiba-Santana, G. (2014). Social innovation: Moving the field forward. A conceptual framework. *Technological Forecasting and Social Change, 82*, 42–51.

Chatterton, P., & Goddard, J. (2000). The response of higher education institutions to regional needs. *European Journal of Education, 35*(4), 475–496.

Crosling, G., Nair, M., & Vaithilingam, S. (2015). A creative learning ecosystem, quality of education and innovative capacity: A perspective from higher education. *Studies in Higher Education, 40*(7), 1147–1163.

Davis, S. N., & Jacobsen, S. K. (2014). Curricular integration as innovation: Faculty insights on barriers to institutionalizing change. *Innovative Higher Education, 39*(1), 17–31.

Dawson, P., Daniel, L., & Farmer, J. (2010). Special issue: Social innovation. *International Journal of Technology Management, 51*(1), 1–8.

Dee, J. R., & Leišytė, L. (2016). Organizational learning in higher education institutions: Theories, frameworks, and a potential research agenda. In *Higher education: Handbook of theory and research* (pp. 275–348). Cham: Springer.

Finch, D., Deephouse, D. L., O'Reilly, N., Massie, T., & Hillenbrand, C. (2016). Follow the leaders? An analysis of convergence and innovation of faculty recruiting practices in US business schools. *Higher Education, 71*(5), 699–717.

Fumasoli, T., Pinheiro, R., & Stensaker, B. (2015). Handling uncertainty of strategic ambitions: The use of organizational identity as a risk-reducing device. *International Journal of Public Administration, 38*(13–14), 1030–1040.

Hasanefendic, S., Birkholz, J. M., Horta, H., & van der Sijde, P. (2017). Individuals in action: Bringing about innovation in higher education. *European Journal of Higher Education, 7*(2), 101–119.

HESA. (2015). *Staff in Higher Education 2013–14.* Higher Education Statistics Agency. Retrieved from www.hesa.ac.uk/data-and-analysis/publications/higher-edu cation-2013-14/introduction

Huq, A., & Gilbert, D. H. (2013). Enhancing graduate employability through work-based learning in social entrepreneurship: A case study. *Education + Training, 55*(6), 550–572.

Ims, J. K., & Zsolnai, L. (2014). Ethics of social innovation. *Society and Business Review*, *9*(2), 186–194.

Ishengoma, E., & Vaaland, T. I. (2016). Can university-industry linkages stimulate student employability? *Education + Training*, *58*(1), 18–44

Jepperson, R., & Meyer, J. W. (2011). Multiple levels of analysis and the limitations of methodological individualisms. *Sociological Theory*, *29*(1), 54–73.

Jones, C. (2010). Entrepreneurship education: Revisiting our role and its purpose. *Journal of Small Business and Enterprise Development*, *17*(4), 500–513.

Kezar, A., & Eckel, P. D. (2002). The effect of institutional culture on change strategies in higher education: Universal principles or culturally responsive concepts? *The Journal of Higher Education*, *73*(4), 435–460.

Kunnari, I., & Ilomäki, L. (2016). Reframing teachers' work for educational innovation. *Innovations in Education and Teaching International*, *53*(2), 167–178.

Lašáková, A., Bajzíková, L'., & Dedze, I. (2017). Barriers and drivers of innovation in higher education: Case study-based evidence across ten European universities. *International Journal of Educational Development*, *55*, 69–79.

Maxwell, R., Irwin, W., & Bennett, S. (2015, October). When education met innovation met employability: The birth of employability plus. In *ECEL2015-14th European Conference on e-Learning: ECEl2015* (p. 347). Academic Conferences and Publishing Limited.

McClure, K. R. (2015). Exploring curricular transformation to promote innovation and entrepreneurship: An institutional case study. *Innovative Higher Education*, *40*(5), 429–442.

Merton, P., Froyd, J. E., Clark, M. C., & Richardson, J. (2009). A case study of relationships between organizational culture and curricular change in engineering education. *Innovative Higher Education*, *34*(4), 219–233.

Parra-Requena, G., Ruiz-Ortega, M. J., & Garcia-Villaverde, P. M. (2013). Social capital and effective innovation in industrial districts: Dual effect of absorptive capacity. *Industry and Innovation*, *20*(2), 157–179.

Peredo, A. M., & McLean, M. (2006). Social entrepreneurship: A critical review of the concept. *Journal of World Business*, *41*(1), 56–65.

Pinheiro, R., Geschwind, L., & Aarrevaara, T. (2014). Nested tensions and interwoven dilemmas in higher education: The view from the Nordic countries. *Cambridge Journal of Regions, Economy and Society*, *7*(2), 233–250.

Pinheiro, R., Geschwind, L., & Aarrevaara, T. (2016). Mergers in higher education. *European Journal of Higher Education*, *6*(1), 2–6.

Pol, E., & Ville, S. (2009). Social innovation: Buzz word or enduring term? *The Journal of Socio-Economics*, *38*(6), 878–885.

Rae, D. (2007). Connecting enterprise and graduate employability: Challenges to the higher education culture and curriculum? *Education + Training*, *49*(8/9), 605–619.

Rae, D. (2010). Universities and enterprise education: Responding to the challenges of the new era. *Journal of Small Business and Enterprise Development*, *17*(4), 591–606.

Rashman, L., Withers, E., & Hartley, J. (2009). Organizational learning and knowledge in public service organizations: A systematic review of the literature. *International Journal of Management Reviews*, *11*(4), 463–494.

Reeve, F., & Gallacher, J. (2005). Employer–university 'partnerships': A key problem for work-based learning programmes? *Journal of Education and Work*, *18*(2), 219–233.

Richmond, R. C. (2015). The future of the university is change. In G. A. Olson & J. W. Presley (Eds.), *Future of higher education: Perspectives from America's academic leaders* (pp. 31–41). New York: Routledge.

Saad, M., Guermat, C., & Brodie, L. (2015). National innovation and knowledge performance: The role of higher education teaching and training. *Studies in Higher Education, 40*(7), 1194–1209.

Shaw, E., & de Bruin, A. (2013). Reconsidering capitalism: The promise of social innovation and social entrepreneurship? *International Small Business Journal, 31*(7), 737–746.

Short, J. C., Moss, T. W., & Lumpkin, G. T. (2009). Research in social entrepreneurship: Past contributions and future opportunities. *Strategic Entrepreneurship Journal, 3*(2), 161–194.

Slantcheva-Durst, S. (2010). Chapter 1: Redefining short-cycle higher education across Europe: The challenges of Bologna. *Community College Review, 38*(2), 111–132.

Slantcheva-Durst, S. (2014). Mechanisms of lifelong learning: The spread of innovative short-cycle higher education qualifications within national systems. *Higher Education, 68*(1), 87–102.

Tranfield, D., & Mouchel, D. D. (2002). *Developing an evidence-based approach to management knowledge using systematic review.* Advanced Management Research Centre: Cranfield School of Management.

Tranfield, D., Denyer, D., & Smart, P. (2003). Towards a methodology for developing evidence-informed management knowledge by means of systematic review. *British Journal of Management, 14*(3), 207–222.

van der Have, R. P., & Rubalcaba, L. (2016). Social innovation research: An emerging area of innovation studies? *Research Policy, 45*(9), 1923–1935.

Van Waarden, F. (2001). Institutions and innovation: The legal environment of innovating firms. *Organization Studies, 22*(5), 765–795.

Windrum, P., Schartinger, D., Rubalcaba, L., Gallouj, F., & Toivonen, M. (2016). The co-creation of multi-agent social innovations: A bridge between service and social innovation research. *European Journal of Innovation Management, 19*(2), 150–166.

Wu, H. Y., Chen, J. K., & Chen, I. S. (2012). Ways to promote valuable innovation: Intellectual capital assessment for higher education system. *Quality & Quantity, 46*(5), 1377–1391.

Yorke, M. (2006). *Employability in higher education: What it is-what it is not* (Vol. 1). York: Higher Education Academy.

6

FACILITATING STUDENTS' (DOCTORAL) TRANSITION TO THE WORKPLACE

A critical review

Arvind Upadhyay, Vikas Kumar and Jose Arturo Garza-Reyes

Introduction

In a highly challenging and uncertain environment, the UK higher education system is going through very difficult times. Tuition fees paid directly by students across UK universities have risen significantly over the last few years, which puts intense pressure on students to excel in their education and to secure a good job after graduation. Within a university setting for an academic career, or in preparation for opportunities in the wider public and private sector workforce, students are seeking additional guidance that will help to prepare them for their future. Hence, universities must make sure that students get their money's worth and offer good career prospects advice after their degree. Doctoral researchers are an integral part of the student community, and they play an important role in carrying out teaching and research activities in UK universities. However, their active roles in teaching vary from university to university. Many fully funded doctoral researchers look to perform teaching-related duties as part of their funding contract, whereas others choose to get involved thinking about their future job prospects. It is well known that teaching experience is essential if one wants to build a career in academia. However, many PhD graduates also transition to jobs in the private corporate sector.

Research shows that the biggest growth in vacancies is expected in public sector organisations and high street and online retailers, which together intend to recruit over 1,200 extra graduates in 2017 (High Flyers Report, 2017). Some other key points from High Flyers reports are:

- In the past year, graduate recruiters made more use of social media, university recruitment presentations, skills training events and campus brand managers and did less advertising in career sector guides (p. 6).

- A total of 3,000 graduate positions will be available in accounting and professional services firms; public sector employers; engineering and private sector; and investment banks (p. 12).
- Over a third of recruiters involved in the research stated that graduates who have had no previous work experience at all are unlikely to be successful in securing a job offer for these organisations' graduate programmes (p. 24).

While some traditionalists uphold the view that the universities' focus should be on developing student researchers' knowledge of the discipline, it is increasingly acknowledged that universities have a responsibility to give opportunities to students to equip them with all necessary skill sets to make them employable in both public and private teaching and non-teaching organisations.

This chapter, therefore, sets out to explore the role that a PhD supervisor can play in responding to the broadening set of learning requirements that will support a successful transition to employment and the challenge facing the universities in equipping them.

From our experiences as academics, we believe it may be useful to explicitly explore behaviour in the context of students' employability. It broadens the CBI (2011) reference to a 'can-do' approach and Yorke's (2010) emphasis on graduate attributes.

There is also a need to focus on softer skills and behaviours in considering successful transition as research suggests: this concept that behaviour is even more important in today's organisations is outlined in three recent reports from the CIPD. *Real-life Leaders: Closing the Knowing-Doing Gap* (Zheltoukhova, 2013); *Managing for Sustainable Employee Engagement: Developing a Behavioural Framework* (Lewis et al., 2012) and *Using the Head and Heart at Work: A Business Case for Soft Skills* (McGurk, 2010) all emphasise the need for managers to recognise 'effective behaviours'. McGurk (2010) argues that it is the role of business schools to provide opportunities for students not only to be book-smart, but also to develop these behaviours for themselves. The Department of Business Innovation & Skills states that:

> Continued strong demand for graduates will rest on whether they are actually perceived as high quality in intellectual terms, but even more importantly whether they have the **communication** and **people skills** plus **positive work** ethics and **commercial attitudes**, which were the *'must have'* behaviours for employers.
>
> *(Pollard et al., 2015, p. 13)*

Supporting a focus on behaviours, Hinchliffe and Jolly (2011, p. 580) identified four types of experiences employers want graduates to demonstrate:

1. **Values** – personal ethical values and social awareness.
2. **Intellect** – covering capabilities such as the ability to think critically, analyse and communicate information, and challenge and bring new ideas.

3. **Performance** – the application of skills and intellect in the workplace.
4. **Engagement** – the willingness to meet personal, employment and social challenges head-on.

We would argue that behaviours are implicitly linked to each of these four areas outlined.

Universities have career services that focus on improving the job prospects of the students, which include careers education and understanding which options best suit them; helping students better understand themselves through self-reflection; learning about their personal drivers and motivation; and practical job application skills. Job competencies are learned through experience and have been defined as "one of the sets of behaviours that the person must display in order to perform the tasks and functions of a job with competence". Each competency is a discrete dimension of behaviour; as Woodruffe (2007, p. 82) states, "The word competency has become an acceptable label for what assessment and development centre measures".

According to the Higher Education Funding Council for England (HEFCE), more than 130 universities have signed up to participate in the Teaching Excellence Framework (TEF). One of the assessment criteria is student experience and employability. As a result, all academic institutions in the UK are concerned about their students' experience and employability. It is widely known in academic spheres that qualifications help people to progress but not in isolation (Blackmore & Kandiko, 2012). Hence, academic institutions are keen on finding innovative ways to improve the employability of their students by improving their transferable skills (Bloxham & Boyd, 2011). Research studies have shown that innovative teaching methods combined with external engagement and internationalisation of the curriculum leads to a smooth transition for students towards a successful career path (Leask, 2008).

Madeleine Atkins, CEO of HEFCE, said that if students seeking employment can display innate capacities for work, communication and leadership skills, analytical thinking and problem-solving, they may be able to gain employment in an environment that will then provide the training they need to become capable in relevant jobs (Brown & Race, 2013; Repko, 2011). All these skills can be developed by proper planning and engaging students in experiences in the early stages of their university career. This might be enough to worry anyone preparing to cope with the overwhelming first weeks at university, but it need not be the case. With a little application in the first year, students can confront and plan for a career without 'cramping their style' (Hunt et al., 2013; Land, 2013). Waters (2009) reported that the employability of young graduates is increasingly dependent upon their ability to maintain 'positional advantage' in a labour market. As a result, a number of students pursue postgraduate qualifications, and many attempt this through the acquisition of an international degree from an overseas institution. The UK, being one of the most popular destinations for overseas students, attracts several thousand students every year. According to the UK Council for

International Student Affairs (UKCISA) in 2015 to 2016, around 438,010 non-UK students entered into UK higher education institutions. Around half of these non-UK students (199,730) were admitted for the higher degrees (postgraduate) (HESA, 2015–2016). Surprisingly, around 11,000 students each from the UK and non-UK obtained higher degrees in research (doctoral degree). This shows that research degrees are equally popular among students regardless of whether they are domestic or overseas students.

It is evident from discussions that it is important for universities to work hard, to develop both hard and soft skills among their students. This will help them to develop once they embark on their careers. This study focuses specifically on the career development of postgraduate research students. There have been some studies that have focused on addressing the support and learning of postgraduate research students (Ali et al., 2016; Grant et al., 2014; Leonard et al., 2006). For example, Grant et al. (2014) attempted to explore the role that postgraduate supervisors play in successful doctoral thesis completion through advising, mentoring and monitoring. The next section describes the methodology adopted in this study, which is followed by findings and discussions.

Methodology

The research methodology adopted a combination of synthesis of literature and face-to-face interviews with students and faculty members. A total number of 28 interviews were conducted with staff and PhD students. This included interviewing 18 PhD students and 10 staff who were involved in the supervision.

The research study was conducted with students and staff from three UK universities. The context for this work is a Business School in a university. The postgraduate research environment is facilitated by the university's Doctoral College, a collective of research degree students, their supervisors, director of postgraduate studies and specialist research degree administrators. All postgraduate research students are members of the Doctoral College.

In the Business School, research is taking the centre stage and various research clusters have developed in recent years (Friga et al., 2003). The Doctoral College Centre within the Business School is focused around different research centres doing research work on contemporary business problems.

The study relies on both primary and secondary data. In order to understand how successful transition of PhD students to the workplace can be facilitated, it was considered important to investigate the role of supervisors. The primary and secondary research was carried out to find out the skills and knowledge necessary to become a good PhD supervisor. The interviews were conducted with PhD supervisors and PhD students within the Business School where most of the data was collected. The secondary research involved a review of academic literature and higher education (HE) and university policy documents.

For the purposes of the study, the PhD supervisor was expected to have adequate subject knowledge. They were required to understand the rules and regulations of a PhD programme, supervision process and academic practices, and also have the interpersonal skills to interact with the students. Research is now seen as an important strategic activity epitomised in the university's Strategic Plan.

Findings and discussion

Skills and knowledge necessary to be a good PhD supervisor

Understanding of a PhD programme's rules and regulations

Our study found that the PhD supervisor's training tends to focus on institutional requirements and the formal aspect of doctoral supervision (Whitelock et al., 2008). This has an impact on PhD students' progress in the PhD programme. Institutional requirements include bureaucratic documentation and red tape, which undermines function, social and project management skills. The complexity of the research development requirements takes its toll on the quality of PhD supervision (Gurr, 2001). However, for the success of any PhD programme, a supervisor should have a thorough understanding of the institution's rules and regulations in context with the specific PhD programme.

PhD supervision process and structure

The critical issue in PhD supervision is how the supervisor and student's research interests match with each other and the way they handle the research. Franke and Arvidsson (2010) introduced a novel concept of different PhD supervision experiences, and they found that there are two broad supervision structures: research practice-oriented and research relation-oriented supervision. The main difference between these two approaches is whether the supervisor and student share a common research goal, objective and practice, or not. If the research goal, objective and practice do not match, then it is difficult for the student to complete the PhD programme in the given time. The need here is to match the supervisor's research goal with the student's research goal, and only then can both work in the same direction (Appel & Bergenheim 2005; Lönn Svensson, 2007). If there are differences between the research approaches of supervisor and student, it becomes difficult to successfully complete the research in the given time frame.

Understating of academic practices

The difference between supervisor and student can emerge not only due to the differences between research approach and goal, but also due to some other factors, as well. Mitchell and Carroll (2007) discussed unacceptable research practices and compromised standards which are unacceptable within the research community, awarding body and wider research context. Then the situations arise where both supervisor and students find themselves in a different type of relationship due to the unacceptable research practices and academic misconduct. New PhD supervisors are poorly trained in dealing with academic misconduct due to lack of engagement with regulatory bodies, lack of cross-cultural understanding (in situations where the PhD supervisor and student are from different cultural backgrounds) and not clearly understanding the meaning of academic theft.

Personal experience as PhD student

Lee (2008) states that a supervisor can make or break a PhD student's research journey. Hence, a supervisor plays a vital role in PhD studies. Lee (2008) further adds that a PhD supervisor's supervision skills are influenced by two key things: firstly, their concept of research supervision, and secondly, their own experience as a doctoral student.

Pearson and Brew (2002) worked on skills and knowledge required by PhD supervisors, and later, Lee (2007) worked on the same issue and developed a framework. Table 6.1 shows the framework adopted and developed from Pearson and Brew (2002) and from Lee (2007) for this work, and it is referenced later in the chapter as a comparator for the findings in our study.

Halse (2011) pointed out that supervising PhD students' theses affects the supervisors' learning. It is not just the PhD student who learns from being supervised but also their PhD supervisor. Increase in the accountability and quality in the HE sector more widely also requires PhD supervisors to learn and update their skill set.

One of our interviewees pointed out that there was not much emphasis on the supervisor's training 25 years ago.

> When I started PhD student supervision 25 years ago, there was hardly anything for new PhD supervisors. It was more like learning by doing and I learned over a period of time sometimes by my own mistakes and sometimes by other's mistakes.
>
> *(Reader, Social Science)*

The above statement is a clear indication of how the academic environment has changed in the UK over the last 25 years. Earlier, there was not much emphasis

TABLE 6.1 Profile compiled for PhD supervisor's skills and knowledge

Profile Compiled for PhD Supervisor's Skills and Knowledge			
Skills $\rightarrow$	*Project Management*	*Critical Analysis/ thinking*	*Building Relationship*
PhD Supervisor (Profile compiled)	Guiding, directing and managing PhD thesis project	Developing arguments, being reflective	Staying emotionally strong, emotional intelligence

Source: Adopted and developed from Pearson and Brew (2002) and Lee (2007).

placed on training PhD supervisors, but now, with growing expectation from students and academic bodies, this is central. The result is clearer guidance and more training available for PhD supervisors: reflected in the training offers made to PhD supervisors in our participating universities.

Another interviewee said,

> I feel myself as a curious student when I go to attend these supervisors' refresher courses and there is always something new to learn. I learnt something new from every refresher course which I attended over the last ten years.
>
> *(Senior Lecturer, Business School)*

It suggests that there is always potentially something new to learn from these refresher courses, and as such, they can add value to the PhD supervisor's portfolio.

Evaluation

The next part of the study consists of the evaluation of skills, knowledge and experience required of supervisors against the emerging profile generated from the literature review and research interviews.

Understating of PhD programme's rules and regulations

As a new employee to the Business School and a PhD supervisor, it is necessary to know the roles and responsibilities of a PhD supervisor. The Doctoral College or equivalent department is the central body of a university which keeps the latest information and updates at a national and international level in doctoral education. They also provide the training and refresher course to new PhD supervisors. The main aim is to inform the new rules and regulations and to discuss new issues. These may include:

- Doctoral College and what can it do for PhD supervisors?
- Research Plan Approval (RPA): how important is this stage of a research degree and what are the key elements of an RPA?
- Update to current processes and protocols: student progression from induction to examination – what has and hasn't changed?
- Fostering researcher development.

Subject specialism of supervisor

For a PhD student, their supervisor is the main source of information for all the queries linked with their research area. Hence, a PhD supervisor should have in-depth knowledge of the research area and also the cognate area (Gill & Burnard, 2008). In the Business School, there is an emergence of cross-disciplinary PhDs having the main focus on management discipline but also linked with other areas, for example, psychology, environment technology, industrial engineering and so on. In such cases, the supervisor's job becomes more challenging to guide the PhD students. As one of the interviewees put forward in their own words,

> The supervision process has changed over a period of time, earlier it was more individual subject-specific research, but nowadays the research is more cross-disciplinary in nature. This change in research pattern is posing a challenge to PhD supervisors in their supervision.
>
> *(PhD Supervisor, Business School)*

PhD supervision process and structure

The Researcher Development Framework (RDF) was developed from empirical studies (Bray & Boon, 2011). These characteristics are placed in four domains and 12 sub-domains encompassing functional knowledge, intellectual ability and professional standards to do research as well as to work with others (Vitae, 2010). Vitae is the first point of contact/guide for anybody who is interested in academic research in the UK. As one of our interviewees points out,

> Vita is the first thing we tell about our research students in the UK. As the number of international students on PhD programmes are increasing, it becomes necessary to inform them about the UK PhD structure and process. The same thing applies to PhD supervisors as well, now there are lots of PhD supervisors who didn't complete their PhD in the UK so they are not familiar with the UK PhD supervision structure. Hence it becomes important to inform them about the UK system of PhD supervision process.
>
> *(Principal Lecturer, Business School)*

Experience of international students in UK context

International students constitute a major strength in postgraduate teaching and research student groups (Ryan & Viete, 2009). One of the universities in the study has an international service desk which helps international students to settle into both the university and the city. International students in the study reported feeling deserted and depressed after a certain period of time. This is illustrated by the quotation below from one of the research students interviewed. Completion of a PhD needs intensive self-study and motivation, which is difficult for some international students who are not settled into student life, and this takes a toll on their studies.

> After arriving in the UK, I had to go through lots of bureaucratic processes, e.g. residence permit, registration with police, finding accommodation, opening bank account etc. and it affected my initial weeks of study period.
>
> *(International PhD Student, Business School)*

Understating of academic practices

To understand the academic practice in a specific university takes time. The academic practices followed by different universities are sometimes different from each other, but in a broad sense, they have very similar structures. Some of these practices may be learned from colleagues (other senior PhD supervisors within the Business School). During the interviews, one of the PhD supervisors pointed out that

> PhD supervision is a learning process and you learn something new with each new PhD student you supervise. So the more you supervise, the more you learn.
>
> *(Senior Lecturer, Business School)*

Cultural differences between supervisors and supervisees

Culture is an understated factor in PhD supervision (Cargill, 1998; Sinclair, 2004), and most of the time, universities do not focus on it. The Doctoral College, which is part of this study, does not have any specific guidelines for addressing cross-cultural issues in supervision. However, international students do feel the cultural differences with their supervisors, as illustrated by the quotation from one student outlined below. In the Business School, there are PhD students from different parts of the world, for example, the Middle East, South America, Africa, Asia and so on, and the culture and teaching atmosphere in their native countries is likely to be quite different from the UK. In such cases, students may feel stressed at times, as they may not be able to understand the non-verbal and local cultural norms.

> The teacher-student relationship is very different here as compared to my home country in the Middle East. Sometimes, it's hard for me to understand non-verbal communication due to the cultural differences.
>
> *(PhD Student, Business School)*

This highlights the need for PhD supervisors to have received appropriate training to understand and be able to support students whose experience prior to their current placement has been different.

Personal experience as a PhD student

Personal experiences as a PhD student play a vital role in taking the position of a PhD supervisor (Gibbs & Griffin, 2013). We can look at and understand the need of a PhD student in a better manner. The UK Professional Standard Framework is really helpful in understanding the UK PhD system, but effective management of the needs of PhD students goes beyond professional standards frameworks. We interviewed some PhD students who are currently enrolled in a PhD programme, and one of them said,

> As an international PhD student, I find it really difficult to understand the expectation of my supervisor. There are certain rules but still, there are lots of unsaid rules and expectations which are prevalent in the UK PhD system. And as English is not my mother tongue so it becomes difficult to read between the lines.
>
> *(PhD Student)*

This highlights the need for research students to specifically focus on research beyond their subject area, also needing to take the time to better understand the different regulatory systems here in the UK. By doing this, they will be in a better position to operate more effectively within these parameters. This requires a proactive mind-set on the part of the student to recognise and acknowledge these cultural differences and then act accordingly, seeking to better understand the local context and how to operate effectively within it. All of this, in turn, will link into the future employability of the student; in particular, it links to the need to focus on behaviour as a key feature of any approach, as referenced earlier in the study.

Move from dissertation to research paper approach

There has been a shift in the PhD programme in the UK over the past decade, a shift from a British approach to PhD programmes to an American approach to the PhD system (Connor, 2016). Largely, the British approach has historically focused on dissertation/thesis work after performing research work for three years. While in the American system of PhD, the focus is on publishing the three papers during the PhD period (Davies & Rolfe, 2009). As mentioned by one of the interviewees,

> Over the last decade I saw the change in the approach of Universities towards the PhD programme, now the focus is more on publishing the papers during the PhD programme and it's affecting the type of supervision. Now I ask my PhD students to focus on a publication from the very first day.
>
> *(Professor)*

In higher academic employment, there is an increasing focus on publication and its benefits to the university through improving reputation and therefore sustainable student recruitment. In the international, competitive market, flexibility and multiple focus is increasingly important.

Doctoral College role

At one university in this study, the Doctoral College has changed the PhD supervision process. Now it is a more structured and continuous overview of a student's progress in the PhD programme. Supervision is more specific and

TABLE 6.2 Evaluation of current knowledge, experience and skills against the profile compiled in Table 6.1 on Role Profile page

Skills →	Project Management	Critical Analysis/ Thinking	Building Relationship
PhD Supervisor (Profile compiled from literature review) (knowledge, experience and skills)	Guiding, directing and managing PhD thesis project **Yes** (Doctoral College helped to gain these skills)	Developing arguments, being reflective **Yes** (Own experience as PhD student)	Staying emotionally strong, emotional intelligence **Ongoing** (Support from peer supervisors/ colleagues)

timely, and continuous review of progress means focus on quality from both sides. One interviewee said,

> The PhD programme at Business School is more structured nowadays, and the credit goes to Doctoral College which streamlined the whole PhD supervision system. It helps both PhD students as well as supervisors to stay focused on their respective roles. Before the Doctoral College, things were not very clear in terms of PhD supervision.
>
> *(Principal Lecturer, Business School)*

This highlights the additional opportunity to reflect on skills development and necessary guidance throughout the process. The whole process is reflective and responsive, enabling continuous skills improvement for both student and supervisor.

Role of Research Excellence Framework

The Research Excellence Framework (REF) has changed the research scenario in UK HE institutions over the past three years. It replaced the RAE (Research Assessment Exercise) in 2014, which itself had been introduced in 1986. Regularly reviewed and updated, it is the new system of assessing the quality of research in the UK. Funding bodies in the UK use the outcome of REF to allocate funding to HE institutions (REF, 2014). Research output from PhD supervision is well considered as part of the REF output. Hence, there is a strong focus on PhD supervision resulting in publications, and supervisors should guide the PhD students in such a way that they can publish in journals which are eligible for consideration in the REF. Table 6.2 illustrates and evaluates the students' learning profiles as identified in the study against the profiles compiled from literature reviews and interviews.

Discussion and implication

The study provides an overview of the challenges facing doctoral students in their transition to the workplace and some of the considerations that can enable positive transition. Many PhD positions are paid (funded scholarships) and hence require doctoral students to undertake teaching/consultancy responsibilities in return, thus providing work experience in an academic environment. Some PhDs are also funded by industry, where students spend a substantial amount of time, providing relevant industrial experience. The PhD journey needs to be managed dependent on students' goals. Who are the key players in this journey? What role do they play in shaping their career pathways? What skill sets do they need?

These considerations are applicable to any HE institution in the UK and to other countries where the academic system is similar. In some academic institutions, student placement is an integral part of both undergraduate and postgraduate programmes. Good guidance prior to placement can lead to a relevant job offer at the end of the placement term. There are specially designed manuals and literature (that are sometimes outdated) available in most universities regarding this. As institutions, we need to keep an eye on new trends in employment and the key skills which employers seek in their employees, and ensure that this is reflected in the student offer, from undergraduate through to PhD level.

Research students are expected to engage in the programme, during which they gain a range of valuable skills in addition to the in-depth knowledge and understanding of their research topic. Skills development and understanding of work culture has a critical part to play in their employability in academia and in industry. It is well recognised that employers both within and outside of academia place great importance in, and recognise the value of, developed transferable skills in prospective employees.

By planning and undertaking the right training, and thinking about their professional personal development, students can significantly improve their transition and employability.

Limitations and future research

The research work is based in only three academic institutions' Business Schools, so the results are likely to be applicable for similar institutions in the UK only. We cannot generalise and assume these results will apply in a wider context, as academic systems are different in different countries. Therefore, future research studies need to include bigger sample sizes to widen relevance. Two potential research areas could be professional doctorate programmes, which is sometimes called a Doctor of Business Administration (DBA), and part-time PhDs.

Students who enrol in a DBA programme are expected to be in employment during the course of their programme. In these cases, students have the challenge of balancing work and academic requirements.

There is a growing number of students who prefer to go for part-time PhD studies because they have competing commitments outside of their academic studies. These students have very different needs compared to their full-time equivalents, but there is not enough research to show the variety of issues and impact on transition, for example, those students already working but in a different field to their studies.

References

Ali, P. A., Watson, R., & Dhingra, K. (2016) Postgraduate research students' and their supervisors' attitudes towards supervision, *International Journal of Doctoral Studies, 11*, 227–241.

Appel, M., & Bergenheim, A. (2005) *Reflecting research supervision*. Lund: Studentlitteratur.

Blackmore P., & Kandiko, C. B. (2012) *Strategic curriculum change: Global trends in universities*. Abingdon, Oxon: Routledge.

Bloxham, S., & Boyd, P. (2011) *Developing effective assessment in higher education: A practical guide*. Berkshire: Open University Press.

Bray, R., & Boon, S. (2011) Towards a framework for research career development: An evaluation of the UK's vitae researcher development framework. *International Journal for Researcher Development, 2*(2), 99–116.

Brown, S., & Race, P. (2013) Using effective assessment to promote learning. *University Teaching in Focus*. London: Routledge.

Cargill, M. (1998) Cross-cultural postgraduate supervision meetings as intercultural communication. In *Quality in postgraduate research: managing the new agenda*, Proceedings of the 1998 Quality in Postgraduate Research Conference, 175–187.

CBI (2011) *Working towards your future: Making the most of your time in higher education*. London: CBI. [online] http://aces.shu.ac.uk/employability/resources/CBI_NUS_Employability%20report_May%202011.pdf [accessed 02/01/13].

Connor, T. (2016) PhD by publication. *The Legal Academic's Handbook, 28*.

Davies, R. E., & Rolfe, G. (2009) PhD by publication: A prospective as well as a retrospective award? Some subversive thoughts, *Nurse Education Today, 29*(6), 590–594.

Franke, A., & Arvidsson, B. (2010) Research supervisor's different ways of experiencing supervision of doctoral students. *Studies in Higher Education, 36*(1), 7–19.

Friga, P. N., Bettis, R. A., & Sullivan, R. S. (2003) Changes in graduate management education and new business school strategies for the 21st century. *Academy of Management Learning & Education, 2*(3), 233–249.

Gibbs, K. D., & Griffin, K. A. (2013) What do I want to be with my PhD? The roles of personal values and structural dynamics in shaping the career interests of recent biomedical science PhD graduates. *CBE-Life Sciences Education, 12*(4), 711–723.

Gill, P., & Burnard, P. (2008) The student-supervisor relationship in the PhD/doctoral process. *British Journal of Nursing, 17*(10), 668–672.

Grant, K., Hackney, R., & Edgar, D. (2014) Postgraduate research supervision: An 'agreed' conceptual view of good practice through derived metaphors. *International Journal of Doctoral Studies, 9*, 43–60.

Gurr, G. M. (2001) Negotiating the "Rackety Bridge": A dynamic model for aligning supervisory style with research student development. *Higher Education Research & Development, 20*(1), 81–92.

Halse, C. (2011) Becoming a supervisor: The impact of doctoral supervision on supervisors' learning. *Studies in Higher Education, 36*, 557–570.

HESA Statistics (n.d.) *Introduction*. [online] www.hesa.ac.uk/data-and-analysis/publications/students-2015-16/introduction [accessed on 02/11/17].

High Flyers (2017) *The graduate market in 2016*. London: High Flyers Research. [online] www.highfliers.co.uk/download/2017/graduate_market/GMReport17.pdf [accessed 11/06/17].

Hinchliffe, G. W., & Jolly, A. (2011) Graduate identity and employability. *British Educational Research Journal, 37*(4), 563–584.

Hunt, L., Chalmers, D., & Macdonald, R. (2013) Effective classroom teaching. *University teaching in focus*. London: Routledge.

Land, R. (2013) Discipline-based teaching. *University teaching in focus*. London: Routledge.

Leask, B. (2008) Internationalisation, globalisation and curriculum innovation. *Researching international pedagogies: Sustainable practice for teaching and learning in higher education*, 9–26. UK: Springer.

Lee, A. (2007) Developing effective supervisors concepts of research supervision. *South African Journal of Higher Education, 21*(4), 680–693.

Lee, A. (2008) How are doctoral students supervised? Concepts of doctoral research supervision. *Studies in Higher Education, 33*(3), 267–281.

Leonard, D., Metcalfe, J., Becker, R., & Evans, J. (2006) *Review of literature on the impact of working context and support on the postgraduate research student learning experience.* New York, NY: The Higher Education Academy.

Lewis, R., Donaldson-Feilder, E., & Tharani, T. (2012) *Managing for sustainable employee engagement: Developing a behavioural framework, CIPD research report.* [online] www.cipd.co.uk/binaries/6067%20Sustainable%20engagement%20RI%20(WEB).pdf [accessed on 02/01/13].

Lönn Svensson, A. (2007) It depends. *Experienced research supervisors' views on good supervision.* Borås: Borås University.

McGurk, J. (2010) Using the head and heart at work: A business case for soft skills. CIPD research report. [online] www.cipd.co.uk/NR/rdonlyres/18616949-CF66-47F8-A088-7C8FF2D864E0/0/HeadandheartguideFINAL.pdf [accessed 30/09/12].

Mitchell, T., & Carroll, J. (2007) Academic and research misconduct in the PhD: Issues for students and supervisors. *Nurse Education Today, 28*(2), 218–226.

Pearson, M., & Brew, A. (2002) Research training and supervision development. *Studies in Higher Education, 27*, vol. 2, 135–50.

Pollard, E., Hirsh, W., Williams, M., Jonathan, B., Marvell, R., Tassinari, A., & Ball, C. (2015) *Understanding employers' graduate recruitment and selection practices. BIS Research Paper 231.* [online] www.employment-studies.co.uk/resource/understanding-employers%E2%80%99-graduate-recruitment-and-selection-practices [accessed 15/12/16].

REF (2014) *Information for research users.* [online] www.ref.ac.uk/users/ [accessed 20/05/14].

Repko, A. F. (2011) *Interdisciplinary research: Process and theory* (2nd ed.). London: Sage Publication.

Ryan, J., & Viete, R. (2009) Respectful interactions: Learning with international students in the English-speaking academy. *Teaching in Higher Education, 14*(3), 303–314.

Sinclair, M. (2004) *The pedagogy of good PhD supervision: A national cross-disciplinary investigation of PhD supervision.* Canberra: Department of Education, Science and Training.

Vitae (2010) *Careers Research and Advisory Centre (CRAC) Limited.* [online] www.vitae.ac.uk/RDF [accessed 17/05/14].

Waters, J. L. (2009) In pursuit of scarcity: Transnational students, 'employability', and the MBA. *Environment and Planning A, 41*(8), 1865–1883.

Whitelock, D., Faulkner, D., & Miell, D. (2008) Promoting creativity in PhD supervision: Tensions and dilemmas. *Thinking Skills and Creativity, 3*, 143–153.

Woodruffe, C. (2007) *Development and assessment centres* (4th ed.). London: Human Assets.

Yorke, M. (2010) Employability: Aligning the message, the medium and academic values. *Journal of Teaching and Learning for Graduate Employability, 1*(1), 2–12. [online] http://jtlge.curtin.edu.au/index.php/jtlge/article/view/7 [accessed 24/09/14].

Zheltoukhova, K. (2013) *Real-life leaders: Closing the knowing-doing gap.* CIPD Research Report. [online] www.cipd.co.uk/binaries/6303%20Leadership%20report%20%28WEB%29.pdf [accessed 26/09/14].

7

LEADING INNOVATION CENTRES IN HIGHER EDUCATION INSTITUTIONS IN DEVELOPING COUNTRIES

Ensuring graduate employability

Val Quimno and Dennis Alonzo

Introduction

The drive for graduate employability and skills alignment to industry needs provided the impetus for many higher education institutions (HEIs) in developing countries to establish innovation centres which aimed at improving institutional research, industry collaboration and the innovation portfolio. Such initiatives are mostly patterned from HEIs in developed countries, adopting their current models and processes. However, despite emulating best practices from the US and UK, HEIs in developing countries are fraught with immense difficulties in leading and managing innovation centres due to the lack of context-based frameworks for successful implementation. This is because there is a dearth of literature around this area in the context of developing countries. Research along this line intensely focuses on the intersection of research, entrepreneurship, consultancy, barriers and advantages, but not in the context of employability (Ashraf et al., 2018).

We present the concept of employability through innovation in HEIs in developing countries to highlight the critical role of university-industry linkages in developing entrepreneurial and leadership skills of students that potentially enhance their employability (Ashraf et al., 2018). Accordingly, there is a big challenge for universities in developing countries to develop competency that translates to employability. In addition, we want to examine the need for further studies in this area in the context of developing countries because, despite the growing interests in innovations, as benchmarked to the successes of this endeavour in developed countries, there is scant literature that focuses on innovation and employability in this context. From our literature search in academic databases (ERIC, Web of Science, Emerald, ScienceDirect, Taylor & Francis, Scopus), no journal article dealing with innovation and employability in developing countries was found from leading education and information systems journals.

The purpose of this chapter is therefore to portray the current landscape of research on innovations and employability in the context of HEIs in developing countries. We examine the theories related to innovation and employability and attempt to analyse the trends by identifying key areas for further research and development. We envisage encouraging future research, aimed at filling the gaps, expanding the coverage of important but relatively neglected topics and stimulating further debate on relevant topics and research approaches under this domain. As such, there are two overarching questions that this chapter aims to uncover: (1) What has existing research in developing countries identified in terms of innovation and employability? and (2) What are the typical characteristics and trends of arrangements for innovation within the higher education and industry sphere within developing countries?

In the succeeding sections, we present our methodology in reviewing the literature. This is followed by discussing the major trends, including the employability and HEIs, innovation and science and technology, and innovation in developing countries. Lastly, the chapter concludes with a recommendation for an innovation and employability framework in HEIs in developing countries.

Method

Systematic review methods allow a comprehensive assessment of a particular topic by applying rigorous, objective and transparent procedures and criteria for reaching conclusions from a body of scientific literature (Petticrew & Roberts, 2006). By conducting a systematic review, intentional or unintentional bias in the selection of publications can be avoided by identifying all potentially relevant literature through transparent and explicit procedures. The systematic approach brings more reliability as the outcome is reproducible. It enables identification of areas where substantial progress has been made and where future research could be directed (De Vries, Bekkers, & Tummers, 2016; Voorberg, Bekkers, & Tummers, 2015).

In this chapter, a systematic approach prescribed by Okoli and Schabram (2010) was used to conduct the literature review. First, the purpose of the review was clearly laid out at the onset. Then, a review protocol was designed to ensure a transparent and rigorous selection of studies related to employability and innovation in developing countries from 2000 to present was covered. The systematic approach helped to locate articles related to innovation and employability in the context of higher education in developing countries. The search terms were kept deliberately broad to cover the full range of studies that address employability and innovation. A Boolean search was carried out using the keywords (employ* AND (developing countr* OR developing nation* OR developing world) AND (innovat*)). This search string was used because there are articles that cloak into some other terms such as employment, employ, employability, employable, innovate, innovation and innovativeness. The authors acknowledge that these terms do not necessarily have the same meaning, but it is crucial to perform the said search to possibly cover a wide range of articles reviewed in this chapter. Further filtering was done in the initial search result, and relevant articles were selected. Articles that have an employability and innovation focus but with a different country setting were excluded from the analysis. However, these articles served as a background reference to support some assertions given that only a few literature was found in the context of developing countries. The searches were made on the title, keywords and abstract only, which yielded 162 articles from eight databases, namely, ERIC, ScienceDirect, Scopus, Sage, Web of Science, Taylor and Francis, Emerald and JSTOR databases. These databases were selected as they offer concise and structured search results related to the topic. The articles' journal outlets are varied. However, leading education journals based on Scimago rankings 2018 – *Research Synthesis Methods*, *Review of Educational Research*, *Educational Researcher*, *Learning and Instruction*, *Internet and Higher Education*, *Sociology of Education*, *Studies in Science Education*, *Journal of Second Language Writing*, *Educational Evaluation and Policy Analysis* and *Educational Research Review* – were included in the review.

The authors brought no *a priori* theory or hypothesis in this research but focused on the content analysis of 162 research papers as the best way of revealing and understanding the current status of employability and innovation research in developing countries. Content analysis has been presented as both a positivist (Neuendorf, 2002) and constructionist (Jankowicz, 2000) technique. The combination of these techniques lends strong support from Heeks and Bailur (2007), who argue that content analysis can be approached from either position. Our approach to content analysis in this research lies in between positivism and interpretivism, which is aligned with our research philosophies.

Employability and higher education in developing countries

Employability is an individual's attribute that makes them marketable and employable based on a certain skill set. Employability "refers to a graduate's achievements and his/her potential to obtain a 'graduate job', and should not be confused with the actual acquisition of a 'graduate job'" (Yorke, 2006, p. 4). In other words, it relates to gaining relevant competencies that enable individuals to obtain initial employment and maintain that employment across varying job roles within an organization (Berntson, 2008). Therefore, employability is not just a transfer of knowledge and skills, but it is a product of complex learning process where students are provided with a range of opportunities to develop also general skills that are necessary for the labour market.

Developing employable citizens who are ready for the competitive global job market remains a big challenge for governments. One of the primary issues of employment in the global job market is attributed to education (Kapoor, Weerakkody, & Schroeder, 2018). In developing countries, for instance, several initiatives have been devised to improve the employability of citizens through educational systems such as those described in the study of Sinha (2018) in Myanmar, Li-Hua, Li, Aouad, and Wilson (2011) in China, Barnard and Van der Merwe (2016a) and Molla and Cuthbert (2016) in South Africa and Gangi (2017) in Qatar. This is because access to good-quality education is one of the most effective ways of preparing the students to become employed or empowering them to be self-employed (Nyika, 2015). Developing an enabling environment that nurtures enterprise creation and investment through innovation centres and technology hubs could propel economic growth enough to create jobs for the growing number of youth (Kararach, Hanson, & Léautier, 2011). It is therefore critical that graduates of HEIs in developing countries are competitive in terms of their job-related knowledge and skills in order to get employment or to create their own employment as entrepreneurs. Matsheke and Dhurup (2017) argued that entrepreneurial education is one of the keys in unlocking the economic and unemployment challenge.

In spite of the potential of relevant and good-quality education to develop the future workforce for industry, this is not always translated into actual employment. For instance, researchers have identified that the future of the Indian Information Technology-Business Process Outsourcing (IT-BPO) industry relies heavily on quality workforce as they drive creativity and innovation (Sharma, 2014). However, it was found that there is a mismatch in knowledge and skills acquired in HEIs and what the industry needs. Industries often require a range of soft skills in addition to other areas such as creativity, communication and analytical and critical thinking skills. As such, HEIs need to integrate the acquisition and development of these skills to their curricula to support the employment of graduates to ensure they are more employable or productive (Kishore, 2013).

Apart from the skills mismatch, most developing countries are experiencing varying levels of employment issues. These are caused by several factors including problems in the supply of skills – attributed to the quality of education systems and low employability of individuals (Valiente, 2014), increasing competition caused by globalization (Jules & Sundberg, 2018) and technological advancements in commercial and industrial processes. To some extent, these trends lead to diminishing worker requirements. In addition, the 'brain drain' in the scientific and technical sectors in some developing countries appears to be problematic as knowledge and technical capabilities seem to veer away outside of the host country due to the disparity of salary packages given by employers in developed countries (Kong, Chadee, & Raman, 2013).

As such, what is needed in developing countries, apart from a well-structured education system that prepares the next generation of employees ready for the job marketplace, is the government's reconsideration of their employment and job policies to retain individuals who have the potential to drive economic growth. In addition, to ensure graduate employability, there is a need for the government to establish an educational system whose curricular offerings are demand driven and responsive to the dynamic needs of the job markets (Nyika, 2015).

Conceptualization of innovation

Everett Rogers, the luminary in diffusion of innovations, posits that an innovation is an idea, practice or object perceived as new by an individual (Rogers, 1995).

Its significance is not whether the idea is objectively new but that the adopter perceives newness and reacts accordingly to that idea (Baskerville & Pries-Heje, 1998). Essentially, it is the perceived newness of the idea which determines it to be an innovation. While research on innovation has grown rapidly in recent years, it is still based on Schumpeter's principle that views innovation as a driving force of economic development (Ishengoma & Vaaland, 2016). Consistent with Roger's idea of innovation, Schumpeter's definition of innovation points to the "new combinations" of new knowledge and resources, the distinction between the invention (i.e. new ideas) and implementation of these inventions in practice, and the classification of innovations into product, process and organizational innovation. The OSLO manual of the OECD (2005) defines innovation as the implementation of a new or significantly improved product, a marketing method or a new organizational method, workplace organization or external relationship. Consequently, the introduction of a new or significantly improved good or service is known as product innovation. The implementation of a new or significantly improved process or method is known as process innovation, and the introduction of a new marketing method (e.g. product design, packaging and pricing) is known as marketing innovation. Lastly, improving a firm's performance in terms of cost and productivity is known as organizational innovation (Ishengoma & Vaaland, 2016).

Despite the emerging understanding about innovation, this concept is always associated with science and technology (S&T). The widely acknowledged conception is that science relates to the scientific examination that produces discoveries to improve lives and society, while technology helps develop products and objects out of scientific discoveries to transform lives and society. According to Burke, Bergman, and Asimov (1985), S&T have had a major impact on society, even until now. Through S&T, many areas have drastically changed, from communication to work and workplace, transportation, food, shelter and almost all aspects of people's lives. The inherent nature of S&T in producing new ideas, practice or objects clearly points to the direction of innovation. As such, S&T and innovation are often interchangeably used to describe new solutions that aim to help people and society. While it is true that it can therefore be argued that as S&T initiatives grow, innovation also flourishes, there is a need to reconsider this concept to include the development in the area of social sciences to account for the socio-cultural and political dimensions of innovation.

Innovation in developing countries

Innovation in developing countries is either home grown or nurtured by overseas donor organizations or companies. An example of the government-led innovation is the Indian IT–BPO industry. It has been a benchmark and often a subject of envy among developing countries in the past two decades. Contrary to common perception, the success of this industry in India is attributed not because of product liberalization, but a long-term vision of organizing S&T soon after the country gained independence in 1947 (Sharma, 2014). In its early years, the 'body shopping' model – where low-cost engineers were sent to work onsite for clients overseas – was the standard. As the industry gained confidence and reputation from its customers overseas, Indian firms pioneered the concept of offshore delivery and development models. These models paved the way for business process outsourcing where Indian firms act as an extension of offshore clients adopting their business processes, policies and standards. Variations of this model have been replicated in other countries, and the number of such destinations continues to grow and emerge as competitors to the Indian industry. With the looming competition from different countries, the Indian industry should diversify into new types of services, new geographies, new verticals and higher end of services. Moreover, the Indian industry can take advantage of a growing domestic market as well as markets that will soon develop in least-developed countries. While India continues to enjoy a large potential workforce, functioning democracy and robust domestic market, it still needs to improve its current educational system at all levels to make it industry-ready, develop an innovation infrastructure with relevant linkages, improve productivity of knowledge workers and nurture domestic markets (Sharma, 2014).

Contrary to the success of India, there are some countries which cannot successfully follow this model. Babb (2003), in her study in the Caribbean, argued that the real barrier to long-term economic, social and political development in the middle- and high-income developing countries of the Caribbean is the lack of social access to the tools, skills and resources they would enable the development, management and diffusion of information, knowledge and innovation at all levels of society. It has been found that for citizens to be competitive in this globalizing economy, societal access to tools and networks of the new economy remains crucial to mould the knowledge-intensive human resources in the region. Advanced forms of access are required to transform and help to diversify stagnating, inefficient economies; to unlock the inherent knowledge and innovative abilities; and to safeguard small states' power, agency and self-determination in a globalizing, socio-political economy – specifically, effective management and use of new ICT networks that could facilitate the physical, financial, secure, cognitive, administrative and operational frameworks capable of maximizing the potential benefits that the new technologies provide. According to Babb (2003), such a six-layered model develops human capacity and the creation of knowledge at the centre of societal development at every level, thereby contributing to stability, security, sustainability and self-determination in the emergent global networked society. A more appropriate approach to innovations in this context is through partnership with donor countries. The international entities enable the host country to not only have more direct or smoother access to existing technological and managerial competencies but to also be part of an international process of knowledge creation and diffusion (Ishengoma & Vaaland, 2016). This provides a direct mentoring from the donor countries for the successful adoption of innovation.

In both approaches of innovation adoption, either home grown or donor-led, developing countries are now investing in training, higher education and innovation practices to improve their knowledge-based economy (KBE) index (Sinha, 2018). KBE is a kind of economy focused on the production and management of knowledge by individuals in a society capable of creating and adapting innovative solutions that can address current challenges in society. Sinha (2018) pointed out that skills development is considered the most important factor in a KBE-empowered nation. Similarly, Babb (2003) argued that the most precious resource that developing countries possess is the human capital. These resources when nurtured are likely to be the most important determinant in maintaining high living standards in the global networked economy.

Innovation and employability in HEIs in developing countries

Ensuring graduate employability in developing countries requires HEIs to establish innovation centres that would allow students to experience job-related assessment tasks which are aligned to what knowledge and skills the industry require to carry out their business processes. According to Ashraf et al. (2018), academia should closely collaborate with the industry for the 'capitalization of knowledge'. This happens when a strong tie between the university and industry exists as economic value is added or produced. The university-industry linkages take inspiration in mutual collaboration between two parties. These linkages can be defined as "bi-directional linkages between the university and industry entities, established to enable the diffusion of creative ideas, skills and people with the aim of creating mutual value over time" (Plewa, Korff, Baaken, & Macpherson, 2013, p. 23). On the one hand, universities take a proactive stance and build relations with industry through establishing mutual agreements (i.e. MoU or MoA), internship programs, meetings and consultations, and collaborative research. On the other, industries, particularly SMEs, communicate to universities to gain the latest knowledge and technology and help improve the future employability of their students (Ashraf et al., 2018).

There are several aspects of collaboration between the university and industry. For instance, in South Africa, the main form of university-industry linkages is financial. Industries support research (postgrad, PhD level) through loans, bursaries and sponsorships (Herman, 2013). In some cases, companies support individual employees who choose to pursue doctoral degrees if there is some form of 'return on investment'.

Although the university-industry linkage model has shown some success, it was found to be weak in the sense that some HEIs are not capable to interface with the corporate sector due to lack of efficient direct mechanisms to encourage university-industry collaboration (Iqbal & Zenchenkov, 2014). What is needed is strong support from the government to mediate the universities and industries by providing platforms for collaboration. This concept of university-industry-government collaboration was named by Etzkowitz and Leydesdorff in 1995 the triple helix model of innovation. The basic tenet for this model is that, as collaborations flourish between these institutions, each helix evolves to adopt some characteristics of the other institution which eventually transforms to hybrid institutions. It is a self-reinforcing spiral model of innovation which analyses the importance of university-industry-government relations in a country's economic growth through the development of relationships. The reciprocal relations of the elements enable internal transformation of each of the 'helices', mutual influence among the three 'helices' and creation of a new super-imposition of trilateral networks and organizations resulting from the interaction of the three 'helices' (Datta, 2018; Villarreal & Calvo, 2015). However, these helices of an innovation system can be expected to entertain a dually layered network: one layer of institutional relations in which they constrain each other's behaviour, and another layer of functional relations in which they shape each other's expectations (Leydesdorff, 2010). Different institutional arrangements can be developed where the function of university-industry relations can be performed such as transfer offices, spin-off companies, licensing agreements and so on.

The Education-Innovation-Employability Framework

Drawing from the industry-education-government collaboration framework, the Education-Innovation-Employability Framework is developed with the intention to improve graduate employability. This requires a significant investment for HEIs through innovation centres. Policies need to be developed to expand the opportunity space and support the development of innovation systems (Kararach et al., 2011). HEIs in developing countries should move away from the general concept of employability; that is, improving competencies for the workplace (Ponnan & Ambalavanan, 2014). While such approach seems to be working to some, HEIs in developing countries has to veer away from that traditional notion by looking at enhancing employability even beyond employment. The framework (Figure 7.1)

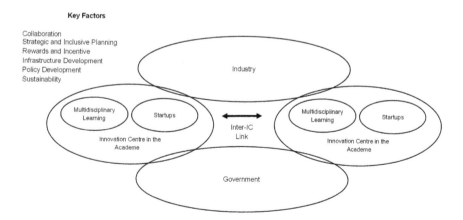

FIGURE 7.1 Education-Innovation-Employability Framework

is crafted as a concept to help HEIs to capitalize on establishing innovation centres that enhance employability of graduates.

The espoused Education-Innovation-Employability Framework shown in Figure 7.1 emphasizes collaboration between and among HEIs' innovation centres, industry and the government. Within the HEI, multidisciplinary learning is an approach that covers multiple knowledge domains that moves away from the isolated nature of innovations. Similarly, inter-innovation centres can be established through partnerships with different universities in the region, nationally or internationally. This kind of innovation centre lends strong support to the concept of complementation to bring together the individual strengths of universities, addressing possible limitations due to resources, curriculum matters and human resources. The complementation strategy blurs the line of competition among universities, and it allows greater focus for the achievement of regional goals for enhancing human resources rather than competing which university produces the best graduates. Furthermore, both the university and the industry can exploit their mutual relationship. This can be achieved through the establishment of research and development programs where people from industry, faculty members and students would engage in a specific research project with the aim of using the product for wider dissemination, patenting and use.

The key factors for the implementation of this framework are as follows:

1. Collaboration. The role of the government is critical for the operationalization of this framework. Research can be stimulated by the government through various support channels such as financial instruments (i.e. grants and tax credits) as well as the creation of a policy and legal environment supporting research and development (Ankrah & Al-Tabbaa, 2015). These can create the platform for collaboration that develops conditions to attract key elements of innovations (Altenburg, Schmitz, & Stamm, 2008). Industry and academe should collaborate in developing curriculum responsive to the challenging needs of the industry, share theoretical and industry knowledge through university-industry immersion, consultancy, access to industry practitioners/ experts, internship, among others.

2. Strategic and Inclusive Planning Research show that innovation in higher education is a result of strategic and inclusive planning borne of collaboration. According to Barnard and Van der Merwe (2016b), conditions for innovation in sustainable development in higher education include decisive leadership on strategic direction; regular, flexible and inclusive planning; regular culture climate surveys; constant monitoring of progress; and strategic agility that is essential to promote innovation among the entire workforce (p. 208).

3. Rewards and Incentives. Reinforcement of efforts on establishment of and participation in innovation centres propels innovation in both the industry and HEI. Innovation centres can leverage innovations through the right kind of fiscal incentives, financial mechanisms, policy support, human capital and state-of-the art infrastructure. Paid internships and other incentives are found

to be important tools that enhance employability of students through the industry-university link (Ashraf et al., 2018; Mazumdar-Shaw, 2018).

4. Infrastructure Development. Developing the necessary infrastructure is key to connecting various institutions to collaborate. For example, infrastructure that improves transport and communication thereby enhancing the mobility of goods and services essentially helps all sectors in this framework. Infrastructure development is also crucial for raising the competitiveness of local producers against competitors (Kararach et al., 2011).

5. Policy Development. Governments play an important role in crafting policies that support innovation. Coulibaly, Erbao, and Metuge Mekongcho (2018) found that due to government-driven innovation policies, monetary investment per capita increased through formal and informal institutions.

6. Sustainability. The design and business operations of innovation centres should have an inherent feature for sustainability. A sustainability plan is needed to coordinate efforts from all parties, monitor progress and gains, and identify critical changes to further improve the innovation centre design and processes.

Conclusion

This chapter has presented a critical study of the current status of research on innovation, employability and higher education in developing countries with the aim of crafting a framework that will serve as a guide for the implementation of innovation centres in this chosen context. Several factors common to most research in developing countries and major gaps were identified, which include reforms in the provision of access to physical, financial, research and academic resources. Specifically, this chapter has identified that there is a need to improve on the technological infrastructure, education and training, industry-academe-government collaboration, incentives, appropriate internship opportunities, research and publication outlets of HEIs in support of the development of innovation centres within their area. These significant transformations are necessary to create a healthy ambience for knowledge and skills development that could pave the way, improving the employability and value of graduates in the HEIs of developing countries.

Given the ever-changing demands for graduate employability and greater focus for leadership, creativity, innovativeness and entrepreneurial skills, HEIs in the developing countries need to establish multidisciplinary, inter-universities and industry-linked innovation centres. A stronger collaboration between HEIs and industry should be enabled and supported by the government by providing a socio-political climate that enables the operationalization of the suggested framework.

References

Altenburg, T., Schmitz, H., & Stamm, A. (2008). Breakthrough? China's and India's transition from production to innovation. *World Development, 36*(2), 325–344. doi:10/cb8d63

Ankrah, S., & Al-Tabbaa, O. (2015). Universities–industry collaboration: A systematic review. *Scandinavian Journal of Management, 31*(3), 387–408. doi:10/gfc4nd

Ashraf, R. U., Hou, F., Kirmani, S. A. A., Ilyas, M., Zaidi, S. A. H., & Ashraf, M. S. (2018). Student employability via university-industry linkages. *Human Systems Management, 37*(2), 219–232. doi:10/gd8dpm

Babb, A. C. (2003). Surfing the knowledge wave: Access for Caribbean development. *Journal of Information, Communication and Ethics in Society, 1*(2), 71–80. doi:10/dh4n2b

Barnard, Z., & Van der Merwe, D. (2016a). Innovative management for organizational sustainability in higher education. *International Journal of Sustainability in Higher Education, 17*(2), 208–227. doi:10/f8vf83

Barnard, Z., & Van der Merwe, D. (2016b). Innovative management for organizational sustainability in higher education. *International Journal of Sustainability in Higher Education, 17*(2), 208–227. doi:10/f8vf83

Baskerville, R., & Pries-Heje, J. (1998). Information technology diffusion: Building positive barriers. *European Journal of Information Systems, 7*(1), 17–28.

Berntson, E. (2008). *Employability perceptions: Nature, determinants, and implications for health and well-being: (529722013-001)* [Data set]. American Psychological Association. doi:10.1037/e529722013-001

Burke, J., Bergman, J., & Asimov, I. (1985). *The impact of science in society.* Washington, DC: Scientific and Technical Information Branch, National Aeronautics and Space Administration.

Coulibaly, S. K., Erbao, C., & Metuge Mekongcho, T. (2018). Economic globalization, entrepreneurship, and development. *Technological Forecasting and Social Change, 127,* 271–280. doi:10/gfc4nm

Datta, P. P. (2018). Developing competencies to lead innovation in Indian manufacturing: An education model. *International Journal of Innovation Science, 10*(4), 475–494. doi:10.1108/IJIS-07-2016-0016

De Vries, H., Bekkers, V., & Tummers, L. (2016). Innovation in the public sector: A systematic review and future research agenda. *Public Administration, 94*(1), 146–166. doi:10/gc5rs6

Etzkowitz, H., & Leydesdorff, L. (1995). *The triple helix – university-industry-government relations: A laboratory for knowledge based economic development* (SSRN Scholarly Paper No. ID 2480085). Rochester, NY: Social Science Research Network.

Gangi, Y. A. (2017). The role of entrepreneurship education and training on creation of the knowledge economy: Qatar leap to the future. *World Journal of Entrepreneurship, Management and Sustainable Development, 13*(4), 375–388. doi:10/gdsm5g

Heeks, R., & Bailur, S. (2007). Analyzing e-government research: Perspectives, philosophies, theories, methods, and practice. *Government Information Quarterly, 24*(2), 243–265. doi:10.1016/j.giq.2006.06.005

Herman, C. (2013). Industry perceptions of industry–university partnerships related to doctoral education in South Africa. *Industry and Higher Education, 27*(3), 217–225. doi:10/gfc4qk

Iqbal, A., & Zenchenkov, M. (2014). Market tested business education: Corporate sector perceptions of Saudi graduate's competencies. *Asia-Pacific Journal of Cooperative Education, 15*(2), 91–106.

Ishengoma, E., & Vaaland, T. I. (2016). University-industry linkages in developing countries: Perceived effect on innovation. *Education + Training, 58*(9), 1014–1040. doi:10/gd8dmv

Jankowicz, D. (2000). Reviews. *Management Learning, 31*(1), 140–143. doi:10/dtpqvk

Jules, T. D., & Sundberg, K. C. (2018). The internationalization of creativity as a learning competence. *Global Education Review, 5*(1), 35–51.

Kapoor, K., Weerakkody, V., & Schroeder, A. (2018). Social innovations for social cohesion in Western Europe: Success dimensions for lifelong learning and education. *Innovation- the European Journal of Social Science Research, 31*(2), 189–203. doi:10/gfc4nx

Kararach, G., Hanson, K. T., & Léautier, F. A. (2011). Regional integration policies to support job creation for Africa's burgeoning youth population. *World Journal of Entrepreneurship, Management and Sustainable Development, 7*(2/3/4), 177–215. doi:10/cdc76x

Kishore, S. (2013). Value-addition for empowerment and employability through intervention of ODL mode of Ignou. *Turkish Online Journal of Distance Education (TOJDE), 14*(1).

Kong, E., Chadee, D., & Raman, R. (2013). Managing Indian IT professionals for global competitiveness: The role of human resource practices in developing knowledge and learning capabilities for innovation. *Knowledge Management Research & Practice, 11*(4), 334–345. doi:10/f5hx6f

Leydesdorff, L. (2010). The knowledge-based economy and the triple helix model. *American Society for Information Science and Technology, 44*(1), 365–417. doi:10/fzp45w

Li-Hua, R., Li, X., Aouad, G., & Wilson, J. (2011). Strategic aspects of innovation and internationalization in higher education: The Salford PMI2 experience. *Journal of Chinese Entrepreneurship, 3*(1), 8–23. doi:10/dp8rgb

Matsheke, O., & Dhurup, M. (2017). Entrepreneurial-related programmes and students' intentions to venture into new business creation: Finding synergy of constructs in a University of Technology. *Science, Technology and Society, 22*(2), 259–283. doi:10/gbfh4x

Mazumdar-Shaw, K. (2018). Leveraging affordable innovation to tackle India's healthcare challenge. *IIMB Management Review, 30*(1), 37–50. doi:10/gfc4nt

Molla, T., & Cuthbert, D. (2016). Re-imagining Africa as a knowledge economy: Premises and promises of recent higher education development initiatives. *Journal of Asian and African Studies, 53*(2), 250–267. doi:10/gc3zx4

Neuendorf, K. A. (2002). *The content analysis guidebook*. Thousand Oaks, CA: Sage Publications.

Nyika, A. (2015). Mother tongue as the medium of instruction at developing country universities in a global context. *South African Journal of Science, 111*(1/2), 1–5. doi:10/f62hqs

OECD. (2005). *Oslo manual: Guidelines for collecting and interpreting innovation data* (3rd ed.). OECD. doi:10.1787/9789264013100-en

Okoli, C., & Schabram, K. (2010). A guide to conducting a systematic literature review of information systems research. *Sprouts: Working Papers on Information Systems, 10*(26). Retrieved from http://sprouts.aisnet.org/10-26/

Petticrew, M., & Roberts, H. (2006). *Systematic reviews in the social sciences*. Malden, MA: Blackwell Publishing.

Plewa, C., Korff, N., Baaken, T., & Macpherson, G. (2013). University–industry linkage evolution: an empirical investigation of relational success factors. *R&D Management, 43*(4), 365–380. doi:10/gfkk4v

Ponnan, R., & Ambalavanan, B. (2014). Innovations to broadcasting curriculum to meet workplace expectations. *Procedia – Social and Behavioral Sciences, 123*, 160–169. doi:10/gfc4nr

Rogers, E. M. (1995). *Diffusion of innovations*. New York, NY: Free Press.

Sharma, D. C. (2014). Indian IT outsourcing industry: Future threats and challenges. *Futures, 56*, 73–80. doi:10/f5wdvc

Sinha, G. R. (2018). Innovation and research skill for knowledge-based economy of Myanmar: Current status and recommendation. *Journal of Science and Technology Policy Management*. doi:10/gfc4mj

Valiente, O. (2014). The OECD skills strategy and the education agenda for development. *International Journal of Educational Development, 39,* 40–48. doi:10/f6wb9v

Villarreal, O., & Calvo, N. (2015). From the triple helix model to the global open innovation model: A case study based on international cooperation for innovation in Dominican Republic. *Journal of Engineering and Technology Management, 35,* 71–92. doi:10/gfgx5n

Voorberg, W. H., Bekkers, V. J. J. M., & Tummers, L. G. (2015). A systematic review of co-creation and co-production: Embarking on the social innovation journey. *Public Management Review, 17*(9), 1333–1357. doi:10/gfb7zv

Yorke, M. (2006). *Employability in higher education: What it is, what it is not.* York, England: Higher Education Academy. Retrieved from www.heacademy.ac.uk/sites/default/files/id116_employability_in_higher_education_336.pdf

8

DEVELOPING BUSINESS-READY GRADUATES

Teaching Inside Out

Christine Rivers and Justin O'Brien

Introduction

The UK Commission for Employment and Skills (2016, p. 3) reports that 'a growing number of jobs are being left unfilled because companies can't find the right people with the right skills'. Fiona Dunsire (CEO, Mercer) defines the concept of *right* people as individuals who can lead change and effectively manage teams (CML Cast Series, 2017). But do we teach or prepare students for that? MacGregor and Semler (2012) believe that management education needs to do a lot more than merely use in-class case studies, an 'innovation' which harks from the 1930s. Some might say that we need to fundamentally rethink our teaching practices (Waddock & Lozano, 2013) if they do not support the development of skills that are needed in the current and future working environments. Others call for actions beyond those of rethinking management education, and in response, they have actually designed and tested new programme structures in practice (Dunne & Martin, 2006; Adams & Morgan, 2007; Manimala & Thomas, 2017). The Higher Education Academy (HEA; n.d.) has also taken a proactive stance and made one of their cross-disciplinary strategic priorities embedding employability in the curriculum. Several useful models and concepts of graduate employability have since been developed, including Graduate Employability in Context (Tomlinson & Holmes, 2016), CareerEDGE (graduate employability development which emphasises emotional intelligence [EI]) (Dacre Pool & Sewell, 2007) and USEM (Understanding, Skills, Efficacy and Meta-cognition) (Knight & Yorke, 2004). While Tomlinson and Holmes (2016) theoretically defined the concept of employability, it was predominantly drawn from secondary data or student experiences. Augmenting employer perspectives more directly as part of their evidence would have strengthened the synthesis of ideas made by the contributing authors, particularly careerEDGE (Dacre Pool & Sewell, 2007; Dacre Pool, 2017). The essence of the 2004 USEM model, while still relevant, also needs to be expanded to fit the current needs of graduates in the workplace, most notably digital skills. So, while there are good models and evidence available to draw from, the question that remains is how we can educate students and equip them with the necessary skills to work in the VUCA environment (Bennett & Lemoine, 2014). Therefore, this chapter aims to:

(1) identify the skills and qualities that are needed and wanted by employers and
(2) provide a framework for detailed implementation at module level in management education.

Theoretical background

Skills development in management education

Research on business curriculum and soft skills blind spots that incorporates industry perspectives appear less developed in literature than may be anticipated (Leisen et al., 2004; Milhauser & Rahschulte, 2010). The small number of studies (e.g. Rao, 2014) that have taken recruiters' perspectives into account are mostly quantitative in nature and use a brief approach to identify the skills that are required (Rao, 2014) or to explain how they would transform in the future. Other studies look at employability from the student perspective. For instance, Tymon (2013) focused on the employability rate of business management students. This study highlighted that the lack of student commitment and engagement has a detrimental effect on soft skills development. The Dictionary of Human Resource Management (Heery & Noon, 2008, p. 1) defines soft skills as 'competencies that employees possess associated with activities such as customer handling, communication, problem-solving and team working'. They emphasised the importance that employers put on soft skills and note that new recruits are 'sadly lacking' such skills. This definition provides a useful starting point to address the question of soft skills development.

Stevens' (2005) research with Silicon Valley employers found that students needed to develop stronger writing skills, learn how to professionally use and write emails, strengthen their self-expression and impression management and avoid the use of slang. Milhauser and Rahschulte's (2010) US study of international team work identified a range of key skills including logistical facilitation, decision making for complexity, leveraging diversity in conflict and effective communication. Knowles and Hensher (2005) identified leadership and communications for special attention, and Leisen et al. (2004) noted the criticality of audience analysis and presentation capabilities. While it is critical to understand what students are lacking, it is equally important to understand an employer's current needs (which is similar to Stage 1 of the HEA employability framework). Lester and Costley (2010, p. 561) emphasised the need to determine capabilities relevant for future roles and warned that programmes should not merely focus on *upskilling* for its own sake, a danger business schools might easily fall into given the pressures of league tables, ranks and the Teaching Excellence Framework (TEF).

In working together, industry stakeholder research (McCracken et al., 2016) and the UK Department for Business, Innovation & Skills (2015) identified that employers value generic leadership abilities (competencies comprising interpersonal and personal behaviours and cognitive ability) and personality (attitudes, values and personal qualities). While these may appear to be useful insights, they fail to provide an in-depth insight into how employers can help business schools implement them innovatively within the curriculum to address future needs and concerns. So what innovative pedagogies have successfully been used to foster soft skills and thereto enhance the development of business graduates more deeply?

Innovative pedagogic practices

The most pertinent approach which appears to address the issue outlined above is the method of problem-based learning (PBL) (Kolmos et al., 2004; Carvalho, 2016; Delaney et al., 2017) and work-based learning (Lester & Costley, 2010; Raelin, 2016) combined with flipped classroom application (Hamden et al., 2013). These pedagogies are not new, yet they do not seem to have been implemented or embedded in the management education curricula to a degree that truly transforms student learning, with the aim to manifestly address the soft skills development expected by employers. Instead, the approaches are often adopted piecemeal, either as a single lesson episode or merely as part of the assessment of a module (Riebe & Jackson, 2014). However, it is less often seen as a learning and teaching strategy for a whole module or programme, with some exceptions, for example, O'Brien and Brown (2017) who focused on off-campus business engagement as experiential learning.

By applying such approaches, the abandonment of traditional lectures (Knowles & Hensher, 2005) and seminar structures (a scenario some might be uncomfortable with) may be required. A flipped classroom (Bergmann & Sams, 2016) means that students learn outside the classroom using instructions and materials provided by the teacher. Students would use the time in the classroom to deepen their understanding through small-group discussions and reflections. The concept of in-class interaction can be as theoretical and/or practical as appropriate. While this notion may seem an effective way to encourage deeper learning, a flipped classroom approach requires careful design that considers soft skills development.

PBL (Delaney et al., 2017) refers to the process of designing programmes or modules based on open-ended problems within a particular context. In such event, students become self-directed problem solvers through active investigation and collaboration. The idea is that students implement their agreed solutions and subsequently discuss the outcome with the teacher leading the in-depth critical evaluation of their own work and the wider class.

In contrast, but not opposition, is work-based learning (Raelin, 2016). Lester and Costley (2010, p. 562) described the term work-based learning as any learning that is situated in the workplace or arises directly out of workplace concerns, different from work-related learning that is concerned with learning about work in class and through field trips (Moreland, 2015). Raelin (2016) emphasised that a work-based approach potentially enables students to gather a real, collective, practical experience, enhancing their team and leadership skills while indirectly supporting skills development. Thus, similar to PBL, this approach takes place within a certain context.

It is clear that innovative practices in management education do exist, are applied and have been tested to some degree. However, less evidence, which focuses on developing business-ready graduates who can deal with the challenges ahead such as the VUCA environment, automation, big data and a dynamic digital economy, is available. The next section will outline the research design of this study in order to answer the three research questions:

(1) To what extent (if any) do business schools prepare students to enter a VUCA environment (Bennett & Lemoine, 2014)?
(2) What are the soft skills and qualities that business schools should be focusing on?
(3) Can employers help guide business schools to develop business-ready graduates?

Research design and methodology

The literature suggests that there is some, albeit mainly quantitative, research in skills development, but this is often conducted without the effective integration of the new pedagogy design. This qualitative study combines the understanding of skills development and presents a pedagogic framework that supports this. The study spanned four years and included three test phases. The framework developed was implemented and tested at undergraduate FHEQ Level 6 in 2016, 2017 and 2018 with an average cohort size of 70 students, and at postgraduate FHEQ Level 7 in 2015 and 2016 in an MBA class with an average cohort size of 32 students. Data was collected over four years by conducting interviews with employers who were co-teaching with the lead academic, and with employers who were not involved in the design process. (Students and employers have given their consent to use their non-anonymised quotations for publication purposes.) Based on our insights, we developed a framework called *Teaching Inside Out* (TIO), which reflects the criticality of employer perspectives.

The data was corroborated with qualitative feedback provided by students through the module evaluation questionnaire (a standard format for collecting feedback from students after teaching has taken place). In total, we collected feedback from 50 students and interviewed eight employers individually, four of whom also participated in a panel discussion focusing on 'developing business-ready graduates'. All interviews and the panel discussion were recorded and analysed using thematic analysis (Braun & Clarke, 2006; Clarke & Braun, 2014).

Analysis and findings

Following the steps of thematic analysis, three notable aspects were found to be of particular interest: (1) employers' concerns and topics students should learn about

TABLE 8.1 Overview of initial coding

Topics students need to learn about	Soft skills students should develop	Integrating soft skills development into the curriculum
Change management	Flexibility	People management
Understanding data	Hard working	Networking skills
Interpretation of data	Public speaking	Having a mentor
Effective (team) leadership	Having an opinion	Understanding the value of management tools for decision making
Can't predict people's reactions	Maintaining focus	Engaging industry projects
People management	Down time	Real-world assessments
Employment and payment	Making mistakes	Client management
Understanding the industry you work in (context)	Embracing silence	Cultural awareness
Understanding funding opportunities	Taking time to make decisions	Emotional intelligence

to further develop their soft skills, (2) what soft skills employers are looking for and (3) what business schools should consider to support soft skills development and integration into curriculum design. Table 8.1 gives an overview of the three aspects and associated themes.

Further analysis of these aspects showed three strong themes: (1) adapting to change and change management, (2) self-awareness and (3) relationship management and networking.

Adapting to change and change management

Employer 1 (BMW Financial Services Ltd) stated, in his view, that employers felt the graduates they interviewed frequently did not seem to understand the effect that constant change would have on organisation(s). For having such a mind-set can help students to think about how they can support and thrive in an organisation that always changes, particularly how to manage and lead people within such an environment. Employer 2 (Farrow Creative) noted that although universities might teach change management as a subject, students are not necessarily exposed to any scenarios that let them experience how to deal with and manage change. This is certainly an aspect that could be implemented as part of the assessment or the learning and teaching strategy.

Self-awareness

Interviewee(s) and panel participant(s) highlighted that graduates often lack self-awareness. This was described as the ability of students to identify their own strengths and areas for development, the ability to possess a responsible work ethic and a level of resilience that informs decision making (Knight & Yorke, 2004; Dacre Pool & Sewell, 2007).

Employer 3 proclaimed, 'Predicting people's behaviour and reactions is not easy, but, if you are self-aware you become more sensitive to other people's behaviour'. Two employers emphasised the need to let students make mistakes and to learn from such mistakes. This experience will enable them to become resilient and increasingly self-aware of their own strengths and weaknesses. Employer 1 pointed out that students are often not aware of their weaknesses or strengths when asked at interview stage, and this is something he found very alarming, as it shows that students have not developed the necessary level of self-awareness to judge their own abilities. Consequently, he questioned how they would judge those of their colleagues. Clearly, self-awareness, patience and resilience are viewed as very important soft skills which graduates essentially need to develop if they are to adapt to an everchanging working environment.

Relationship management and networking

In addition to dealing with work in a fast-changing environment, employers also emphasised the need to develop relationship and networking skills. While technological advances drive the need for people to develop better digital skills, which higher education providers can address, for example, interpreting data and dealing with big data, the more intangible 'people side of things' is often important for businesses to be truly effective. These relationships skills are necessary both inside and outside a company and include, for instance, clear communication skills and evidence-based decision-making skills. For example, Employer 5 stated:

> The beginning of one's career is about leading by example. But as you grow, you actually need to learn [how] to lead a team effectively, especially through change. This is the most important skill in a well-functioning team. This is not necessarily a comfortable position, because it means that there are tensions and different ideas and points of views. It is about how you model these different stages as a leader while the environment is constantly changing around you.

Even if you have developed those soft skills, employers recommend that graduates network with influencers early on, either within or outside a company. Employer 6 emphasised the power of social network platforms by stating, 'It is really important for students to start building their networks . . . The earlier in their career they can do that the better, utilise platforms to show off capabilities and skills, that's what employers are looking for'.

Employer 7 recommended utilising social media platforms to develop a personal brand: 'If you are passionate about virtual reality in advertising then demonstrate that: collect evidence, comment on developments in the field, start a blog and build your network before you enter the industry'. Employer 5 also highlighted the importance of developing networking skills early and making contacts which will help students engage with people from various industries before they even start working. In turn, this could lead to job opportunities and help expand the industries' insight. Networks can also be built through mentors, although these relationships need nurturing with appropriate skills and resources. Providing students with industry mentors would also support the development of those soft skills.

Integration of soft skills development into the curriculum – TIO framework

It is clear that topics such as change management, people management and leadership are currently a cause of major concern for employers. The way the curriculum in many business schools is structured does not necessarily embrace these aspects directly. Instead, it was found that these three subjects are either taught in isolation or embedded in assessment components, such as group work, although not directly assessed either. Figure 8.1 illustrates the siloed curriculum structure typically offered by business schools:

Interviewees suggested that those in the industry should be more engaged in the curriculum design process. Employer 8 said,

> We need to integrate soft skills development and diverse ways of thinking into graduate learning as early as possible, – not as explicit points of "assessment" but as hygiene factors (in the same way they are in the world of work). Ask: what does the world require from our graduates, then think inside out: what do we need to change internally to accommodate these needs?

Employer guided curricula input – TIO

So how do you think 'inside out'? Could a programme start with soft skills development and then branch out into knowledge acquisition? Would it be possible to move away from subject-based, module-specific teaching towards project-based

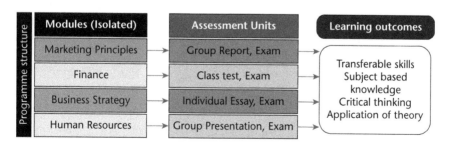

FIGURE 8.1   Current programme structures (isolated modules with separate assessment units and learning outcomes for each module)

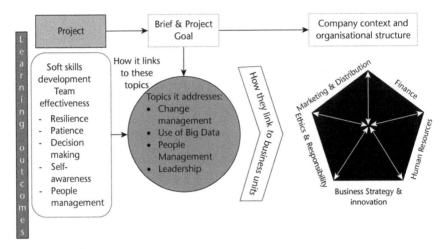

FIGURE 8.2 Teaching Inside Out framework

aggregated teaching? Figure 8.2 visualises the inside out approach to curriculum design based on our research.

Instead of offering isolated, siloed, functional modules, educators could develop projects in these areas with specific learning outcomes around real business problems from a soft skills development perspective. For example, a capstone live consultancy project is often used in this way in MBA programmes. However, the difference between a consultancy project and the proposed TIO framework is that the project design does not necessarily serve the company. Instead, projects are designed to address wider issues in the workplace or of a specific industry at programme level (project- and work-based learning). In addition, the industry partner is fully immersed in the project design and acts as a coach and mentor for students along the way.

Employer 7 found the label 'building new context around old lessons' an effective descriptor for this innovative approach to learning. Projects are developed with industry partners and focus on stories of effective team leadership or failure but are firmly anchored on concepts of change management, people management, big data and leadership and then linked to conventional business units, although knowledge acquisition is left to the students to explore in their independent study time, as seen in flipped classroom learning (Herreid & Schiller, 2013). This enables students to lay down the foundations of a strong business acumen right from the start, which gets shaped by further learning and by doing iterations during their studies. We found that using TIO supported not only the development of soft skills but also the wider life skills (e.g. self-management) and at the same time facilitated effective knowledge acquisition.

This means assessments would also need to be adaptable in order to focus on three key questions: (1) What did you learn about yourself? This could be a reflective piece of work, including a self-evaluative report of weaknesses and strengths and/or suggestion(s) for improvement that the students can expand on throughout their studies. If offered online, it would enable students to build a portfolio of their soft skills development that, for instance, can be shared with employers; (2) What did you learn about the industry? Demonstrating industry context and knowledge is vital as pointed out by the interviewees, and this would enable students to find their own specialism supported by evidence; and (3) What did you learn about the business, and what are your insights and suggestions for future projects to succeed? Again, this enables students to build a portfolio and knowledge base of what they have learnt and at the same time help them become reflective critical thinkers who can embrace the changes happening around them.

Impact of TIO on students and employers

We found that TIO enhanced student soft skills development, learning and student experience. Business Management Graduate 4 (2017) wrote on LinkedIn:

> The structure of the course is refreshingly different with a clear focus on practical application of learnings, something that is often absent from other university modules . . . The assessment methods are highly relevant to working within a real-life context . . . To sum it up, immersive and practical as well as highly enjoyable.

Practitioner Stephen Leigh, co-teacher on the MBA in 2015 to 2016, said:

> I've had the pleasure of co-lecturing on both Full-Time and Executive MBA programmes, and have been impressed by the TIO approach in providing the best learning experience – from both an academic and personal development perspective. A great experience for all concerned.

The partner's involvement increased their company's corporate social responsibility footprint, and they felt that they had gained the relevant new skills required when working with a younger generation, and understanding how to teach soft skills. Students felt more self-aware and confident to enter the world of work, and employers who co-taught on the module felt that it helped raise student awareness to the challenges that the new generation entering the workplace face.

Concluding remarks

The major findings of this research are twofold: teaching practice and theory. Firstly, it was found that employers do not necessarily want the finished product, but they want business-ready graduates. That means that businesses and organisations will favour those students who acquire skills that help them navigate effectively in a VUCA environment. These skills include self-awareness, resilience, decision making, people management skills and patience. Employers want graduates to understand the bigger picture and within that understand aspects of change management, big data use, people management and leadership, rather than have a highly theoretical knowledge of isolated subjects.

Secondly, TIO influences pedagogic theory and research on soft skills development in management education (ME). TIO could be used to expand that which is currently limited – for example, the use of flipped classroom concept (Hamden et al., 2013) from a micro (module) to a macro (programme) level – and question the use of online and offline spaces in ME (Jones & Bennett, 2017). TIO offers a new pedagogic exploration and conceptual framework for curriculum design in ME beyond subject areas such as entrepreneurship education (Manimala & Thomas, 2017). TIO builds on existing research in soft skills development (e.g. Tymon, 2013; Waddock & Lozano, 2013; Ingols & Shapiro, 2014) and explains what these soft skills are and how these can be 'taught' or 'developed'. Finally, TIO enables close collaboration and knowledge exchange between industry and academia. In doing so, TIO challenges the view that universities are the sole providers of knowledge and questions current programme structures of isolated subject-based modules (e.g. Kek & Huijser, 2017). It reaffirms Dyllick's (2015) view that business schools are neglecting soft skill development and that university educators are acting irresponsibly by providing a solution.

It should be made a requirement that business schools and higher education institutions (HEIs) embrace the changes discussed above. HEIs are no longer the sole source of knowledge, and it seems paramount for higher education educators to understand that one's access to knowledge has expanded and changed. TIO provides a solution to help meet the requirements of the VUCA working environment, which in turn transforms how students learn and engage with new information. The implication(s) of adopting such an approach can be wide reaching, questioning the efficacy of module, programme and curriculum design. It also raises questions as to the role of the teacher in the future. Is it possible that a cultural change is required at all levels? This is probably the biggest challenge HEIs currently face.

References

Adams, J. and Morgan, G. (2007). "Second generation" e-learning: Characteristics and design principles for supporting management soft-skills development. *International Journal on E-Learning*, 6(2), 157–185.

Bennett, N. and Lemoine, G. J. (2014). What VUCA really means for you. *Harvard Business Review*, Jan–Feb.

Bergmann, J. and Sams, A. (Eds.). (2016). *Flipped learning for elementary instruction* (1st edition). Eugene, OR: International Society for Technology in Education.

Braun, V. and Clarke, V. (2006). Using thematic analysis in psychology. *Qualitative Research in Psychology*, 3(2), 77–101.

Carvalho, A. (2016). The impact of PBL on transferable skills development in management education. *Innovations in Education and Teaching International*, 53(1), 35–47.

Centre of Management Learning (CML) Cast Series (2017). My industry with Fiona Dunsire, Mercer CEO (September, Clip 1). Retrieved from www.cmlsurrey.co.uk/casts/industry-fiona-dunsire-mercer-ceo-september-clip-1/

Clarke, V. and Braun, V. (2014). Thematic analysis. In *Encyclopedia of critical psychology* (pp. 1947–1952). New York, NY: Springer.

Dacre Pool, L. (2017). Developing graduate employability: The CareerEDGE Model and the importance of emotional intelligence. In M. Tomlinson and L. Holmes (Eds.), *Graduate employability in context* (pp. 317–338), London: Palgrave Macmillan.

Dacre Pool, L. and Sewell, P. (2007). The key to employability: Developing a practical model of graduate employability. *Education and Training*, 49(4), 277–289.

Delaney, Y., Pattinson, B., McCarthy, J. and Beecham, S. (2017). Transitioning from traditional to problem-based learning in management education: The case of a front-line manager skills development programme. *Innovations in Education and Teaching International*, 54(3), 214–222.

Department for Business, Innovation & Skills (2015). *Understanding employers' graduate recruitment and selection practice*. BIS Research paper no. 231. Retrieved 25 Sept 2017 from www.gov.uk/government/uploads/system/uploads/attachment_data/file/474251/BIS-15-464-employer-graduate-recruitment.pdf

Dunne, D. and Martin, R. (2006). Design thinking and how it will change management education: An interview and discussion. *Academy of Management Learning and Education*, 5(4), 512–523.

Dyllick, T. (2015). Responsible management education for a sustainable world: The challenges for business schools. *Journal of Management Development*, 34(1), 16–33.

Hamden, N., McKnight, P. E., McKnight, K. and Arfstrom, K. (2013). *A review of flipped learning. Flipped Learning Network*. Upper Saddle River, NJ: Pearson Education.

Heery, E. and Noon, M. (2008). *A dictionary of human resource management* (3rd edition). Oxford, England: Oxford University Press.

Herreid, C. and Schiller, N. (2013). Case studies and the flipped classroom. *Journal of College Science Teaching*, 42(5), 62–66.

Higher Education Academy (n.d.). Embedding employability in higher education. Retrieved 20 Sept 2017 from www.heacademy.ac.uk/individuals/strategic-priorities/employability

Ingols, C. and Shapiro, M. (2014). Concrete steps for assessing the "soft skills" in an MBA program. *Journal of Management Education*, 38(3), 412–435.

Jones, A., and Bennett, R. (2017). Reaching beyond an online/offline divide: Invoking the rhizome in higher education course design. *Technology, Pedagogy and Education*, 26(2), 193–210.

Kek, M. and Huijser, H. (2017). Agile PBL and the next generation of learners. In M. Y. C. A. Kek and H. Huijser, *Problem-based learning into the future* (pp. 31–48). Singapore: Springer.

Knight, P. and Yorke, M. (Eds.) (2004). *Learning, curriculum and employability in higher education*. London: Routledge Falmer.

Knowles, L. and Hensher, D. (2005). The postgraduate business curriculum: The frontline in the war between professionalism and academic irrelevance. *The International Journal of Management Education*, 4(3), 31–39.

Kolmos, A., and Fink, F. K. (2004). *The Aalborg PBL model: Progress, diversity and challenges*. L. Krogh (Ed.). Aalborg: Aalborg University Press.

Leisen, B., Tippins, M. J. and Lilly, B. (2004). A broadened sales curriculum: Exploratory evidence. *Journal of Marketing Education*, 26(3), 197–207.

Lester, S. and Costley, C. (2010). Work-based learning at higher education level: Value, practice and critique. *Studies in Higher Education*, 35(5), 561–575.

McCracken, M., Currie, D. and Harrison, J. (2016). Understanding graduate recruitment, development and retention for the enhancement of talent management: Sharpening 'the edge' of graduate talent. *The International Journal of Human Resource Management*, 27(22), 2727–2752.

MacGregor, S. and Semler, K. (2012). Towards whole person learning through sustainable executive performance. *Journal of Management Development*, 31(3), 231–242.

Manimala, M. J. and Thomas, P. (Eds.) (2017). *Entrepreneurship education: Experiments with curriculum, pedagogy and target groups*. Singapore: Springer.

Milhauser, K. and Rahschulte, T. (2010). Meeting the needs of global companies through improved international business Curriculum. *Journal of Teaching in International Business*, 21(2), 78–100.

Moreland, N. (2015). *Work related learning in higher education*. Retrieved 2 Nov 2017 from www.heacademy.ac.uk/system/files/id370_work-related_learning_in_higher_education_582.pdf

O'Brien, J. and Brown, D. (2017). Business engagement: Lessons learnt from experiential learning approaches with management students. *Journal of Learning Development in Higher Education*, 12(6). www.journal.aldinhe.ac.uk/index.php/jldhe/article/download/395/pdf

Raelin, J. A. (2016). Work-based (not classroom) learning as the apt preparation for the practice of management. *Management Teaching Review*, 1(1), 43–51.

Rao, M. S. (2014). Enhancing employability in engineering and management students through soft skills. *Industrial and Commercial Training*, 46(1), 42–48.

Riebe, L. and Jackson, D. (2014). The use of rubrics in benchmarking and assessing employability skills. *Journal of Management Education*, 38(3), 319–344.

Stevens, B. (2005). What communication skills do employers want? Silicon Valley recruiters respond. *Journal of Employment Counseling*, 42(1), 2–9.

Tomlinson, M. and Holmes, L. (Eds.) (2016). *Graduate employability in context: Theory, research and debate*. London: Palgrave Macmillan.

Tymon, A. (2013). The student perspective on employability. *Studies in Higher Education*, 38(6), 841–856.

UK Commission for Employment and Skills (2016). UKCES Employer Skills Survey 2015: UK report. Retrieved from www.gov.uk/government/publications/ukces-employer-skills-survey-2015-uk-report

Waddock, S. and Lozano, J. (2013). Developing more holistic management education: Lessons learned from two programs. *Academy of Management Learning and Education*, 12(2), 265–284.

9

ENGAGEMENT WITH ASIA VIA THE NEW COLOMBO PLAN

Impact on Australian students' career directions and employability

Ly Thi Tran, Glen Stafford, Thao Thi Phuong Vu and Mark Rahimi

Introduction

Over the past decade, the number of Australian students undertaking study or internships overseas has significantly increased, reaching more than 49,000 in 2017 (AUIDF, 2018). One in five Australian domestic undergraduate students were engaged in international learning experience in 2017, with the participation rate of almost 23%. The number of Australian students studying in Asia increased by more than 30% within just two years between 2014 and 2015 (AUIDF, 2016). The latest data shows that New Colombo Plan (NCP) students have been the main growth driver in the number of study abroad students in 2016 to 2017, while there was very little growth in non-NCP students (Ilieva, 2018). By 2018, the NCP had funded 40,000 students from 40 Australian universities to study and undertake internships across 35 locations in the Indo-Pacific (Australian Government, 2018a).

The NCP is considered the Australian government's premier student mobility and public diplomacy initiative. The key goals of the NCP are to 'broaden and deepen' Australia's engagement in the Indo-Pacific region through 'people-to-people connections' (Australian Government, 2016) and to provide Australian students with the opportunity to establish learning experiences in the Indo- Pacific region as a 'rite of passage'. Such an opportunity takes them beyond the traditional classroom settings into communities, workplaces and other experiential environments (Harrison & Potts, 2016). This is in line with the literature, which indicates study abroad is or is expected to increase students' professional competence and prospects for employability after graduation (Di Pietro, 2013; Nerlich, 2013; Potts, 2015).

The NCP is well funded, with a budget of AUD 50.93 million pa across 2018 to 2022 (Australian Government, 2018b) by the federal government and strongly supported by Australian universities. Yet, little is known about the impact of students' international experience through the NCP on their development of career choices, career transformations and life goals, despite the program being positioned as a 'rite of passage' between higher education and employment for Australian's young generations. Such knowledge is important to test the intention or claim that NCP participation boosts students' employability. Such knowledge is also essential for developing sustainable effective mobility programs integral to the government agenda to strengthen national human capital. This chapter is based on a study that responds to this knowledge gap by generating fresh insights into the relationship between participation in the NCP and employability, viewed from the students' perspectives. The study shows that exposure to different ways of constructing disciplinary knowledge, direct professional and personal experiences in Asia, new outlooks, skills and attributes, fostered via the NCP experience, have the potential to benefit students' long-term career development and, in particular, enhance their readiness for a future in relation to Asia. The findings point to many instances in which students' professional and personal selves have been shaped and reshaped through engagement with the host communities. However, how to maximise the potential benefit of study abroad via the NCP into students' future career outcomes and bridging the gap between students' self-perceived employability and actual employment outcomes remains a critical question. This chapter puts forward a number of practical recommendations for universities and related stakeholders to assist students in translating the experiences, learning and connections gained through the NCP into real career outcomes for students. It stresses the need to ensure that there is a close relationship between the student mobility unit and the career support service. It also underscores the importance of a coordinated and systemic framework to integrate study abroad experiences into pedagogy and other support services rather than treating them as stand-alone add-ons.

In this paper, the term 'Asia' is used in relation to this research, which focuses on Asian countries, while 'Indo-Pacific' is used to refer to policies on the NPC, which focuses on the Indo-Pacific region, including Asia, the Pacific and the sub-continent (Tran & Vu, 2018).

Study abroad and employability

The European Council (2012, p. 4) defined employability as "a combination of factors which enable individuals to progress towards or enter employment, to stay in employment and to progress throughout their careers". Various studies indicate the impact of the transformative experiences gained through study abroad on participants' career choices and employability. Focusing on the expansion of the European ERASMUS student exchange program, Parey and Waldinger (2010, p. 220) found that mobility programs may have a potentially large impact on "affecting students' behaviour in their labour market mobility decision". The authors (2010) argue that students with study abroad experience are more likely to follow their career in the country of their program or even in a different overseas destination. Such tendencies towards working abroad post-graduation can be attributed to either students' skill sets in relation to a particular context (i.e. language and knowledge of the labour market) or the overall impact of the overseas experience on widening students' horizons.

Gaining global work-ready skill sets is often regarded as an advantage that can potentially be achieved through either acquisition of overseas learning/work experience or graduation from overseas universities. Potts (2018) identifies and analyses 10 studies published between 2014 and 2018, which explore the link between learning abroad and employability. Based on her analyses, the author (2018, p. 19) concludes that "learning abroad facilitates skills development and provides an environment for applying new and existing skills". Potts points out that learning abroad can "provide a competitive edge in the graduate employment market" in some Anglophone contexts and foster particular skill sets such as "developing capacity in a second language" in some contexts such as Europe and Japan. A study by Matherly (2005) shows that study abroad experiences result in developing various employability attributes, including "increased confidence, adaptability and creativity in problem solving" in alumni (p. 30). Similarly, a study by Doorbar (2003) indicates the association of study abroad with interpersonal communication development in participating students.

Scholars (for example, Harder et al., 2015; Orahood, Kruze & Pearson, 2004; Trooboff, Vande Berg & Rayman, 2008) show that employers value study abroad experiences listed on graduates' resumes. Trooboff et al. (2008, p. 29) state in the US, "employers in general, and some classes of employers in particular, place significant value on studying abroad". Another US-based research by Harder et al. (2015) reported that the majority of employers in the agriculture and natural resources industries would prefer to recruit candidates with previous study abroad experience. In the field of business, graduates emphasised that mentioning study abroad experience on their CVs greatly grasps the attention of employers at job interviews (Orahood et al., 2004). From this perspective, study abroad is a "symbolic capital" (the term coined by Bourdieu, 1986) that improves the position of graduates in an increasingly competitive global employment market.

Bourdieu's theory as a conceptual frame

In this chapter, Bourdieu's concepts of capital and habitus are used to interpret students' perceptions of the potential impact of the NCP experience on their career directions and employability. Three forms of capital, social, cultural and economic, were classified by Bourdieu (1986; Bourdieu & Wacquant, 1992). Social capital refers to the social assets arising from social memberships, networks and relationships. Cultural capital is understood as the skills, knowledge, titles and sensibilities people possess. The concept of cultural capital encompasses the embodied (including language competence and style), the institutionalised (e.g. educational qualifications) and the objectified (including books and artwork) (Bourdieu, 1986). Economic capital is associated with the access to material and financial resources.

In the Bourdieuian scheme, habitus refers to "deeply internalised dispositions, schemas, and forms of know-how and competence, both mental and corporeal, first acquired by the individual through early childhood socialisation" (Swartz, 2002, p. 625). As an individual might possess or aspire to possess a different capital, habitus is also distinct for each individual.

Research design

The research focuses on two universities across South Australia and Victoria, Australia: one is part of the Group of Eight (Go8), which is a coalition of elite research-intensive Australian universities, and another is a 'young' university among the world's top universities under 50 years old. Fifty-two semi-structured interviews with NCP students, academics, mobility coordination staff and policy-makers were conducted over the two sites. Critical discourse analyses of national and institutional policy texts and policy settings and program were also conducted (Gribble & Tran, 2016; Tran & Rahimi, 2018).

After gaining the ethics approval from the university where the research was based, the researchers asked the director of mobility program and student mobility coordinators from each university to invite undergraduate students who were taking part in the NCP mobility program, academics, and outbound mobility staff to participate in the study. This paper, however, focuses mainly on the perspectives of NCP students. Student participants came from a range of disciplines, including science, health, humanities, education and business. Participants were involved in either mobility or scholarship program. A total of 35 NCP students participated in this study. Both pre-departure and re-entry interviews were conducted with 12 students (n = 24). Re-entry interviews alone were conducted with 23 other students. The recruitment of participants was based on their availability, access and willingness to share their experiences and offer sufficient information. Each interview lasted from 45 to 60 minutes. The participants' names and institutions are kept anonymous to protect their identity. The interview with NCP students focused on their motivations to undertake international mobility through the NCP, types of learning and engagement in Asia, effects of learning in Asia on their career pathways and access and equity.

All the interviews were audio recorded with participants' consent. They were then transcribed, entered into NVivo and analysed using *open coding* of responses to interview questions. This open coding method via NVivo enabled thematic analysis to identify patterns and different stakeholders' perspectives.

Discussion of findings

Existing literature on outbound mobility of students' career outcomes and employability is mainly restricted to research in the European contexts, especially ERASMUS programs (Potts, 2016). The current study provides an Australian perspective about this aspect of mobility programs through the perceptions of NCP student participants, who are generally positive about the effects of the program on their *career orientation* and *employability prospects*.

Career orientation

In this study, NCP student participants provided vivid accounts of how their abroad sojourn contributed to the (re)orientation of their future career:

> [Going over] there made me more excited about moving overseas to teach. It was always a dream of mine to move overseas and teach anyway but I guess *going to Malaysia enhanced that dream that little bit more because it made me think, "Well you know what, this is the focus, I'm still going to go overseas"*. It's not really my plan to teach in Australia, probably not until I've got that experience then I'll come back. So in that sense *I guess teaching overseas rather than here that's just where I see myself in life.*
>
> (Ingrid, Teacher Education, Malaysia, emphasis added in italics)

> *It was really eye opening in the fact that I realised how much international business actually interests me.* I think it was probably the most interesting subject that I've done at university so far. Like just seeing how this economy is—it's a completely different emerging economy and how they face different struggles compared to what we face in Australia. I feel like I've got a much more—*my career focus will be more focused on international business now that I've done a study tour like this.*
>
> (Jane, International Business, Thailand)

> Also, actually for me *it's more opened up the doors to one day want to teach in Asian countries*, because prior to this I was more inclined to move away to go to English speaking countries, so across to Europe, England or the Americas. But that's opened up Asia and I think I do want to go back to Malaysia or somewhere close, somewhere near there. *So it definitely changed my views on where I want to be in the future, what I want to do as well.*
>
> (James, Teaching Science, Malaysia)

In light of Bourdieu's theory, students' 'new' experience of discipline/profession-related engagement in transnational fields integrates with their habitus ("a dream of mine"—Brigid or "prior" inclination to teach in Anglo countries—Scott) and exerts different influences. The interview excerpts above indicate multiple ways in which the students' habitus about their future career has been affected following their NCP participation. Specifically, the NCP experience is reported to *enhance* their career habitus ("made me more excited about moving overseas to teach . . ."—Ingrid), *transform* the habitus ("it was really eye opening . . . I realised how much international business actually interests me . . . my career focus will be more focused on international business"—Jane) or *modify* the habitus ("it definitely changed my views on where I want to be in the future, what I want to do as well"—James). By looking at students' habitus, these research findings lend a new perspective to support previous studies that endorse the positive effects of the sojourn abroad, such as fostering students' motivation for their chosen career direction (Potts, 2015) or clarifying their imagination about their future career (Brandenburg et al., 2014) and decision about their future professional pursuits (Ingraham & Peterson, 2004).

In addition, it is shown from the current study that the NCP experience drew students' attention to Asia as 'where' they see their future career to be ("I guess teaching overseas rather than here that's just *where* I see myself in life"—Ingrid; "it definitely changed my views on *where* I want to be in the future, what I want to do as well"—James). This finding reinforces the association between international study experiences and an international career that has been suggested in various prior studies (Jahr & Teichler, 2007; Norris & Gillespie, 2009; Wiers-Jenssen, 2008).

The current research highlights that there could be a possible linkage between the destination of abroad learning and future career, as the NCP experience in Asian countries apparently encourages students to develop *Asia*-oriented career plans. The students' accounts also point to the interconnection between mobility, sense of place, growing understanding and connection to the host country and their professional identity. In this regard, the students reveal how their professional identity attached to their career aspiration is refined and redefined due to their exposure to and increased connection with the host country. The NCP experience thus provides students the cultural capital to pursue careers beyond the traditional ones, which are often defined by national parameters given their pre-existing habitus and its connection to their place of origin. A growing sense of place, growing awareness of the 'other' culture, hands-on experience and growing connections with Asia seem to open up a space of 'new normal' for career aspirations and trajectories for the students.

For some students, the international experience has the potential to spark a new interest in a career direction (Dwyer, 2004):

> It was definitely a worthwhile experience. I learnt a lot about India and I also learnt stuff that I hadn't even asked questions for, I learnt about and it opened my eyes to different areas of work in international health. And like things that I might be interested in *pursuing in my career at some* point.
>
> (*Kristine, International Health, India*)

> Well, now I understand that it's really beneficial for people like me. I don't think it's really all that beneficial for the place I go to at the time. *It's more beneficial for me when I come back and I have these I guess inspiring ideas and more understanding about maybe where I want to go and do in the future.* It could also just be more of a deterrent for teaching as I learn more about I guess the bad constructions there are in all education systems. But, really this gives me, it more just opened my eyes up I guess would be the best thing out of it.
>
> (*James, Teaching Science, Malaysia*)

Interestingly, as shown in the second quotation above, the student indicated that the change or the new interest in career orientation did not take place during the in-country experience but after he came back to Australia. This shows the importance of developing a pedagogy underpinning the whole cycle of study abroad including the re-entry stage to guide and support students in engaging in critical reflection, specific activities and explicit thinking about the effects of study abroad on their professional growth, their awareness of the professional self and career possibilities. This finding aligns with Tran and Rahimi's (2018, p. 13) argument about the critical need to develop "a more structured and coherent approach to learning abroad that involves not only students but also mobility offices and academics from both the home and host universities/organisations to support deep and continuing engagement, learning, and capacity building during and after international mobility experiences".

Ways of interpreting disciplinary knowledge and international outlooks

A distinct effect of engagement in study abroad via the NCP indicated by some students is how it helps to provide them with an exposure to different approaches to disciplinary knowledge and instil an international outlook on their discipline-specific learning and professional field:

> [N]ow *having gone to China I think that I'm interested in the context of public health in an international sense* as well. So maybe that's something I will pursue as a career later on in life.
>
> *(Laura, Law-Health Sciences Double Degree, China)*

> Differences between research they do in Japan compared to Australia, research skills, things that are good for my employability . . . the study tour helps with my academic learning because [I am exposed to] different kinds of oceanography in Japan.
>
> *(Melissa, Science, Japan)*

> I thought it was a really great opportunity thinking about *my future career*, seeing as you know the world becoming so globalised I guess. I just wanted a bit of an *experience and an insight* into another country's health issues, and how they're going about tackling their issues pretty much, and then hopefully I'll be able to have some knowledge that can sort of be applied in an Australian setting, or be more knowledgeable about health on a more international scale I guess.
>
> *(Paul, Health Sciences, India)*

Being exposed to alternative approaches to disciplinary knowledge and possibly some contrasts in professional practices in Asia may stimulate students' minds and provoke new thoughts in how things can be done differently in different contexts.

Such an exposure fosters the condition to nurture the development of students' international perspectives to disciplinary learning, different or alternative approaches to curriculum-specific issues, international outlooks and comparative and reflective capabilities that are of growing importance for a career in an increasingly globalised work environment. However, professional learning may not occur naturally during the international experience without appropriate and purposeful pedagogy to engage students in learning. Tran (2013) stresses the need to design specific learning activities across different stages of learning, including the re-entry, to assist students with the development of international outlook and productive comparative perspectives that are useful to their professional learning. These activities should focus on engaging students in discussing and comparing the professional practices shaped by the different national, political and socio-cultural context to which students are exposed and draw implications for their professional development.

Development of experiential learning, networking and cross-cultural understandings

Students highlighted that study abroad through the NCP provides them with the opportunity to develop international hands-on experience and overseas networking that could help enhance their employability:

> Yeah, because it's all about making connections and getting your name out there so that when you graduate *it's all about who you know*, so that's really what's motivating me.
>
> *(Janet, Primary Education, Malaysia)*

> Well that was definitely a plus but I think for me, it was the real world experience. Because I don't really get placement in my course unless I do an internship or something like that. So to be able to study and get *real world/ hands on* experience, that was a definitely win win situation for me. Also the *networking with people overseas, I feel like that could be very beneficial for graduands*, like me, at the end of the year.
>
> *(Helen, Environmental Health, India)*

> I guess the main thing was to get some *hands-on experience* and to grow as a health professional. I just think it'd be a really, really good experience and to open my mind to the health issue, as there's such a difference between the health issues, between Australia and abroad.
>
> *(Caitlin, Health Science, India)*

International experience clearly provides students with rich authentic learning environments. In this case, students are provided with the opportunity to be exposed to what is actually happening in a real context related to their study subject but in an overseas setting. International situated learning presents enormous potential for students to develop professional and cultural capitals, ranging from hands-on experience to disciplinary-specific knowledge, international perspectives, cultural understanding and networking. However, learning is not simply achieved through observation or engagement in the experience but more from opportunities for them to engage in analysis, discussion and critical reflection of the context.

Other students referred to the development of cross-cultural understandings and professional and personal self as potentially enhancing their employability:

> I know it's two completely different worlds but it's allowed me to kind of be more mindful of other people and their cultures and yeah.
>
> *(Mary, Health, India)*

> And I guess *I'll just grow professionally* and as a person, to be able to do something like this . . .
>
> *(Caitlin, Health, India)*

NCP experience as value for employers

A distinctive value of the NCP experience on the students' employment and professional competence is their perception of its attractiveness to employers. In the following excerpts, the students elaborated on how they perceived their engagement in the NCP program would be valued by employers:

> I think *employers want to know that* you've got that experience, *you've been outside of Australia as well, you've seen diversity, you've seen culture and you can bring that knowledge and experience straight into the work field as well.* Like even in, just like working in Geelong or Bendigo, there's always diversity and you've got to learn to work with people with all different backgrounds and abilities.
>
> *(Joe, Health, India)*

> I remember when I had my interview over the phone, both *people that I spoke to were quite impressed about that and they thought, "Wow, what an amazing opportunity you got to go somewhere, like a different country to teach for three weeks. I think that's fantastic".* And because London is so multi-cultural as well with kids from different backgrounds *it's good to bring that to the table and be able to*, you know, when I go there and teach there *I'll be more culturally sensitive around those kids because I've been around it before.*
>
> *(Ingrid, Teacher Education, Malaysia)*

> Anyone who I've spoken to so far about getting a job as a nurse next year said that *my experience in Nepal will stand out, because no one would have had an opportunity like that in my course, because not many people do the double degree . . . my ability to transfer the skills that I learnt over there, like overcoming challenge*s and stuff like that, I know that that will *bring confidence into my nursing practice* as well.
>
> *(Charlotte, Nursing, Nepal)*

These students, of different disciplines, all contend that the intercultural and professional experience gained from their NCP participation adds value to their employability. They are or become aware that their acquisition of 'professional capital' such as knowledge, skill and attributes related to their profession, intercultural competence ("diversity, culture") (Joe), cultural sensitivity (Ingrid) and self-confidence (Charlotte) can potentially be valued by future employers. Janet, particularly, was successful in her job application. In particular, a student links the development of flexibility and adaptability to her potentially enhanced employability. She explicitly mentioned "the flexibility in working in different environments and in different countries" gained through the mobility program will make her more work ready in today's changing and globalised work environment.

Students also made links between the international work placement and the enhancement of their resumes:

> And having it on *my resume* is such a great thing to show that, you know, I really do care about what I want to do and that I will go the extra lengths.
>
> *(Janet, Primary Education, Malaysia)*

> The key benefits? It was insightful. It provided me with just a good opportunity so it looks good *on a resume* and I've just had a placement and stuff like that, so it's kind of all led onto that.
>
> *(Mary, Health, India)*

The participants see international internships as not only enabling them to have insights into the real-world practices overseas but interestingly as an indication of their positive attitude towards their professional learning and willingness to go extra miles to develop their professional capabilities and experiences. In other words, an international experience in this case is regarded as a symbolic capital that helps to present themselves positively for prospective employers. Existing literature also suggests students are attracted by the value of study abroad on their resumes (Chew & Croy, 2011; Mulvey, 2012).

Concluding remarks and practical recommendations

The findings from this study show that NPC students see their employability being potentially enhanced thanks to the development of new or different perspectives on disciplinary knowledge, new outlooks, experiential learning, networking, cross-cultural understandings in Asia and critical skills and attributes, in particular, the flexibility to operate in different environments. There is initial evidence that effective engagement with Asia through the NCP and continuing learning post return enables the development of an Asia-oriented/Asia-aware mindset in students' career directions. Meaningful engagement and sustainable learning in Asia and beyond the mobility experience helps to foster students' motivation for their chosen career direction, ignite new interest in a career direction or clarify their imagination regarding their future career. Participation in a well-designed mobility program or internship provides students with the opportunity to acquire important disciplinary knowledge and practical experience potentially valued by employers. Increasingly, employers are seeking graduates who have relevant discipline-related work experience, and the internship component of NCP is regarded as a distinct strength of the program. While study abroad has the potential to enhance graduate employability, more structured and sustainable support and guidance are required in order to equip students with the capability and approaches to translate their mobility experiences into the skills, attributes and competencies valued by employers and meaningful to their life and communities with which they engage. Study abroad can only be regarded as a 'rite of passage' for students if they are supported to use "these experiences to better effect into the future" (Forsey et al., 2011, p. 37). Tran and Rahimi (2018) stress the importance to "move beyond the ideological frame and normative assumption that increased understanding of the Indo-Pacific, learning and engagement with it will automatically happen" (p. 13), and employability will automatically be enhanced simply by sending students to the region. Reflection, continuing learning and sustaining connections are among the key features to truly realise the maximum impact of these experiences for the students.

Recommendations for practice

Institutions have a key role to play in ensuring the experiences gained through the NCP are translated into real career outcomes for students. This study further reinforces the need to integrate study abroad experiences into pedagogy and other support services rather than treating them as stand-alone add-ons.

As study abroad experiences are still only available to a small but growing minority of students, institutions should pay close attention to continuing to build participation. If participation does not increase (including to under-represented groups), the employability benefits demonstrated in this study will continue to be unavailable to most students. This represents an ongoing equity concern.

Strategies for institutions to consider may include:

> At this institutional level, ensuring study abroad is considered alongside other initiatives intended to boost employability such as internships and work integrated learning.

> Explicitly promoting study abroad experiences as career development opportunities in addition to their benefits in terms of discipline content, global experience and intercultural development.

> Ensuring there is a close relationship between the student mobility unit and the career support service. Employability programs for students before their study abroad experience can help them understand the employment value of experiences before and as they occur, and support post return can help students

understand and enhance their ability to articulate their own growth and transferrable skills as they relate to their future employment.

Building opportunities for critical reflection of students' learning and experiences into the NCP programs, with explicit guidance provided around employability.

Finding opportunities for students to use the specific experiences and learnings of their NCP experience in courses/subjects undertaken after they return. Such opportunities may include classroom activities where NCP students are invited to reflect on and share their experiences, case studies and assessments building on the insights they gained during their NCP experience.

Where possible, including exposure to international work environments in study abroad experiences. Institutions' international alumni networks can provide a useful resource for this.

DFAT's increased support for alumni through the NCP Alumni Program is a welcoming move in boosting alumni's ongoing connections with the region and their employability. There is scope for DFAT and institutions' mobility unit, career service and faculty to work more closely together in optimising the benefits of professional development and networking events and learning opportunities for alumni into real employment outcomes. The combined expertise of these key stakeholders, if effectively tapped on, is crucial to realise the maximum impact of NCP experiences on participants' employability.

Limitation of the research: This study offers valuable insights into NCP students' perspectives on how their short-term mobility or internship has helped them shape or reshaped their career aspirations and potentially enhanced their employability. However, further investigation into the long-term impact of the NCP experience on students' career prospects and outcomes after their graduation is recommended to have a more nuanced understanding of the causal relationships between study abroad and employability. A follow-up longitudinal study (2017–2021) by the research team funded by the Australian Research Council is an attempt to respond to this gap.

References

Australian Government (2016). *New Colombo Plan: Connect to Australia's future – study in the region.* Canberra: DFAT.

Australian Government (2018a). *An infographic on the NCP.* Canberra. Retrieved from https://dfat.gov.au/people-to-people/new-colombo-plan/resources/Documents/an-infographic-on-the-ncp.pdf

Australian Government (2018b). *New Colombo Plan Guidelines Mobility Program 2019 Round.* Canberra: DFAT. Retrieved from https://dfat.gov.au/people-to-people/new-colombo-plan/mobility-program/Documents/ncp-mobility-program-guidelines-2019.pdf

Australian Universities International Directors Forum (AUIDF) (2016). *Learning abroad 2015.* Newcastle, Australia: Author.

Australian Universities International Directors Forum (AUIDF) (2018). *Learning abroad 2017 (in 2018)*. Canberra: AUIDF.

Bourdieu, P. (1986). The forms of capital. In J. Richardson (Ed.), *Handbook of theory and research for the sociology of education* (pp. 241–258). New York, NY: Greenwood Press.

Bourdieu, P., & Wacquant, L. (1992). *An invitation to reflexive sociology*. Cambridge: Polity.

Brandenburg, U., Berghoff, S., Taboadela, O., Bischof, L., Gajowniczek, J., Gehlke, A., & Petrova, D. (2014). *The ERASMUS impact study. Effects of mobility on the skills and employability of students and the internationalisation of higher education institutions*. Publications office of the European Union, Luxembourg. Retrieved from http://ec.europa.eu/education/library/study/2014/erasmus-impact_en.pdf

Bretag, T., & van der Veen, R. (2015). 'Pushing the boundaries': Participant motivation and self-reported benefits of short-term international study tours. *Innovations in Education and Teaching International*, 1–9.

Byrne, C. (2016). Australia's New Colombo Plan: Enhancing regional soft power through student mobility. *Intl. J.: Canada's J. of Global Policy Analysis, 0*(0), 1–22.

Chew, A., & Croy, W. G. (2011). International education exchanges: Exploratory case study of Australian-based tertiary students' incentives and barriers. *Journal of Teaching in Travel & Tourism, 11*(3), 253–270.

Di Pietro, G. (2013). Do study abroad programs enhance the employability of graduates? *IZA Discussion Paper, No. 7675*.

Doorbar, A. (2003). The US study abroad market: What are the barriers to purchase? *Networker (Fall)*, 58–60. Institute of International Education (IIE).

Dwyer, M. M. (2004). More is better: The impact of study abroad program duration. *Frontiers: The Interdisciplinary Journal of Study Abroad, 10*, 151–164.

European Council (2012). *Council conclusions of 11 May 2012 on the employability of graduates from education and training*. OJ 2012/C 169/04, 15.6.2012. Brussels.

Forsey, M. G., Broomhall, S., & Davis, J. (2011). Broadening the mind? Australian student reflections on the experience of overseas study. *Journal of Studies in International Education, 16*(2), 128–139.

Gribble, C., & Tran, L. T. (2016). *International trends in learning abroad: Information and promotions campaign for student mobility*. Melbourne: Universities Australia & IEAA.

Harder, A., Andenoro, A., Roberts, T. G., Stedman, N., Newberry III, M., Parker, S. J., & Rodriguez, M. T. (2015). Does study abroad increase employability? *NACTA Journal, 59*(1), 41

Harrison, L., & Potts, D. (2016). *Learning abroad at Australian universities: The current environment*. IEAA. Retrieved from www.ieaa.org.au/documents/item/752

Ilieva, J. (2018). Outward mobility: Comparative evidence; *mimeo*. Bristol, UK.

Ingraham, E. C., & Peterson, D. L. (2004). Assessing the impact of study abroad on student learning at Michigan State University. *Frontiers: The Interdisciplinary Journal of Study Abroad, 10*, 83–100.

Jahr, V., & Teichler, U. (2007). Graduates' international experience and mobility. *Careers of University Graduates*, 211–224.

Matherly, C. (2005). Effective marketing of international experiences to employers. In M. Tillman (Ed.), *Impact of education abroad on career development*, pp. 9–10. Stamford, CT: American Institute for Foreign Study.

Mulvey, L. (2012). Why study abroad? Why not! *Educational Research and Innovation*, 319–332.

Nerlich, S. (2013). Australians as international students–where they go, what they do and why they do it. *Journal of Higher Education Policy and Management, 35*(4), 386–395.

Norris, E. M., & Gillespie, J. (2009). How study abroad shapes global careers: Evidence from the United States. *Journal of Studies in International Education, 13*(3), 382.

Orahood, T., Kruze, L., & Pearson, D. E. (2004). The impact of study abroad on business students' career goals. *Frontiers: The Interdisciplinary Journal of Study Abroad, 10*, 117–130.

Parey, M., & Waldinger, F. (2010). Studying abroad and the effect on international labour market mobility: Evidence from the introduction of ERASMUS. *The Economic Journal, 121*(551), 194–222.

Potts, D. (2015). Understanding the early career benefits of learning abroad programs. *Journal of Studies in International Education, 19*(5), 441–459.

Potts, D. (2016). *Outcomes of learning abroad programs*. Melbourne: International Education Association of Australia (IEAA). Retrieved from www.ieaa.org.au/documents/item/750

Potts, D. (2018). Learning abroad and employability: Researching the connections. *Research Digest, No. 13*. Melbourne, Australia: International Education Association of Australia. Retrieved from www.ieaa.org.au/documents/item/1267

Swartz, D. L. (2002). The sociology of habit: The perspective of Pierre Bourdieu. *OTJR: Occupation, Participation and Health, 22*(1 suppl), 61S–69S.

Tran, L. T. (2013). *Teaching international students in vocational education and training: New pedagogical approaches*. Camberwell: ACER Press.

Tran, L. T., & Rahimi, M. (2018). New Colombo Plan: A review of research and implications for practice. *Research Digest, No. 14*. Melbourne, Australia: International Education Association of Australia. Retrieved from www.ieaa.org.au/documents/item/1448

Tran, L. T., & Vu, T. T. P. (2018). Beyond the 'normal' to the 'new possibles': Australian students' experiences in Asia and their roles in making connections with the region via the New Colombo Plan. *Higher Education Quarterly, 72*(3), 194–207.

Trooboff, S., Vande Berg, M., & Rayman, J. (2008). Employer attitudes toward study abroad. *Frontiers: The Interdisciplinary Journal of Study Abroad, 15*, 17–33.

Wiers-Jenssen, J. (2008). Does higher education attained abroad lead to international jobs? *Journal of Studies in International Education, 12*(2), 101.

10

TEACHING TOWARDS GRADUATE ATTRIBUTES

How much does this approach help Australian graduates with employability?

Thanh Pham and Eisuke Saito

Introduction

Graduate attributes have become the focus of Australian higher education during the past two decades. However, 'graduate attributes' is yet to be defined because there is a great deal of variation in the way universities and academics interpret and work on graduate attributes. Graduate attributes are also referred to as 'soft skills', 'graduate competencies', 'work-ready skills', 'generic skills' and 'transferable skills' (Tomlinson, 2012). In Australia, the concept of graduate attributes was introduced into the higher education agenda by the West Review in 1998 (Department of Education, Training and Youth Affairs [DETYA], 1998). This review provided a list of generic attributes that university graduates should obtain during their tertiary study. In the following years, there were various studies investigating the skills and attributes that university students are believed to be equipped with. Barrie (2004) emerged as one of the leading researchers in graduate employability. She identified four levels or clusters of graduate attributes, including:

1. necessary precursor skills and abilities (mainly reading, writing and arithmetic);
2. skills that complement discipline knowledge;
3. abilities to translate or apply disciplinary knowledge; and
4. abilities that infuse and enable all scholarly learning and knowledge.

Since then, Barrie's attribute clusters have largely influenced the establishment of specific skills and attributes that many Australian universities have attempted to embed into their programmes and courses.

Australian universities and their engagement with the graduate attributes agenda

Australia initiated the idea of matching knowledge and skills produced in universities and those required by employers during the mid-1990s. This agenda emerged due to various factors, among which Leoni (2012) identified the reason being that this period was characterised by heavy organisational and technological shocks because of the emergence of new types of firms (e.g., lean production, internally flexible firm, modular firm) and the rapid development of ICT. These changes led to a high unemployment rate because workers failed to meet the new requirements of employers. European governments, therefore, initiated the 'Bologna Process' that required higher education providers to match students' learning outcomes with the requirements of employers (Leon, 2012). An important aspect of the Bologna initiative is that it emphasises generic skills and general knowledge more than specialised knowledge and degrees.

Australia then quickly showed its impetus towards the Bologna agenda (Jackson, 2009). This support was shown via the establishment of the Committee for Quality Assurance in Higher Education and then the Tertiary Education Quality and Standards Agency (TEQSA), formerly known as the Australian Universities Quality Agency (AUQA) in early 2000. TEQSA strongly supports the development of graduate attributes in higher education, and so it requires evidence of industry engagement in course development (TEQSA, 2012). TEQSA mandates that Australian higher education providers can only maintain their accreditation if they comply with TEQSA's Higher Education Standards Framework (Threshold Standards). Therefore, the Framework requires higher education providers to mention their graduate attributes in their curricula and how they teach to meet these attributes explicitly.

All universities have to take a serious approach when embedding these attributes in their programmes and courses because both the government and accrediting organisations make it a requirement that universities must show how their students are learning the skills and attaining the attributes that are claimed. Also, the employment success rate is now used to justify the quality of higher education (Bath, Smith, Stein, & Swann, 2004). One significant condition of assessment for public funding requires Australian higher education providers to demonstrate how they are engaged in embedding graduate attributes in their courses and programmes. The government makes public funding for universities partially contingent upon demonstrable graduate outcomes, with an emphasis on the production of 'work-ready' graduates who are competent within their disciplinary fields and possess the abilities necessary to negotiate a world of work that is in constant flux (Bowden, Hart, King, Trigwell, & Watts, 2000). To respond to the requirements of TEQSA's Higher Education Standards Framework, researchers, academics, industries and Australian universities have attempted to identify specific graduate attributes that they believe university students need to develop during the course of their studies. Many programmes have used a mapping approach to show

how each graduate has embedded these attributes in their units and programmes (Thompson, Treleaven, Kamvounias, Beem, & Hill, 2008).

However, as discussed previously, although Barrie's (2004) attribute clusters provide an outline of key attributes, there is, at present, no agreeable definition of each graduate attribute. The concept is fluid depending on how each university, faculty, department, programme of study and academic interprets it. The attributes are even sometimes interpreted in opposing ways. For instance, 'critical thinking' is often interpreted as 'asking many questions', but it can also be seen as a 'more cognitive-centred' process, with the meaning of thinking quietly (Jin & Cortazzi, 1995). This variation has made it hard for all stakeholders to ensure whether graduates have achieved satisfactory attributes even when they are assessed and measured in assignment rubrics. Furthermore, attributes are abstract and tend to be subjective, so the question as to how much they should be embedded in each unit is contentious among academics, faculties and universities.

As Australian universities are currently under great pressure to produce employable graduates (Bridgstock, 2009), there is an increasing focus on how to match graduate attributes and employability; universities and academics are certainly interested in knowing whether their graduates have been equipped with sufficient attributes. Barrie (2004) claimed that a sound strategy that could measure the success of the graduate attributes approach is to obtain feedback from industries and employers about the quality of graduates when they enter the workforce. However, to date, surprisingly, there has been a lack of an effective methodology to gain useful feedback from employers. Very limited attempts have been made to find out if graduates are actually demonstrating those attributes in the workplace using employer feedback. The predominant current research method is online, one-off surveys. They have yet to use well-established approaches to gathering continuous feedback from industries and employers. In addition to this, graduate attributes and employability are complicated concepts. Besides this, no attempt has been made to reveal the potential uses of the findings reported in different studies.

This chapter attempts to fill this gap by reviewing the literature to reveal the relationship between graduate attributes and employability skills through an exploration of key attributes that are currently emphasised by Australian universities and those key employability skills required by employers. This exploration will provide some insights into whether Australian universities are preparing their graduates with the right skills and attributes that industries and employers are looking for. The chapter also examines feedback of employers about the quality of Australian graduates in the labour market. This examination aims to determine whether graduates are equipped with the attributes and skills at a level that satisfies employers and industries. This would give some evidence indicating the effectiveness of the graduate attributes approach.

Data collection and analysis

The project is based on existing documentation research whereby the authors conducted a qualitative literature review of relevant documents and reports. Relevant studies included in this investigation were identified through a thorough search for relevant published studies. To do so, first of all, we utilised electronic databases, including Educational Resources Information Centre (ERIC), Psychological Abstracts (PA), Dissertation Abstracts International (DAI) and the Social Sciences Citation Index (SSCI). Second, we examined relevant bibliographies, searched reference sections of the studies included in this study to identify further relevant studies and contacted relevant researchers and organisations for supplementary data. The search used a combination of keywords, such as 'Australia', 'graduate attributes', 'employers', 'employability skills', 'employability', 'university', 'higher education', 'work-ready', 'soft skills' and 'graduates'. To ensure high-quality resources and a sharp focus, the review set the following inclusion and exclusion criteria:

- The review only included published documents. This aims to enable the audience to access the original sources for further interaction should such needs arise. For this reason, a few unpublished reports and or theses in the field were excluded from consideration in this study.
- Within the scope of this paper, the review only included research in the Australian context. This criterion excluded a large amount of research on graduate attributes and employability skills in other countries, especially in European countries where a lot of research on higher education and graduate employability has been done.
- To ensure the rigor of the reviewed studies, the paper only selected projects with a large scope such as at the faculty, university or national level.

We acknowledge the absence of access to internal reports of universities, faculties and companies which might have provided additional details. Besides this, we are also aware that since this chapter only includes research conducted in Australia, it may show a different or narrower perspective than if it had been conducted on a broader scale.

Findings

Graduate attributes at Australian universities

There is much variation in the types and interpretation of graduate attributes identified by Australian universities and academics. The literature has, so far, reported three large projects that have attempted to identify the most common attributes that university students need to develop during their university programme. Brief details of these projects are (1) the ALTC national 'Graduate attributes project' (GAP) (2009), (2) the 'B factor project: understanding academic staff beliefs about graduate attributes' (De la Harpe et al., 2009) and (3) the 'Proclaimed graduate attributes of Australian universities: patterns, problems and prospects' project by Donleavy (2012). The graduate attributes identified in these projects are provided in

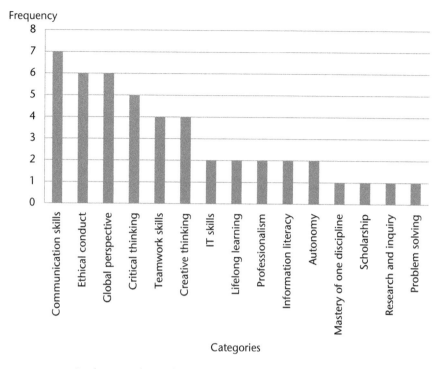

Frequency

Categories

FIGURE 10.1 Graduate attributes disclosed by key research in Australia

Figure 10.1. In this figure and those following, the 'X' axis represents the categories of items that those reports referred to, and the 'Y' axis represents the frequencies of references on those categories.

Findings of Figure 10.1 show that almost all universities and academics selected 'communication' and 'global perspective' as the key graduate attributes. Beyond this similarity, there was a variance in the selection of other attributes among universities and academics and among the different types of universities. Surprisingly, 'IT skills' and 'problem-solving skills' have been widely emphasised in teaching and learning at universities but were not selected as key attributes of the majority of universities and academics. Further, 'academic results' were not mentioned by all universities and academics. A group of regional universities in Donleavy's (2012) research selected 'in-depth mastery of one discipline', but it was unclear if this attribute meant 'academic results'.

Skills and attributes expected from Australian employers

After screening research on the skills and attributes that employers expected from graduates, six projects met the selection criteria: (1) the 'Employability skills for the future framework' project, (2) the Graduate Outlook Survey (GOS), (3) Shah and Nair's (2011) project, (4) Scott, Chang, and Grebennikov's (2010) project, (5) the

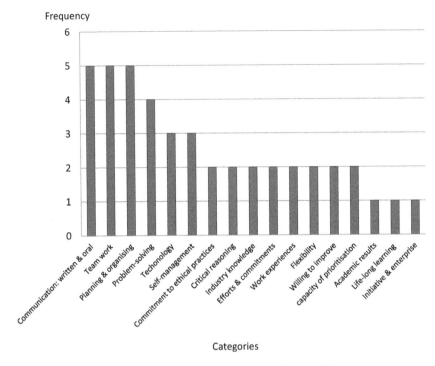

FIGURE 10.2 Employability skills and attributes required by employers

University of South Australia's (UniSA) survey (2009) and (6) McArthur, Kubacki, Pang, and Alcaraz's (2017) research. The skills and attributes required by employers in these projects are provided in Figure 10.2.

The findings of Figure 10.2 show that almost all employers selected 'communication' as a strong requirement of graduates. Following this, emphasised skills were 'teamwork', 'problem-solving' and 'planning and organising'. Although not being selected by the majority of employers, 'IT skills', 'industry knowledge' and 'work experience' appeared as strong areas that employers expected to see from graduates.

Skills and attributes of graduates that employers were NOT satisfied with

The review process revealed six projects that revealed employers' feedback about the qualities of graduates that they were not satisfied with. Among these projects, three projects (Graduate Outlook Report, 2015; Shah & Nair, 2004, 2008; UniSA, 2009) were the same as reported in Figure 10.2. Three new projects were (1) the Department of Education, Science and Training's (DEST, 2002) project, Jackson and Chapman's (2012) project and (3) Australian Industry Group's (2008) project. The skills and attributes that employers in these projects were not satisfied with are reported in Figure 10.3.

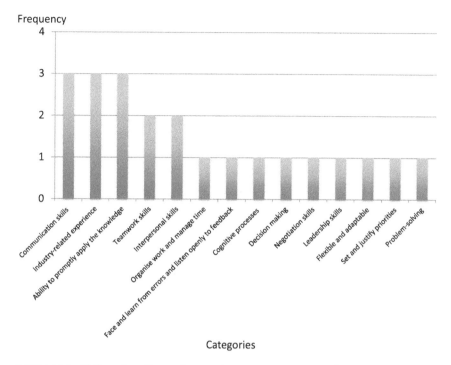

FIGURE 10.3 Skills and attributes that employers were NOT satisfied with

Discussion and implications

Key points drawn from a comparison of findings reported in Figure 10.1, Figure 10.2 and Figure 10.3 are discussed below.

Why do Australian graduates lack 'application skills and industry knowledge'?

As shown in Figure 10.3, one of the areas that employers were not satisfied with in graduates were application skills and industry knowledge. So, what can be done? It is obvious that Australian universities have been equipping students with industry and applicable knowledge through work-integrated learning (WIL) programmes (e.g., placement, internship). The benefits of these programmes are obvious. For instance, Crebert, Bates, Bell, Patrick, and Cragnolini (2004) clearly evidenced that these programmes could enhance students' employability because students could obtain a set of 'real-world' skills. Jackson (2016), in turn, further claimed that experiences obtained in these programmes could help students learn in their disciplines more effectively because they could become more critical by using their problem-solving and analytical skills obtained in the real world. Universities, academics and students expect these programmes to support students' knowledge about industry.

However, leaving the development of students' knowledge and skills about industries to only these programmes has some limitations due to three main reasons. First, WIL programmes are often organised over a short period (ranging from a few days to weeks), meaning that students have limited time and opportunities to learn real-world knowledge and apply their conceptual knowledge in real situations. Second, students have been reported to have various issues while on these programmes, among which, poor communication at the workplace has emerged as a paramount issue (Jackling & Natoli, 2015; Jackson, 2016; Tran & Soejatminah, 2016). This means that students' learning in these WIL programmes can be hindered in terms of developing communication skills.

Issues discussed previously indicate that 'industry knowledge and skills' should not be perceived as what Gilbert, Kristjuhan, Winkler, and Svejstrup (2004) and Sandberg (2000) described as 'reductionist' and 'instrumentalist' that could be developed as extra skills beyond the disciplinary subjects. To better develop in these areas, students should be given more chances to interact with employers and industries – such as having employers join in on teaching the units, or interacting with students at informal on- and off-campus events. Moreover, as Thompson et al. (2008) pointed out, students are often not keen on working on what they are not explicitly required to. Consequently, higher education institutions could include these knowledge and skill areas explicitly on their attribute lists and in their programmes and units. This will ensure that students are aware of the need to work on these areas during the whole university programme and not just on one-off WIL programmes.

Finally, there is a need to embed industry knowledge and skills in teaching and assessment activities. If teaching and assessment are adjusted as to become more hands-on activities, students would be given a better chance to investigate and then improve their possession of skills and knowledge. It is certainly challenging to teach and learn knowledge application into practices within a couple of years while engaging students in various courses. However, this may suggest that faculty members need to investigate issues that practitioners face within their industries more and theorise on those practical issues.

Why are employers dissatisfied with graduates' communication and other non-technical skills?

Employers' dissatisfaction with graduates' communication and other non-technical skills may arise for various reasons. First, at a conceptual level, there is currently a lack of shared understanding of attributes and skills across and between stakeholder groups (academics, industry and students) (Pellegrino & Hilton, 2012). Jackson (2009) evidenced a range of different interpretations of an attribute or skill depending on the background, expertise and position of the interpreter. This leads to confusion among universities and academics and so may embed unnecessary or insufficient attributes in programmes and courses. Pellegrino and Hilton (2012) found that the lack of a shared understanding of attributes and skills has exacerbated the lack of engagement among various groups to the extent that it has been claimed that 'employers, education providers and the youth live in parallel universes' (Mourshed, Farrell, & Barton, 2012, p. 12).

Second, at the implementation stage, there are obstacles facing university, faculties and academics in equipping students with these attributes. At university level, while the quality assurance process in course development requires an employer engagement, the process is questionable because there have not been clear requirements of the industries and employers who could be seen as 'representatives' of an industry. Even if these requirements were issued, the next question would be how many representatives, and how much of their input is enough. A decade ago, Barrie (2006) identified flaws in this process when claiming that the employer representatives in course advisory committees were close allies of individual academics, which limited course development and external input. Massy (2003) and Swift (2012) found another issue with this process when arguing that it was costly and complicated. For example, some universities did not take it seriously and just ticked the boxes. Consequently, some new courses were approved without proper collaboration and discussion between university and employers.

At the programme and course level, the structure consists of several levels so it is hard to make a clear division as to how much should be done at each level. Then at each level, it is impossible to know and divide clearly which aspect of the attributes should be done by whom and where. This often leads to confusion and repetition among courses and units. Consequently, some attributes might be emphasised while others are ignored. More problematically, various studies have found that the implementation of the graduate attributes process is mostly hindered at the academic level (Barrie, Hughes, & Smith, 2009; Jones, 2014). This is because such attributes are often seen as extra skills and qualities that students need to achieve beyond their discipline knowledge. Therefore, academics often see this task as additional work, on top of their main duty which is teaching disciplinary knowledge, leading to their lack of seriousness in working with their students to achieve attributes. Furthermore, a common issue is that even if academics take the graduate attributes approach on board, many of them do not have the capacity to be able to teach and assess these attributes. At the level of the curriculum, academics are uncomfortable teaching skills beyond their discipline-specific experience (Barrie et al., 2009; De la Harpe et al., 2009). This is a big concern for 'hard' disciplines like STEM because there still appears to be an emphasis on their acquisition of content knowledge (Jones, 2014; Wieman, 2007) at the expense of more work-relevant skills and capabilities applicable to real-life settings. The difficulty of finding the optimal balance between knowledge acquisition and skills development is that many university STEM educators are themselves scientists and engineers, and not necessarily skilled in pedagogy and course design that incorporates more work-related skills and capabilities. Consequently, STEM undergraduates may be lacking opportunities to apply their content knowledge to contextually relevant situations. Nagarajan and Edwards (2014) have therefore claimed that at some universities, graduate attributes remain at the level of intended or desired outcomes for students.

This discussion has drawn out the main issues that have hindered the graduate attributes approach. This explains why some attributes, especially the 'communication' attribute, are presented as key areas that the academic world is keen on working on but do not satisfy employers. Issues discussed previously have brought about a problem that many universities and academics may only have superficial engagement with the graduate attributes approach, which may be a contributory factor to the poor outcomes of graduates. Rather than designing courses that are highly valued by academics, there is an urgent need for Australian universities to liaise and communicate much more effectively with industry and employer groups. Understanding how skills are described and applied in industry is an important step in deriving shared understanding and meanings between stakeholders.

Conclusion

The aim of this chapter was to reveal the relationship between graduate attributes and employability skills through an exploration of key attributes that are currently emphasised by Australian universities and the key employability skills required by employers. Key findings, as above, are (1) graduates lack the industrial knowledge and experiences and inevitably applicable knowledge and (2) employers have found the graduates' communication and other non-technical skills as insufficient, as well. This is partly due to a dearth of (a) exposure by the graduates to industries, (b) the consensus among the stakeholders as discussed above about definition of attributes, (c) the complexity of course and programme development and (d) clear requirements of industries and employers.

As found in the literature, graduates are likely to be insufficiently equipped with not only specific job-related attributes, but also with 'soft skills' (Bowden et al., 2000; Tomlinson, 2012). This would suggest that there is a strong question on how much graduates can adapt themselves with fast-paced changes in the industries and how much Australian universities have been successful in teaching them from industrial perspectives, although it has been on the agenda in national higher educational policies since the 1990s (DETYA, 1998).

These findings show that although graduate employability has become an issue of increasing importance for higher education providers (Rae, 2007; Rampersad & Patel, 2014), still the trajectory on this is very new and has to be further developed, and the efforts should be made by multiple stakeholders. There should be closer consultation among stakeholders on, for example, agreeable definitions of graduate attributes to reduce widening gaps in the way of interpretations on graduate attributes within universities and academics. Rather, their efforts need to be towards largely agreed ones, or at least mutually complementary to target them by utilising their unique strengths.

The situation hitherto would be still one of huge confusion without anyone having clear-cut strategies: although Australian universities are under great pressure to produce employable graduates (Bridgstock, 2009), no stakeholders have a clear idea about how to implement such an idea. An effective strategy would be to obtain feedback through closer consultation with industries and employers about the quality of graduates when they enter the workforce. Australian universities have for many years embedded graduate attributes into the curriculum (Hager, Holland, & Beckett, 2002). However, the findings in this review have revealed that there is a considerable risk for such a curriculum to not appropriately address the needs and demands held by employers. Therefore, closer dialogues between universities and industries need to be attempted through various formal and informal channels.

References

Australian Industry Group (AIG) (2008). *Skilling for innovation*. Australian Industry Group and Deloitte. North Sydney, Australia: Australian Industry Group.

Barrie, S. C. (2004). A research-based approach to generic graduate attributes policy. *Higher Education Research and Development, 23*, 261–275. doi:10.1080/0729436042000235391

Barrie, S. C. (2006). Understanding what we mean by the generic attributes of graduates. *Higher Education, 51*(2), 215–241.

Barrie, S. C., Hughes, C., & Smith, C. (2009). The national graduate attributes project: Integration and assessment of graduate attributes in curriculum: ALTC Final Report. Document Number). University of Sydney and Australian Learning and Teaching Council. Retrieved from www.itl.usyd.edu.au/projects/nationalgap/introduction.htm

Bath, D., Smith, C., Stein, S., & Swann, R. (2004). Beyond mapping and embedding graduate attributes: Bringing together quality assurance and action learning to create a validated and living curriculum. *Higher Education Research and Development, 23*(3), 313–328.

Bowden, J., Hart, G., King, B., Trigwell, K., & Watts, O. (2000). *Generic capabilities of ATN university graduates*. Retrieved from www.clt.uts.edu.au/ATN.grad.cap.project.index.html

Bridgstock, R. (2009). The graduate attributes we've overlooked: Enhancing graduate employability through career management skills. *Higher Education Research & Development, 28*(1), 31–44. doi:10.1080/07294360802444347

Crebert, G., Bates, M., Bell, B., Patrick, C. J., & Cragnolini, V. (2004). Developing generic skills at university, during work placement and in employment: Graduates' perceptions. *Higher Education Research and Development, 3*(2), 147–165. doi:10.1080/0729436042000206636

De la Harpe, B., Radloff, A., Scoufis, M., Dalton, H., Thomas, J., Lawson, A., . . . Girardi, A. (2009). *The B factor project: Understanding academic staff beliefs about graduate attributes*. Australian Learning & Teaching Council. Retrieved from www.altc.edu.au/resource-b-factor-academic-beliefs-graduates-rmit-2009

Department of Education, Science and Training (DEST) (2002). *National report to Parliament on Indigenous education and training, 2001*. Canberra, ACT: Department of Education, Science and Training. Retrieved from www.dest.gov.au/sectors/indigenous_education/publications_resources/profiles/national_report_indigenous_education_and_training_2001.htm.

Department of Education, Training and Youth Affairs (1998). *Learning for life: Review of higher education financing and policy*. Canberra, Australia: AGPS.

Donleavy, G. D. (2012). Proclaimed graduate attributes of Australian universities: Patterns, problems and prospects. *Quality Assurance in Education, 20*(4), 341–356. doi:10.1108/09684881211263984

Gilbert, C., Kristjuhan, A., Winkler, G. S., & Svejstrup, J. Q. (2004). Elongator inter-actions with nascent mRNA revealed by RNA immunoprecipitation. *Molecular Cell, 14*(4), 457–464.

Graduate Attributes Project (2009). *Key issues to consider in the renewal of learning and teaching experiences to foster graduate attributes.* Retrieved from www.itl.usyd.edu.au/projects/nationalgap/resources/discussionpapers.htm

Graduate Outlook Report (2015). *The report of the 2015 graduate outlook survey.* Melbourne: Graduate Careers Australia.

Hager, P., Holland, S., & Beckett, D. (2002). *Enhancing the learning and employability of graduates: The role of generic skills.* Retrieved from www.bhert.com/Position%20Paper%20No%209.pdf

Jackling, B., & Natoli, R. (2015). Employability skills of international accounting graduates Internship providers' perspectives. *Education + Training, 57*(7), 757–773. doi:10.1108/ET-08-2014-0093

Jackson, D. (2009). Undergraduate management education: Its place, purpose and efforts to bridge the skills gap. *Journal of Management & Organization, 15*, 206–223.

Jackson, D. (2016). Re-conceptualising graduate employability: The importance of pre-professional identity. *Higher Education Research & Development, 35*(5), 925–939.

Jackson, D., & Chapman, E. (2012). Non-technical skill gaps in Australian business graduates. *Education + Training, 54*(2/3), 95–113.

Jin, L., & Cortazzi, M. (1995). A cultural synergy model for academic language use. In P. Bruthiaux, T. Boswood, & B. Du-Babcock (Eds.). *Explorations in English for professional communication.* Hong Kong: University of Hong Kong.

Jones, S. M. (2014). Assessing the science knowledge of university students: Perils, pitfalls and possibilities. *Journal of Learning Design, 7*(2), 16–27.

Leoni, R. (2012). Workplace design, complementarities among work practices and the formation of key competencies. Evidence from Italian employees. *Industrial and Labor Relations Review, 65*(2), 316–349.

Massy, W. F. (2003). Balancing cost and quality. In W. F. Massy (Ed.), *Honoring the trust: Quality and cost containment in higher education* (pp. 12–23). San Francisco, CA: Jossy-Bass.

McArthur, E., Kubacki, K., Pang, P., & Alcaraz, C. (2017). The employers' view of "Work-ready" graduates: A study of advertisements for marketing jobs in Australia. *Journal of Marketing Education, 39*(2), 82–93.

Mourshed, M., Farrell, D., & Barton, D. (2012). *Education to employment: Designing a system that works.* McKinsey Center for Government. Retrieved from http://mckinseyonsociety.com/education-to-employment/report/

Nagarajan, S., & Edwards, J. (2014). Is the graduate attributes approach sufficient to develop work ready graduates? *Journal of Teaching and Learning for Graduate Employability, 5*(1), 12–28.

Pellegrino, J. W., & Hilton, M. L. (2012). *Education for life and work: Developing transferable knowledge and skills in the 21st century.* Washington, DC: The National Academies Press.

Rae, D. (2007). Connecting enterprise and graduate employability: Challenges to the higher education culture and curriculum? *Education + Training, 49*(8/9), 605–619.

Rampersad, G., & Patel, F. (2014). Creativity as a desirable graduate attribute: Implications for curriculum design and employability. *Asia-Pacific Journal of Cooperative Education, 15*(1), 1–11.

Sandberg, J. (2000). Understanding human competence at work: An interpretative approach. *Academy of Management Journal, 43*(1), 9–25.

Scott, G., Chang, E., & Grebennikov, L. (2010). Using successful graduates to improve the quality of undergraduate nursing programs. *Journal of Teaching and Learning for Graduate Employability, 1*(1), 26–44.

Shah, M., & Nair, C. S. (2011, 1–2 February). *Employer satisfaction of university graduates: Key capabilities in early career graduates*. Proceedings of the 20th Annual Teaching Learning Forum, Edith Cowan University, Perth, Australia. Retrieved from http://otl.curtin.edu.au/tlf/tlf2011/refereed/shah.html

Swift, L. (2012). Assessing the financial viability of academic programmes. *Journal of Higher Education Policy and Management, 34*(3), 259–272.

Tertiary Education Quality and Standards Agency (2012). *Application guide: Application for accreditation of a higher education course of study (AQF qualification)*. Retrieved from www.teqsa.gov.au/sites/default/files/GuideCourseAccreditationUpdatedDec2012.pdf

Thompson, D., Treleaven, L., Kamvounias, P., Beem, B., & Hill, E. (2008). Integrating graduate attributes with assessment criteria in business education: Using an online assessment system. *Journal of University Teaching and Learning Practice, 5*(1), 34–48.

Tomlinson, M. (2012). Graduate employability: A review of conceptual and empirical themes. *Higher Education Policy, 25*, 407–431. doi:10.1057/hep.2011.26

Tran, L. T., & Soejatminah, S. (2016). "Get foot in the door": International students' perceptions of work integrated learning. *British Journal of Educational Studies, 64*, 337–355.

University of South Australia (2009). UniSA employer feedback survey external report. Retrieved from http://w3.unisa.edu.au/gradquals/employerreport.pdf

Wieman, C. (2007). Why not try a scientific approach to science education? *Change: The Magazine of Higher Learning, 39*(5), 9–15.

11

EMBEDDING ENTREPRENEURIAL SKILLS WITHIN COMPUTING

Mark Zarb, Chevonne Brady and Roger McDermott

The Scottish government launched a nationwide drive to increase entrepreneurial skills, looking to become a world-leading entrepreneurial and innovative nation. Within this context, entrepreneurship is considered a mind-set of seeking new opportunities which can be turned into sustained business growth. One of the key ambitions of this drive is to build an education system with entrepreneurship and innovation at its core, which would promote creativity and ambition within the curriculum. The Quality Assurance Agency (QAA) for Higher Education defines entrepreneurship education as a way of equipping students with "the additional knowledge, attributes and capabilities required to apply [the ability of generating ideas and the skills to make them happen] in the context of setting up a new venture or business" (QAA, 2012).

Within computing degrees, there is traditionally a focus on preparing students for employment within industry rather than preparing them with an entrepreneurial skillset, despite content taught within entrepreneurship education being directly applicable to computing (e.g. project management, prototyping). This chapter discusses lessons learnt from the design and implementation of an entrepreneurship module taught to final-year computing students during the 2016 to 2017 academic year and defines a proposed framework showcasing its future implementation.

The main question targeted by this research was as follows: How do we best support the development of entrepreneurial skills to Computing students? To answer this question, a literature search was undertaken and combined with a qualitative analysis of 18 student responses from a prior run of an existing module. The results of this informed the creation of a series of workshops which could be used to support the development of entrepreneurial skills within a computing-related degree.

The study was undertaken to address the lack of entrepreneurial skills being embedded into computing-related degrees. Historically, within the School of

Computing Science and Digital Media at the Robert Gordon University (RGU), the subject of entrepreneurship has been typically restricted to a single module that takes place in the final semester of the final year within the larger context of the undergraduate curriculum. The proposed framework considered how to best support the development of these skills and whether it would be possible to successfully embed them throughout the curriculum.

The main objective of the study was to consolidate literature on entrepreneurship education curriculum development and run a qualitative analysis on responses gathered from a 2016 to 2017 module on entrepreneurship, run with final-year undergraduate students at the School of Computing Science and Digital Media. A framework would be generated from the consideration of these two data points to inform how to best embed entrepreneurial skills in a computing context. Future work would include informal interviews with experts, such as tutors at organisations such as the Scottish Institute for Enterprise (SIE) or Elevator UK, and a plan for evaluating its success once it has been rolled out in a wider context.

Literature review

What is entrepreneurship?

The topic of entrepreneurship is one that spans across many disciplines and consists of a number of definitions. Research conducted by Davidsson (2004) shows that "entrepreneurship" could be used to describe a number of topics, including new enterprise, new organisations, innovation, taking advantage of opportunity and production methods. This view is shared by Shane and Venkataraman (2007), who call it "a broad label under which a hodgepodge of research is housed". The umbrella term "entrepreneurship" usually consists of skills that promote idea development, communication, creativity and business flair, typically taught in a constructivist manner, with many educators acting as guides and mentors, rather than instructors (Powell, 2013). The QAA (2012) succinctly sums up enterprise skills as "having an idea and making it happen", with entrepreneurship building upon these skills in the context of setting up new ventures or developing existing organisations.

Entrepreneurship education

Whilst it is difficult to define exactly what is meant by the term entrepreneurship, over the past three decades, entrepreneurship has become an academic discipline that is taught across a variety of courses in higher education. Research by Piperopoulos and Dimov (2015) has shown that entrepreneurship education "can contribute to the development of students' entrepreneurial attitudes, abilities, and skills [as graduate outcomes] and hence enhance their intentions to launch new ventures". These graduate outcomes can be expanded into terms such as opportunity recognition, problem solving, personal awareness and creativity (QAA, 2012).

A systematic literature review by Blenker et al. (2014) showed that entrepreneurship education is a growing field encompassing papers based on both qualitative and quantitative data analysis techniques. Studies in this field often focus on student intention and perception of the subject, typically showcasing that students initially have a negative attitude or perception towards entrepreneurship (Fayolle & Gailly, 2015; Zhang, Duysters, & Cloodt, 2014) – this is posited to be for a number of reasons, including the student's perception of a mismatch, or a gulf, between their current self and their image of a "successful" entrepreneur, often portrayed (both using in-class examples and in the media) as well-spoken/rich/successful.

The research between entrepreneurship education and pedagogy is poorly defined. Some researchers question the legitimacy of the field as a whole due to a lack of actual entrepreneurs teaching the field as academics (Blenker & Christensen, 2010). This is a challenging aspect to address given the fact that some also view entrepreneurship as an innate skill, rather than a subject that can (or, in some instances, should) be taught (Haase & Lautenschläger, 2011; Lans, Blok, & Wesselink, 2014).

Across multiple fields, educators are "challenged with designing effective learning opportunities for entrepreneurship students" (Kuratko, 2005). A number of papers have been found that discuss entrepreneurship pedagogies, with certain journals devoted to researching and analysing the topic (e.g. the *Journal of Entrepreneurship Education*). The QAA (2012) contrasts two types of entrepreneurial teaching – study of the theoretical topic (underpinned by traditional pedagogies) or learning how to do (focusing on developing the entrepreneurial skills and mind-set within students in a more constructivist manner) – concluding that as an academic discipline, an ideal curriculum would combine both theory and practice. Within the wider literature, there is little that discusses entrepreneurship pedagogy, and no literature was found specific to the intersection between entrepreneurship education and computing.

An attempt at refining a subject-specific search using keywords such as "enterprise", "education", "teaching model", "framework" and "pedagogy" resulted in a number of papers. After a review of abstracts, the ones considered irrelevant were discarded, leaving only two papers for discussion, as detailed below.

The first paper (Hannon, 2005) indicates that supporting the development of entrepreneurship outside its usual business context (e.g. within a computing course) could have "potential utility in a post-university environment". There is no mention of pedagogy and no course structure in this paper.

The second paper (Doboli, Kamberova, Impagliazzo, Fu, & Currie, 2010) presents three computing/entrepreneurship modules that were ran in the same university, developed by "experienced local entrepreneurs". There is little indication of module content, no mention of pedagogical awareness, and a post-module survey shows mixed results. The paper concludes with an indication of further study which, as yet, does not seem to have been published.

The gaps identified in this literature led to the following research question being identified: How do we best support the development of entrepreneurial skills to computing students?

A review of the literature indicated that whilst entrepreneurship education is a growing field, there is general consensus that this is normally learnt by doing, with instructors acting as advisers and supporting its development in a constructivist manner. There is no evidence-based, subject-specific literature on suggested frameworks which place entrepreneurship education within the specific subject context, suggesting that this area is ripe for future research.

Methodology

Institutional context

This research was primarily conducted in the United Kingdom, within the School of Computing Science and Digital Media at RGU in Aberdeen, Scotland. The university has a strong focus on professional education, directly leading to very high employment rates for graduates.

As part of School policy, students are asked to anonymously fill in mid-semester feedback sheets on every module. The results of such a survey conducted during an existing entrepreneurship module (now discontinued) in the 2016 to 2017 teaching session was used in an approach inspired by grounded theory (Myers, 2008) to understand issues found with the module. Findings from the literature review were used to provide context to the qualitative analysis, and from this, a number of workshops were proposed.

The module

An existing module (Entrepreneurship and Enterprise Development) was used as the basis for this study. The module was delivered as a core component during the final semester of the final year of most BSc degrees taught within the School of Computing Science and Digital Media at the time, all of which fall under the broader umbrella term of "computing". It had an existing module descriptor with learning outcomes and indicative module content; however, there was no historical developed content, and the module guide contained little detail aside from a proposed overall structure.

Due to the lack of suitable frameworks resulting from the literature review, an approach inspired by Doboli et al. (2010) was taken to populate the module guide. Whilst the original study had "experienced local entrepreneurs" develop the modules, this module was developed in close collaboration over a series of focus groups with key instructors from organisations that deliver unstructured workshops on entrepreneurship education, such as the SIE and Elevator UK, with local business owners invited to give guest lectures where appropriate. This ensured that whilst the module contained topics deemed important by industry experts, it was still structured, delivered and assessed in a constructivist manner. This was achieved by designing the module as an avenue for students to sandbox a business idea: it allows for practical freedom as they are learning by doing, but also gives a safe space to

TABLE 11.1 The module guide for Entrepreneurship and Enterprise Development

Week	Topic
1	Introduction to Entrepreneurship
2	Idea Generation – Disrupting Technologies
3	Elevator Pitches
4	Finance and Costing
5	Prototyping and Wireframing
6	Business Strategies
7	Business Model Canvas
8	Delivering Pitches
9	Building a Business Plan
10	Assessment
11	Assessment
12	Assessment

fail and iterate on existing products based on feedback gained by the teaching staff. A full discussion on the development of the module lies outside the remit of this paper; however, a copy of the redeveloped module guide is given in Table 11.1 for reference.

Participants

The module was delivered as a core component of the final year within a variety of courses delivered at the School of Computing Science and Digital Media, including BSc Business Information Technology, BSc Computer Science and BSc Computing (Graphics & Animation). All students were invited to complete an optional mid-semester survey on their experience of the module. As per School policy, the invite was verbally issued once during Week 6 of the semester and followed up by a notice on the virtual learning environment. Of the 86 students within the module, 18 responded to the survey (20.9%), with this being inside standard limits found by Baruch and Holtom (2008) for preliminary studies. Analysis, therefore, continues based on the acceptability of this response rate.

The survey, known internally within the School as the Module Evaluation Questionnaire, is an optional tool used within all modules delivered within the School of Computing Science and Digital Media. It is deployed at Week 6 of each semester so that module leaders can react appropriately to student feedback. To retain complete anonymity, the survey does not collect identifying data such as name, student number or course studied, and these items are therefore not available for further analysis (e.g. whether the feedback differed depending on the degree path that a certain student was undertaking, for example, whether a Computer Science student was more likely to enjoy or appreciate the module over a Computing (Graphics and Animation) student). This qualitative analysis used responses to Questions 24 ("Please identify three things you think are good about this module") and 25 ("What changes to the module would improve your experience of it?") of the survey, which were the only two questions allowing students to give free-text feedback.

Ethical considerations

There was limited contact with participants in this study, and as such, there was little ethical consideration. Whilst student feedback was used as part of the analysis of the study, this feedback was collected anonymously, with no identifiers on the virtual learning environment, and was therefore acceptable to be used in this research.

Data analysis

Thematic analysis is a qualitative methodology that has become one of the most widely used frameworks for analysing qualitative data (Bryman, 2012). It involves an analysis of data through materials gathered by researchers, splitting that data into core themes (e.g. how to identify categories and how to establish relationships between them). A key process in thematic analysis is analytic coding, where segments of the collected data are assigned to categories with descriptive labels or keywords ("codes"), which in turn leads to an emerging understanding in the form of themes. The researcher's interpretations of the data shape his or her emergent codes (Bryman, 2012).

Instances of the feedback reflecting teaching style were removed (e.g. "[the lecturer] made sure we had plenty of feedback"), and an analytic coding process was applied to the remaining feedback gathered from the open-text responses of Questions 24 and 25 of the survey, resulting in the following coding scheme:

- Variation of topics
- Industry professionals
- Creativity
- Real-life application
- Not suited to final year.

A disadvantage of thematic analysis is that it is susceptible to a single researcher's abilities and understanding, and that the derived core themes might be biased based on the researcher's perception of the results. To counteract this possibility, an inter-rater reliability was performed with an academic colleague who was provided with a list of the analytic codes, and asked to ascribe these codes to the set of completed student feedback.

The reliability between the two raters was Kappa = 0.615 (p < 0.001), 95% CI (0.343, 0887). This indicated a substantial agreement across raters, allowing for the coding scheme to be used to infer conclusions based on the overall student feedback.

Analysis and findings

The agreed coding scheme helped to identify core topics and trends in the received feedback from students. In order to understand these topics and trends, each analytic code was analysed in further detail with respect to the student feedback.

Variation of topics

The proposed module was built in conjunction with key institutions that promote entrepreneurship in Scotland, with the goal of providing an overview of entrepreneurship to a non-traditional demographic of students. As it was not possible to assume any prior knowledge of entrepreneurship, enterprise or business, a variety of topics needed to be covered within the module. Through instances of the analysed feedback, it can be seen that students appreciated the variation of topics taught under the entrepreneurship umbrella (e.g. "There is plenty of variation in lectures"). The designed module led students from idea generation to the creation of a prototype and a business model canvas, effectively allowing students to develop a business idea in a "safe" environment, with constant feedback and guidance. This was considered successful and was reflected in the student feedback (e.g. "It was a good preparation for my own entrepreneurship – this module allowed me to sandbox a business idea").

Industry professionals

As the module was being developed, it became clear that some of the topics should be delivered by experts in the field. This follows the approach proposed by Doboli et al. (2010). Whilst industry professionals used as guest lecturers were appreciated by the students (e.g. "Guest speakers are friendly and eager to help"), feedback indicated that these sessions did not always work as lectures. This is attributed to the fact that industry experts do not necessarily have the pedagogic knowledge to deliver a lecture: "E.g. [the guest lectures] don't really work in the lecture hall [. . .] – there's not enough room to work interactively". Following the constructivist approach discussed in the literature review, these sessions would work best as smaller groups, where guest members from industry could act as mentors, rather than lecturers, and run interactive workshops based on their knowledge base and skillset. This could be supported by an academic member of staff to ensure suitability to the curriculum.

Creativity

Based on the definition proposed by the guidance document written by the QAA (2012), it is important for any module teaching entrepreneurial skills to promote creativity and creative thinking within its content. Creativity is an ongoing theme in the subject area in which this module is contained (Computer Science), and opportunities for personal projects and creativity were provided to students.

For example, students had three opportunities to present business ideas: first as an elevator pitch, then as a prototype and finally as a business case. For each of these, students were encouraged to think of their own idea and retroactively build on this initial idea based on formative feedback. Furthermore, through deliverables such as stand-up presentations and video-based prototypes, students were encouraged to use technology in ways that empowered creativity. The analysed feedback indicated that the module was an "opportunity to be creative" and that it "specified a vital detail: trying and failing is not a bad thing".

Real-life application

Students indicated that the module content was relevant to the real world; for example, "It motivates me to start up my own business in the future" and "It is nice to learn another side of computing that we could put into practice outside of university". This was achieved through the presence of industry members throughout the module and through the fact that students were asked to produce their own ideas and reflect upon them throughout the various assessment points. The relevance of the taught content to potential real-world application was made clear at several points throughout the module.

Not suited to final year

Whilst the module was delivered as a core component in the final semester of the final year in an undergraduate degree, respondents indicated that they were not convinced at the module's suitability in the curriculum, suggesting that it may work best as a non-core topic delivered outside of the final year.

Summary

It is clear through an analysis of the gathered feedback that students found the module content useful, and that there was a clear link between the module content and real-world application. It is also clear, however, that students were not convinced that the module was delivered at a suitable point within their curriculum. Whilst this work is based on a small sample of respondents of one cohort and is not generalisable, this work may be used as a basis to plan and prototype further developments to support entrepreneurship education within higher education environments. For example, within the existing context, this could take the form of a set of optional workshops offered to students across all taught years, allowing them the chance to pilot and sandbox a business idea.

Conclusions and future work

The research question posed at the start of this research project will be discussed as preliminary conclusions below in order to evaluate the success of this research project. The results from this study are encouraging but limited to the context within which this study was run. The small participant numbers mean that the results cannot be widely generalised. The implications of these findings are used to inform the direction of current and future work, which will help in the further validation of these results.

Research implications

How do we best support the development of entrepreneurial skills to computing students?

Whilst an established, peer-reviewed framework could not be found in the existing literature, it is clear that an attempt at supporting the development of entrepreneurial skills should be done in a constructivist manner, allowing students time to learn by doing. This approach was used to develop the module content and to structure the module around the idea of sandboxing a business idea. Post-semester feedback from the students suggested that the module supported the development of entrepreneurial skills, particularly when focusing on creativity, interaction with industry and real-world application. It was clear that some students did not feel comfortable having entrepreneurial skills embedded within the curriculum as a core component. Further work with a wider sample needs to be carried out before concrete conclusions can be put forward for recommendation.

Current work: SEED

The work reported in this paper is preliminary, and further work needs to be carried out in order to establish how to best support the development of entrepreneurial skills – not just within computing, but also across other non-traditional subjects.

Following on from this work, discussions were undertaken with colleagues in Medical Education at the University of Dundee to develop a solution that would allow for entrepreneurial skills to be delivered across institutions and disciplines. These discussions resulted in the creation of SEED (**S**kills in **E**ntrepreneurship **Ed**ucation), a series of workshops which can be delivered as optional components across year groups within courses to interested students.

Following on from the seminal work discussed in this chapter, a SICSA (Scottish Informatics & Computer Science Alliance) education grant was awarded to the authors to run a workshop in September 2017. The purpose of this workshop was to introduce SEED to invited academics, key organisations such as Elevator UK and the SIE, and other stakeholders. The workshop initiated discussion on the need of such a process and consisted of small-group sessions where it was critically evaluated and refined to its current iteration. At this stage, SEED was initially proposed to consist of the following six workshops, which drew upon the sandbox structure of the original module and could be made subject-specific depending on the context in which they were being presented:

- 1: Introduction to Non-Traditional Skills & Idea Generation
- 2: Elevator Pitches
- 3: Managerial Skills
- 4: Prototyping – From Concept to Creation
- 5: The Business Model Canvas
- 6: Student Presentations

Future work

A number of aspects of the research described here could be further researched. First of all, the SEED needs to be formally verified and refined – the authors are currently in discussion with colleagues across a network of Scottish institutions. A proposed pilot aims to run the proposed set of workshops with a number of student cohorts across the different institutions. Data gained from this pilot will be used to further develop SEED.

A theme that emerged from the workshop was the use of language when running events that attempts to support the development of entrepreneurial skills to students and recruiting students to attend such events. Initial observations by the authors, discussions with colleagues at the workshop and existing research discussed in the literature review (Fayolle & Gailly, 2015; Zhang et al., 2014) indicate that the use of certain terms considered to be business-related, for example, "entrepreneurship", "enterprise", "business plan" and so on elicit certain concerns in prospective students that cause them to disengage from the subject before they attempt it. A longer term comparative study could closely explore this area and establish what effect language has on student engagement and long-term satisfaction.

Bibliography

Baruch, Y., & Holtom, B. C. (2008). Survey response rate levels and trends in organizational research. *Human Relations, 61*(8), 1139–1160.

Blenker, P., & Christensen, P. R. (2010). Hunting the entrepreneurial expertise: Entrepreneurs in education. In A. Fayolle (Ed.), *Handbook of research in entrepreneurship education* (pp. 43–53). Cheltenham: Edward Elgar.

Blenker, P., Elmholdt, S. T., Frederiksen, S. H., Korsgaard, S., Wagner, K., Harry Matlay, P., . . . Wagner, K. (2014). Methods in entrepreneurship education research: A review and integrative framework. *Education and Training, 56*(8/9), 697–715.

Bryman, A. (2012). *Social research methods*. New York, NY: Oxford University Press. Retrieved from http://books.google.co.uk/books?id=MzuxygAACAAJ

Davidsson, P. (2004). *Researching entrepreneurship*. New York, NY: Springer.

Doboli, S., Kamberova, G. L., Impagliazzo, J., Fu, X., & Currie, E. H. (2010). A model of entrepreneurship education for computer science and computer engineering students. *2010 IEEE Frontiers in Education Conference (FIE)*, T4D–1–T4D–6.

Fayolle, A., & Gailly, B. (2015). The impact of entrepreneurship education on entrepreneurial attitudes and intention: Hysteresis and persistence. *Journal of Small Business Management, 53*(1), 75–93.

Haase, H., & Lautenschläger, A. (2011). The "Teachability Dilemma" of entrepreneurship. *International Entrepreneurship and Management Journal, 7*(2), 145–162.

Hannon, P. D. (2005). Philosophies of enterprise and entrepreneurship education and challenges for higher education in the UK. *The International Journal of Entrepreneurship and Innovation, 6*(2), 105–114.

Kuratko, D. F. (2005). The emergence of entrepreneurship education: Development, trends, and challenges. *Entrepreneurship Theory and Practice, 29*(5), 577–597.

Lans, T., Blok, V., & Wesselink, R. (2014). Learning apart and together: Towards an integrated competence framework for sustainable entrepreneurship in higher education. *Journal of Cleaner Production, 62,* 37–47.

Myers, M. D. (2008). *Qualitative research in business & management.* London: Sage Publications Ltd.

Piperopoulos, P., & Dimov, D. (2015). Burst bubbles or build steam? Entrepreneurship education, entrepreneurial self-efficacy, and entrepreneurial intentions. *Journal of Small Business Management, 53*(4), 970–985.

Powell, B. C. (2013). Dilemmas in entrepreneurship pedagogy. *Journal of Entrepreneurship Education, 16,* 99–112. Retrieved from http://proxy.lib.odu.edu/login?url=http://search.ebscohost.com/login.aspx?direct=true&db=bth&AN=87744094&site=ehost-live&scope=site

QAA (2012). *Enterprise and entrepreneurship education: Guidance for UK higher education providers.* England: QAA.

Shane, S., & Venkataraman, S. (2007). The promise of entrepreneurship as a field of research. In *Entrepreneurship: Concepts, theory and perspective* (pp. 171–184). doi:10.1007/978-3-540-48543-8_8

Zhang, Y., Duysters, G., & Cloodt, M. (2014). The role of entrepreneurship education as a predictor of university students' entrepreneurial intention. *International Entrepreneurship and Management Journal, 10*(3), 623–641.

12

ENTREPRENEURSHIP EDUCATION AND EMPLOYABILITY AGENDA IN MALAYSIA

Jane Chang and Ainurul Rosli*

Introduction

Universities are expected to actively embed entrepreneurship education (EE) as part of their new employability initiative in order to create value as part of supporting the employability agenda. The often repeated argument, that by embedding EE, universities' focus on employability through EE can bring about greater economic prosperity, has underpinned what has been described as the 'entrepreneurial turn' phenomenon (Cox and Rigby, 2013). Although some literature emphasises the importance of universities acting innovatively and proactively, common characteristics that entrepreneurial universities share include entrepreneurial pedagogy that focuses on developing useful and entrepreneurial skillsets in students (Ratten, 2017). With so much riding on universities' role in supporting employability and transforming the societal attitude (Ratten, 2017), universities mostly jump on the bandwagon towards embedding entrepreneurship as a way for individuals and graduates to be more business savvy (Palalić et al., 2017).

Times Higher Education reported recently (2018) on the universities' struggle with graduate employability, even though most universities in East Asian countries have been rated highly by employers for the graduates they produced. With so many conflicting institutional strategies, pedagogic aims and unclear vision towards supporting employability (Mok, 2005), it is essential to see how a specific policy approach to encourage entrepreneurial education contributes to how universities teach and view entrepreneurial education to support graduate employability.

We consider the case of Malaysia, one of the East Asian countries that can be seen active in the EE landscape (Iqbal and Rasli, 2014; Abdul et al., 2018) with so much investment and support by the government. The massive investment by the Ministry of Education (MoE) on EE policy highlights its importance to the nation (Rahim et al., 2015). We explore how the EE system in Malaysia has come into being, and we discuss how we can encourage universities to behave in ways that are aligned with their employability goals.

Analysing this issue is important, not just to identify potential strengths and weaknesses in the Malaysian system that is being studied, but also to derive lessons that may be useful to policymakers elsewhere who are considering implementing similar approaches.

Entrepreneurship education

Research on EE does not give us a coherent picture of what it means and what to expect from it. Current literature highlights that EE encompasses the development of entrepreneurial attitudes and skills (as well as personal qualities and abilities), emphasising more on the specific concept of "new venture creation-oriented training" (Fayolle and Gailly, 2008) rather than merely focusing on new venture creation (Lackéus, 2015). This is also supported by Chang and Rieple (2018), advocating that EE is for the enrichment of students' mind-sets, attitudes and characteristics necessary to manage the uncertain environment, rather than merely venture creation. Literature has also shown that EE does not have a universal form and involves different processes and practices for educators to act on opportunities through co-creation (Chang et al., 2014; Lackéus, 2015; Chang and Rieple, 2018). Perhaps this poses a challenge, with no clear output and impact measurement mechanism, for what kind of EE to promote to support employability.

Graduates leaving universities to become self-employed is low (Marzocchi et al., 2018) due to the challenge in navigating the uncertain future that we know nothing about to take jobs that do not yet exist. Interestingly, government policy assumes that EE curriculum taught in universities can positively influence graduates' attitudes towards an alternative career path and simultaneously equip them with skills to enable them to become an entrepreneur (Marzocchi et al., 2018).

Nevertheless, Ahmad and Buchanan (2015) reported that academics in higher education found the lack of clarity and the concise guide in embedding entrepreneurship in the curriculum contributed to the differing definition of entrepreneurship (Fayolle and Gailly, 2008; Lackéus, 2014). From this perspective, the provision of EE can be seen as an incentivising factor 'for' and 'of' entrepreneurial competencies (Marzocchi et al., 2018) which not only supports an individual's tenacity to become an entrepreneur, but also provides knowledge of the entrepreneurial institutional framework which could affect the development of a local economy (Fayolle, 2013). Lackéus (2014) argues that the process of value creation for students requires two types of competencies development, namely, operational and entrepreneurial development. Operational competencies concern certainty in focusing on doing routine work such as process management and execution, optimisation and incremental improvements as an entrepreneur. On the other hand, entrepreneurial competencies embrace the elements of risk, ambiguity and exploration which cover new ways of working, explorative value creation, continuous learning and method development. The different aspects and types of EE can be seen in contrasting different modes of teaching, based upon a paradigmatic change between the notion of supporting education 'for' entrepreneurship, 'through' entrepreneurship or 'about' entrepreneurship (Lackéus, 2015).

There is a distinctive approach for the three categories of education: 'about' entrepreneurship instigates entrepreneurship as a societal and economic phenomenon, mostly based upon theoretical discussion; education 'for' entrepreneurship is about the acquisition of skills and knowledge of relevance when creating value (e.g. starting an enterprise); and education 'through' entrepreneurship uses the entrepreneurial process as a tool to achieve a particular set of learning objectives/outcomes. These processes vary from concrete entrepreneurship processes aimed at developing an enterprise (for example, student companies) to projects that work on a case (for example, pupil enterprises) or participation in other interdisciplinary projects combining practical and theoretical learning (for example, collaboration between schools and local businesses) (Chang et al., 2014; Chang and Rieple, 2018). While the 'about' and 'for' approaches are relevant primarily to a subset of students in secondary and higher levels of education, the embedded approach of teaching 'through' entrepreneurship can be relevant to all students and at all levels of education. Some important challenges have been identified when trying to embed entrepreneurship into education this way, such as resource and time constraints, resistance from academics, assessment challenges and cost implications. Understanding the distinctive approach and process of EE helps academics to design effective entrepreneurial pedagogic delivery to achieve the learning outcomes, taking into consideration students' entrepreneurial roles in different disciplines.

Entrepreneurship education and employability agenda in Malaysia

The relevance of entrepreneurship in Malaysian education has been primarily driven from the economic point of view of job creation, which is evident in the high proportions of entrepreneurship courses available in most higher education in Malaysia (Kamaruddin et al., 2017). EE policy in Malaysia has been developed as part of the government initiatives to create more jobs and increase the number of graduate work-readiness (GWR) (Salleh et al., 2019) with the belief that entrepreneurship can act as a significant catalyst for economic growth and job creation (Rahim et al., 2015; Kamaruddin et al., 2017; Salleh et al., 2019). As a response to the increasingly globalised, uncertain and complex world in which we live, in 2010, Malaysia established a policy focusing on the development of an entrepreneurial mind-set of students as well as academics to improve the number of graduate entrepreneurs. This requires the practice approach where both students and academics embody the process of enterprise skills (Chang and Rieple, 2018). Nevertheless, this proved to be challenging despite the terminology of entrepreneurship is spelt out in the EE policy in Malaysia.

In 2013, they introduced a strategic action focusing on EE policy requiring all people and organisations in Malaysia to be increasingly equipped with entrepreneurial competencies (Salleh et al., 2019). The strong emphasis on economic success and job creation has indeed propelled entrepreneurial education to a prominent position at the higher education level with the introduction of a core module for first-year students (Kasim, 2011; Ahmad and Buchanan, 2015) but not as an integrated pedagogical approach for all students on all levels.

According to Kasim (2011), Malaysia's public universities offer entrepreneurship courses as a core subject at the first-degree level. This is in line with the educational goals of the universities, designed to assist the economic development of the country. Though the strategic plan for EE emphasis on the need for the citizen to be entrepreneurial by 2020, globalisation and increasing market uncertainty has spurred significant activity on a policy level but has not yet transferred into broader adoption among teachers on all levels of education.

Literature has also acknowledged that EE can play an important role in societal transformation (Rae et al., 2012; Chang et al., 2014). Therefore, this has positioned

TABLE 12.1 Relevance and the impact of entrepreneurship in Malaysia

Level	Individual	Organisations	Societal
Job Creation	Willingness and capable of creating jobs	Growing organisations generate more jobs	Entrepreneurship and innovation are primary paths to growth and job creation
Economic Success	Entrepreneurship can give individuals financial success	Organisational renewal is fundamental to every firm's long-term success (Rosli et al., 2018)	Renewal processes are fundamental to the vitality of economies
Globalisation & Innovation	People need entrepreneurial skills and abilities to thrive in an ever-changing world	Entrepreneurial firms play a crucial role in changing market structures	A deregulated and flexible market requires people with higher level general skills
Passion & Creativity Work Attachment	Creation/value creation/creativity is a main source of satisfaction	Employee creativity and joy is essential for the performance of new and existing	Economic wealth of nations correlates with the happiness of its citizens
Social Transformation	People can make a difference in society, and marginalised people can achieve economic success	Organisations Corporations can collaborate with small social entrepreneurship initiatives to create social value	Social entrepreneurship addresses problems in society that the market economy has failed to address

entrepreneurial education as a pathway to empower people and organisations to create value through social innovation. There is also an increasing emphasis on the effects entrepreneurial activities can have on students' perceived relevance, engagement and motivation in education (Chang and Rieple, 2013). Table 12.3 provides the connection and the impact of entrepreneurship through education across different level of individuals in Malaysia.

Can entrepreneurship education support the pursuit of the number of GWR in Malaysia?

This might be possible as long as the system provides clear policy guidelines and incentives for universities to develop EE strategies that best exploit their relative strengths and competitive advantages and, within those strategies, to shape students to be job creators, not job seekers.

Here, we outline four challenges which are present in the current system implemented in Malaysia.

(i) Difficulty in identifying which perspective of entrepreneurship education should be promoted

There is a need for policymakers to understand the impact and outcome of the different types of EE. The different perspective on what EE is – either about, for and through entrepreneurship (Levie, 1999) and its implications – prove to be unclear in EE implementation in Malaysia. This is because in order to focus on the employability agenda, the way entrepreneurship is being taught needs to be experiential beyond 'about' entrepreneurship (Lackéus, 2015; Nabi et al., 2017). The Malaysian EE policy has been long connected with the narrow definition of EE, focusing on encouraging students to start up formation (Kamaruddin et al., 2017). Similar to various universities across the globe, teaching about entrepreneurship in Malaysia is content driven, aiming for knowledge acquisition of the phenomenon (Ahmad and Buchanan, 2015), focusing on encouraging students to start a business. One notable early initiative was the establishment of the Malaysian Entrepreneurship Development Centre (MEDEC) at the MARA Institute of Technology (ITM) in 1975 to help develop entrepreneurship and train the indigenous population. It also emphasises until now the training of EE for teachers and students. Another early initiative was KEMUSA by the same institution in 1982, which later influenced other universities to start offering similar courses along the years, where entrepreneurship was taught concerning theory about entrepreneurship and should go beyond profit oriented with social ethos.

Another example is the entrepreneurship programme targeted for students' introduced by The Universiti Utara Malaysia (UUM) called the Student Enterprise Program (SEP). The aim is to increase the number of entrepreneurs in Malaysia by inculcating entrepreneurial values among students. By training students to run their own business and become entrepreneurs, it allows them to experience real-world practices, which they will then be able to gain entrepreneurial skills as part of their own their business learning (Mansor and Othman, 2011).

(ii) Concentrating on prescriptive education models

Research has shown that for sustainable entrepreneurialism to be materialised, innovation must not be mechanistic (Yu Cheng et al., 2009) nor instructional from the top. Given that EE is a social phenomenon process, prescriptive education models become counterproductive to implementation as academics need to develop non-cognitive skills such as being passionate about the role of entrepreneurial educator to make the policy a success (Chang and Rieple, 2013). The challenge at hand is the debate on the effectiveness of pedagogical delivery of EE in shaping students to be job creators, not job seekers.

Realising the setback, the Ministry of Higher Education created an entrepreneurial module called the Basic Culture of Entrepreneurship Module (APK), introduced in 2007 as an entrepreneurship module in all postgraduate courses. This was part of the project 'Projek Tunas Mekar', with the primary objective of providing entrepreneurship exposure to graduates through a compulsory course of two (2) credits for Year 1 in all higher education institutions in Malaysia (Mohammed Lame, 2015).

To foster the culture of entrepreneurialism in higher education in Malaysia, the ministry also established the University Enterprise Networks (UENs) in November 2008 as part of the first EE network managed by the National Council for Graduate Entrepreneurship (NCGE). The UENs aim to establish a culture of enterprise in universities. Examples of services include training provision, advice and encouragement to students and graduates who want to develop and actualise their business ideas, supported by privately owned companies and Regional Development Agencies (RDAs) (Kasim, 2011).

The Ministry also introduced the strategic plan, the Higher Education Entrepreneurship Development Policy, in April 2010: an entrepreneurial development plan for universities to enhance the implementation of EE and to ensure the success of the EE policy implementation. The whole initiative is to increase awareness of the importance of EE and to increase the participation of students in the entrepreneurship programme and activities. Moreover, an Entrepreneurship Awareness Component (EAC) was also introduced with the aims to bring awareness to students on the importance of entrepreneurship learning and inculcate entrepreneurial values to start at an early stage in the students' learning (Mohammed Lame, 2015).

The Malaysian government firmly believes that innovation and entrepreneurship are catalysts for economic growth by setting up the ecosystem for the implementation of EE at the university level. It is crucial in the government agenda with the creation of the Entrepreneur Development Ministry (MED), responsible for the development of inclusive national entrepreneurial development to encourage greater competitiveness for the nation (*The Star*, 2018) and also promote a more aligned entrepreneurial initiative among local universities, polytechnics and diploma colleges in the country in order to attain these entrepreneurial objectives (Mohammed Lame, 2015).

(iii) Difficulties in assessing the effects of entrepreneurship education

Venture creation takes many years to reach success. The challenge here is to prove that it was the entrepreneurial education that caused the successful entrepreneurial behaviour. Emphasis on the EE module in Malaysia on venture creation makes it difficult to isolate the role of entrepreneurial education compared to others. Self-selection bias aggravates this problem, making it difficult to rule out the possibility that the entrepreneurial individual is already attracted to entrepreneurial education, causing these higher levels of entrepreneurial activity (Bager, 2011). Moreover, regardless of whether these students would have acted entrepreneurially or not without educational treatment, it is difficult to deny the benefits that these practising entrepreneurial individuals have received some degree of preparedness through entrepreneurial education. In most other professions, it is generally accepted and unquestioned that training is provided.

(iv) The fixation with science and engineering policy goals

Malaysia has been promoting competitiveness through science, technology and innovation (Razak and Saad, 2007; Mohammed Lame, 2015). The national commitment to science and technology translates nicely towards their goal, aiming to achieve more than 60% of all high school graduates in Malaysia to specialise in STEM subjects by 2020. At the moment, only 40% of students specialise in STEM. To achieve that, the investment made by both the government and industry partners encourages the adoption and creation of new technologies to enhance competitiveness (Razak and Saad, 2007).

For example, all top public universities in Malaysia have their own technology transfer offices (TTO) set up to commercialise academic work and also generate income from external sources. With university strategy emphasising technology transfer, somehow the exploitation of external sources of funding through the TTO also facilitates access to R&D finance, to materials and equipment and specialist expertise and complementary knowledge. These have benefited the students who are encouraged to embark into a technology-based start-up, with the support of university incubation programmes as technology transfer is an important factor in the positive relationship between industrial innovation and the various types of knowledge spill-overs (Rossi et al., 2017).

The incubation support in Malaysian universities serves as centres of excellence for small businesses, fostering students' ability to develop and promote technological innovation and business to achieve a commercial and industrial community by 2020, for example, the Entrepreneurship Development Institute at UUM, the Malaysia Entrepreneur Development Centre (MEDEC) at UiTM, the Small Business Development Centre at the Universiti Putra Malaysia (UPM), the Bureau of Innovation and Consultancy (BIP) at Universiti Teknology Malaysia (UTM) and the Innovation and Consultancy Centre at Universiti Sains Malaysia (USM).

Nevertheless, there is a need for policymakers to understand that entrepreneurship is more than the commercialisation of products, and not many students are capable enough to do a technologically based start-up. Moreover, when borrowed heavily from the sciences and engineering, entrepreneurship was viewed as a substantially linear process, involving incubation of ideas and commercialisation of products. The interest in social transformation (Chang et al., 2014) may also strike the interest of EE. Young teenagers in the country have good altruistic values and a desire to make Malaysia a better place on the global stage.

A missionary approach to support graduate employability in Malaysia

The adoption of EE in Malaysia has been a missionary and is slowly in the process of integrating the importance of understanding the spirit of embodying the process

TABLE 12.2 Academia-industry collaboration to support graduate employability in Malaysia

Targeted area for graduate employability	Initiatives at the national level
• Structured Internship	• Ind-E-Zone – industry engagement zone (a zone within the campus solely dedicated to encouraging direct interfacing between the host university and its students with the industry)
• Practical Training	• Industry-University corporate social responsibility program – big corporation working closely with a university in delivering community projects • Industry Centre of Excellence (ICOE) Program – a mechanism that links education to jobs where industries cooperate with education providers to prepare students with the skills required in the job • Knowledge transfer programme (KTP) – a mutually beneficial collaboration between university and industry, including graduate internship
• Industry-Led Curriculum	• Bridging the Gap Program – bringing together employers, academics and national agencies to tackle the gap in skills development among graduates • Entrepreneurship Programme
• Adjunct Lecturers / Entrepreneurial Academics	• CEO@faculty Programme – mentoring programmes between top local and international CEOs and industry players with emerging young academics
• Professional Qualification	• Professional Exam Programme • Scholarship Award

of entrepreneurship within the EE community system. To start with, Malaysia has been advocating and championing university-industry engagement both at the academic (e.g. CEO@faculty programme) and graduate level (2u2i: two-year university and two-year industry study). The emphasis on industry exposure is crucial as part of the Ministry effort to increase graduate employability. It can be seen from the initiatives run by the Ministry of Higher Education that aims include integrated learning by doing framework: working with different stakeholders through different efforts as part of a closer industry engagement agenda. What is missing is the crafted curriculum at the university level, which we will discuss in the next section.

Nevertheless, what is required is a clear understanding at the university level of how all of these innovative programmes initiated at the national level can be used by relevant universities to connect and link to each other as part of its integrated outcome approach in supporting students' employability agenda.

Although the initiatives highlighted in Table 12.2 have been part of the Malaysia Education Blueprint (2013–2025), the implementation process is still in its infancy as it focuses on supporting both academics and students through events, training and workshops.

Centre of community learning: integrating university-level curriculum with national programmes to support the employability agenda

The previous section highlighted national initiatives to support the graduate employability agenda in Malaysia. What is missing is an integrated curriculum at the university level (which we will discuss in the next section) to provide a pragmatic microcosm of situated learning for students and relevant stakeholders to embody themselves in their respective entrepreneurial roles and to allow emergence of opportunities for socially impactful innovation through the network of relationship (Chang and Rieple, 2018). The integration at the micro level is important, as it provides the clear relationship link between students and academics learning together in the classroom.

Recent political pressure to increase emphasis on entrepreneurship in education in the country has prompted the private sectors to aggressively set up entrepreneurship academies based on an entrepreneurial style choreographed by the progressive constructivist philosophy of education known as 'Powerpreneurs', although at the primary to secondary education (*The Star*, 2018). The majority of the Malaysian public universities fall in the traditional education of standardised, content focused, passive and single subject-based curriculum (Ahmad and Buchanan, 2015), and only a few public universities such as UTM (Rahim et al., 2015), Universiti Sains Islam Malaysia (USIM) and Universiti Kebangsaan Malaysia (UKM) (Kamaruddin et al., 2017) practice individualised, active, process-based, project-centric, collaborative, experiential and multidisciplinary approaches in EE. Most of their discussion does not look into the interpretive nature of the debate but uses a reductionist approach to measure the effectiveness of implementation. Correspondingly, the EE policy has been mooted by the positivistic approach as most of these researches have been based on cross-sectional quantitative analysis instead of following a qualitative approach. Empirical evidence focusing on measurement and performativity of EE also shows that there is no sign of weakening (Salleh et al., 2019).

Aligning with the policy agenda, Malaysian EE scholars have also started to research on how "hands-on" projects based on the learning by doing approach to create value for other people provides higher level engagement, becoming more aware of the skills required to be entrepreneurial. Some of the empirical examples of such models of education in Malaysia include problem-based learning (Zabit, 2010), project-based learning (Yasin and Rahman, 2011) and service-learning (Huda et al., 2018). Project-based learning allows students to create an artefact to a problem in the form of a final product such as a report, a model, a video and many others (Yasin and Rahman, 2011).

On the other hand, there are approaches used where students do not have artefacts but instead discuss possible solutions and guiding students' further study in helping their critical thinking skills (Zabit, 2010). This concept is similar to the teaching 'for' entrepreneurship, an occupationally oriented approach aiming at giving budding entrepreneurs the requisite knowledge and skills. It is important that students assess the skills needed to embark on the entrepreneurial journey (Chang and Rieple, 2013).

Moreover, initiatives also have been put in place to involve and connect students with SMEs as apprentices for a period of one to two years. In this way, they learn by valuable first-hand experiences, which stimulate their interest to concentrate on choosing to become entrepreneurs as a career choice (Kasim, 2011). This initiative can also be part of service-learning: defined as classroom instruction integrated with community service such as cleaning parks, visiting the elderly and providing food to people in need (Huda et al., 2018). Service-learning works best when students participate in the planning of the project, when the duration is one semester or longer, and when student reflection is explicitly facilitated. This approach is in consensus with studies by Chang and Rieple (2013, 2018) when students embodied their entrepreneurial roles when immersed in the interaction with relevant stakeholders in the production of the social course for a period of a semester. This can also be linked to teaching 'through' entrepreneurship, which means a process-based and often experiential approach where students go through an actual entrepreneurial learning process (Levie, 1999; Lackéus, 2015). This approach often leans on the broader definition of entrepreneurship and can be integrated into other subjects in general education, connecting entrepreneurial characteristics, processes and experiences to the core subject.

Rahim et al. (2015) reported how UTM, which reformed its traditional approach into the paradigmatic entrepreneurial approach in 2010, has increased the number of entrepreneur graduates from 2011 to 2013. Indeed, literature shows that learning by doing is a grounded approach (Chang et al., 2014: for example, students work in teams to create revenue for social enterprise). EE as a pedagogical intervention

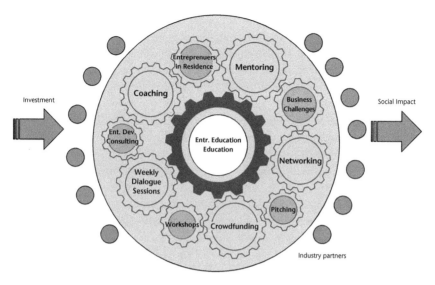

FIGURE 12.1   Synergistic learning platform to practice entrepreneurship

can provide an exciting mechanism to let students create value for other people. This educational approach requires students to know how to create value for other people with the assessment of skills needed for the value creation. More importantly, students immerse themselves through the process of allocation of resources to create value. Different approaches could increase entrepreneurial competencies and a better understanding of the context in which social value creation operates (Gibb, 2002; Lackéus, 2015). Most EE programmes engage students in isolation at the classroom level, with negligible opportunities for students to learn how to create value or take risks (Chang and Rieple, 2018). Being able to cope with emotions such as fear of failure and the ability to deal with uncertainty are also critical entrepreneurial attributes that classroom teaching barely addresses (Lackéus, 2014).

Since the entrepreneurial ecosystem is indeed contextual (Autio et al., 2014), and there is a greater need to understand and research how to establish models for entrepreneurial education that meets the requirements of different educational levels, resource availability and context, rather than continuing the quest for a 'one size fits all' approach to EE. This will improve the relevance of entrepreneurship subject with the aims to inculcate the awareness of entrepreneurial competencies needs to create values in different contexts. It is suggested that a synergistic learning platform to practice entrepreneurship (Chang et al., 2015) in value creation involves various stakeholders – in this case, students, social entrepreneurs, facilitators and business sponsors (see, for example, Professional Practice Entrepreneurship programme www.ppewestminster.com; see Figure 12.1), bringing their own respective knowledge, skills and experiences to the learning path. This type of learning environment allows for the exploration of opportunities and the implementation of value creation (Rae et al., 2012; Lackéus, 2015), but in which unsuccessful value creation is not penalised as it would be in the real world, which requires a university to have close engagement with the industry partners.

The key to propelling academics to adopt effective and efficient entrepreneurial education pedagogy is to know their roles in the professional practice of teaching entrepreneurship within an integrated framework, involving various stakeholders such as students, parents, principals, policymakers, alumni, non-government organisations, charities, local businesses and local communities. Learning by doing is gaining popularity to practice entrepreneurship; however, it must be carefully crafted with a learning environment that allows students to practice being entrepreneurs intrapreneurs, thereby crafting the value creation into start-up or employment in the relevant business sectors. This requires students to work in interdisciplinary teams and interact with people outside school/university, a particularly powerful way to develop entrepreneurial competencies among students. However, this kind of experiential learning-based activity is innovative, and some types of value needs are created for the individuals outside school or university in the process. For the practice to happen, academics must not fear the process of value creation with students, and relevant stakeholders must realise the idea into enterprise and job creation.

It is about physically, mentally and emotionally enacting the entrepreneurial role of the production of value creation. This can be done with the correct support and environment as a result of iterative experimentation in collaboration with committed stakeholders. It also includes the newness or innovativeness of the value creation. The situated learning is the consistent interaction of the value ecosystem developed in dialogue with the objective to complete the process of value creation. This encompasses members to learn from each other and leverage the resources. The relationality is the network of people interacting generally, solving real problems of external stakeholders, interacting with the outside world, in particular, business mentors that are relevant to the said value creation. These features explain why EE can trigger a higher level of motivation, relevant experience, engagement and critical reflexive learning as a community of practice. This entrepreneurial community of practice signals the spirit of entrepreneurialism that creates values.

EE should be embedded over time (Chang and Rieple, 2018) as students become highly engaged by creating value for other people based on the knowledge they acquire to catalyse the critical entrepreneurial learning which illustrates the practical relevance of the knowledge in question. These students pick up the aptitude for value creation to pursue entrepreneurship courses relevant to them and will focus on how to organise the value creation process as part of their entrepreneurial journey as start-ups or intrapreneurial careers in organisations. This has far-reaching implications in curriculum design on how to plan, execute and assess entrepreneurship in education.

Conclusion

This chapter discussed the issues of EE and the employability agenda in Malaysia. The Malaysian government's support at the institutional level towards EE has been tremendous, with lots of investments and incentives as part of embedding entrepreneurial education with the outcome of start-up formation or/and as a way to support and increase students' employability. Indeed, Malaysia is in a good position with great progress as research has shown that EE can be used as a means to achieve more interest, engagement and creativity among students to build employability skillsets (Chang and Rieple, 2013; Lackéus, 2014).

However, despite the substantial investment at the institutional policy and national levels, very little emphasis has been placed on how to improve students' engagement to achieve altruistic values (Kasim, 2011; Mansor and Othman, 2011) at different levels of education through entrepreneurial pedagogic delivery, which is correlated highly with the altruistic values of the teachers. To trigger entrepreneurial learning and inculcate engagement, motivation, confidence and feelings of relevancy among students, there is a need to relook into how EE is perceived, and what kind of outcome should be the focus. We put forward value creation as the centre of entrepreneurial education using the learning by doing approach pedagogy. We propose a more synergistic learning platform to practice entrepreneurship as part of models for entrepreneurial education that meet the requirements of different educational levels, resource availability and context to help integrate university-level curriculum with national programmes to support the employability agenda.

Note

* All parties equally contributed to the work of the chapter.

References

Abdul, Z., et al. (2018). "Students spin-off intentions in Malaysian higher educational institutions: Founders characteristics and university roles." *Journal of Entrepreneurship Education* **21**(3): 1–15.

Ahmad, S. Z. and R. F. Buchanan (2015). "Entrepreneurship education in Malaysian universities." *Tertiary Education Management* **21**(4): 349–366.

Autio, E., et al. (2014). "Entrepreneurial innovation: The importance of context." *Research Policy* **43**(7): 1097–1108.

Bager, T. (2011). "The camp model for entrepreneurship teaching." *International Entrepreneurship and Management Journal* **7**(2): 279–296.

Chang, J. and A. Rieple (2013). "Assessing students' entrepreneurial skills development in live projects." *Journal of Small Business Enterprise Development* **20**(1): 225–241.

Chang, J. and A. Rieple (2018). "Entrepreneurial decision-making in a microcosm." *Management Learning* **49**(4): 471–497.

Chang, J., et al. (2014). "Learning-by-doing as an approach to teaching social entrepreneurship." *Innovations in Education Teaching International* **51**(5): 459–471.

Chang, J., et al. (2015). "Practice based curriculum for effective entrepreneurship education in HE." *Research in Management Learning and Education*.

Cox, D. and J. Rigby (2013). *Innovation policy challenges for the 21st century*, Routledge.

Fayolle, A. (2013). "Personal views on the future of entrepreneurship education." *Entrepreneurship Regional Development* **25**(7–8): 692–701.

Fayolle, A. and B. Gailly (2008). "From craft to science: Teaching models and learning processes in entrepreneurship education." *Journal of European Industrial Training* **32**(7): 569–593.

Gibb, A. (2002). "In pursuit of a new 'enterprise' and 'entrepreneurship' paradigm for learning: Creative destruction, new values, new ways of doing things and new combinations of knowledge." *International Journal of Management Reviews* **4**(3): 233–269.

Huda, M., et al. (2018). Empowering Civic Responsibility: Insights From Service Learning. *Engaged Scholarship and Civic Responsibility in Higher Education*, IGI Global: 144–165.

Iqbal, M. J. and A. Rasli (2014). "Role of civil society in economic transformation in Malaysia." *Pakistan Journal of Commerce Social Sciences* **8**(1).

Kamaruddin, H., et al. (2017). The Government's Role in the Importance of Entrepreneurship Education Amongst University Students in Malaysia. *Leadership, Innovation and Entrepreneurship as Driving Forces of the Global Economy*, Springer: 579–587.

Kasim, R. S. R. (2011). "Malaysian higher education institutions: Shaping an entrepreneurial agenda." *International Journal of Information and Education Technology* **1**(2): 163.

Lackéus, M. (2014). "An emotion based approach to assessing entrepreneurial education." *The International Journal of Management Education* **12**(3): 374–396.

Lackéus, M. (2015). *Entrepreneurship in education: What, why, when, how*. B. paper. Paris.

Levie, J. J. U., the Department for Employment (1999). Entrepreneurship education in higher education in England: A survey. The Department for Employment, the Department for Employment and Education.

Mansor, M. and N. Othman (2011). *Consulting-based entrepreneurship education in Malaysian higher education institutions*. International Conference on Social Science and Humanity.

Marzocchi, C., et al. (2018). "Evolving missions and university entrepreneurship: academic spin-offs and graduate start-ups in the entrepreneurial society." *The Journal of Technology Transfer*: 1–22.

Mohammed Lame, S. (2015). An examination on entrepreneurial competencies between lecturers of higher learning institutions in Malaysia and Nigeria, Universiti Tun Hussein Onn Malaysia.

Mok, K. H. (2005). "Fostering entrepreneurship: Changing role of government and higher education governance in Hong Kong." *Research Policy* **34**(4): 537–554.

Nabi, G., et al. (2017). "The impact of entrepreneurship education in higher education: A systematic review and research agenda." *Academy of Management Learning* **16**(2): 277–299.

Palalić, R., et al. (2017). "Entrepreneurial intentions of university students: A case-based study." *Journal of Enterprising Communities: People Places in the Global Economy* **11**(3): 393–413.

Rae, D., et al. (2012). "Enterprise and entrepreneurship in English higher education: 2010 and beyond." *Journal of Small Business Enterprise Development* **19**(3): 380–401.

Rahim, H. L., et al. (2015). "Entrepreneurship education in Malaysia: A critical review." *Journal of Technology Management Business* **2**(2).

Ratten, V. (2017). "Entrepreneurial universities: The role of communities, people and places." *Journal of Enterprising Communities: People Places in the Global Economy* **11**(3): 310–315.

Razak, A. A. and M. Saad (2007). "The role of universities in the evolution of the Triple Helix culture of innovation network: The case of Malaysia." *International Journal of Technology Management & Sustainable Development* **6**(3): 211–225.

Rosli, A., et al. (2018). "The long-term impact of engaged scholarship: how do SMEs capitalise on their engagement with academics to explore new opportunities?" *International Small Business Journal* **36**(4): 400–428.

Rossi, F., et al. (2017). "Academic engagement as knowledge co-production and implications for impact: Evidence from Knowledge Transfer Partnerships." *Journal of Business Research* **80**: 1–9.

Salleh, N. M., et al. (2019). Graduate Work-Readiness in Malaysia: Challenges, Skills and Opportunities. *The Transition from Graduation to Work*, Springer: 125–142.

The Star (2018). Growing a generation of pioneers. *The Star.*

Yasin, R. M. and S. Rahman (2011). "Problem oriented project based learning (POPBL) in promoting education for sustainable development." *Procedia-Social Behavioral Sciences* **15**: 289–293.

Yu Cheng, M., et al. (2009). "The effectiveness of entrepreneurship education in Malaysia." *Education + Training* **51**(7): 555–566.

Zabit, M. N. M. (2010). "Problem-based learning on students' critical thinking skills in teaching business education in Malaysia: A literature review." *American Journal of Business Education* **3**(6): 19–32.

13

GRADUATE EMPLOYABILITY IN VIETNAM

An initial study on responding of policy makers

Ly Thi Pham

Introduction

In recent years, graduate employability has become an issue of intense public concern in Vietnam. An unexpected rise in the national rate of graduate unemployment has sparked a public outcry, regarding not only the worth of completing a degree, but also about the teaching quality provided by many higher education institutions. In an attempt to quell public disquiet, the Ministry of Education and Training has hastily passed a number of new regulations that are likely to have a significant impact on the higher education system. The issue of graduate employability in Vietnam has not, however, been subjected to close scholarly scrutiny, and the prospective impact of the recently approved regulations have not been critically assessed. This chapter presents a review of this issue and of the Ministry's policy response.

The context

Over the past 30 years, Vietnam has undergone a remarkable economic transformation. In the mid-1980s, Vietnam had one of the poorest economies in the world, with almost 60% of the population living in poverty (World Bank, 2013). By 2016, GNI per capita had climbed reaching 2,050 USD, and less than 14% of the national population of 92.5 million was living below the national poverty line (World Bank, 2017). Vietnam's economy remains fragile, as does its capacity for further sustained economic growth. For example, in 2016, Vietnam ranked 47th in the world in terms of the size of its economy, but it ranked poorly at 115th in the world on the UNDP's Human Development Indicator (HDI) index.

Vietnam identifies itself as a "socialist-oriented market economy", meaning that, although there is a flourishing private sector, many areas of national economic activity remain directly or indirectly under government control. Though private institutions accounted for approximately 14% of all higher education students, the higher education sector is one area of the economy that strongly remains under government control, making the role of policy makers significantly important.

Vietnam's higher education system has grown spectacularly since the early 1990s. This can be seen in the higher education gross enrolment rate, which in 1990 stood at only 2.8%, but nevertheless reached 28.26% in 2016 (Ministry of Education & Training [MOET], 2016). Most of this expansion is attributable to the government's willingness to invest heavily in the public sector of higher education, but the emergence of a private higher education sector has also been a contributor. The rapid expansion of the higher education system has given rise to recent concern about its overall quality (see, for example, Do & Do, 2014). It is certainly the case that some parts of the system have experienced reputational problems, most likely associated with poor quality.

The rising incidence of graduate unemployment is a relatively recent phenomenon in Vietnam. In March 2017, the national rate of graduate unemployment reached an exceptionally high level of 17.5%, compared to the national unemployment rate of only 2.09% and a national rate of youth unemployment of only 7.29%. The high graduate unemployment rate is extremely challenging for the majority of Vietnamese people because it completely overthrows the expectation that having a university qualification will improve one's opportunities of finding work and one's chances of earning a higher income. Not surprisingly, parents and recent graduates have expressed grave concern about the situation.

For policy researchers, a broad set of questions is raised: What are the characteristics of the recent trend? Does the incidence of graduate unemployment relate to the discipline studied or the type of university attended? Is there a correlation between academic grades achieved and the incidence of graduate unemployment? What policy initiatives can be used to reduce graduate unemployment, and what changes can be made to the higher education system to improve the employability of recent graduates? Some of these questions are addressed in this chapter, but it should be noted that it is not possible to address them all because of limitations in the available research.

The literature

The notion of employability is variously defined in international literature. At a general level, it is defined as "the capacity of getting and keeping satisfactory work". Or to be more simplistic, it refers to "the skills and abilities that allow you to be employed".[1] However, these definitions are criticised for being too narrow. Employability therefore has also been defined as "a set of achievements, understandings and personal attributes that help make individuals more employable and successful in their chosen occupations".[2] McQuaid and Lindsay (2005, p. 199) argued that employers have a tendency to view employability primarily as a characteristic of the individual. From the employer's perspective, employability is one's possession of such qualities and competencies required to meet the changing needs of employers and customers. But we should consider both demand and supply factors, as the structural shifts have created mismatches between labour, supply and demand towards various service industries. This has resulted in the increasing demand of interpersonal skills and communication skills, which are increasingly valued. Also, a shift towards part-time and more flexible work/employment practices may change our traditional perception of employability as the "capacity to get a job". Therefore, Cole and Tibby (2013) in Stage 1 of the HEA framework brought employees, students and other stakeholders together to identify key features of employability and then consider how these are being addressed both in the curriculum and beyond.

Employability is clearly not the same as employment, and this distinction can have implications on how successful educational training programs are viewed and measured (Coffield, 1997). The extent to which employability is meant to overlap with employment is also not understood universally in the same way. It should be noted that in recent years, the debates taking place in Vietnam mostly surround matters of employment rather than employability, which is a broader concept and has important implications for university performance.

Knight and Yorke (2003) have compiled a list of 39 attributes that are important for employability. They also identify four methods to enhance graduate employability, including promoting work experience; establishing entrepreneurship modules; providing careers consulting; and assisting students to develop portfolios, profiles and records of achievement. Other studies have pointed to the need for graduates to meet employer expectations in abilities including teamwork, communication, leadership, critical thinking, problem solving and general management (Lowden, Hall, Elliot & Lewin, 2011). A study supported by the Australian government found that international students were unaware of the importance of employability skills (soft or transferrable skills, understandings and personal attributes), and that there was a disparity between employer and graduate perceptions of key employability attributes (Jones, 2013). The Australian study, which drew upon data collected in 2013, also pointed to the fact that stakeholders, from across a range of industry groups, often perceive employability to be enhanced when graduates actively participate in learning, particularly by means of engagement with internship opportunities when available; being selective in choosing prospective employers; doing research to tailor job applications to employer needs; participating in industry initiatives specifically aimed at graduates; and practising the articulation of their personal employability strengths.

Vietnam's academic community has never had a scholarly discussion about the concept of employability and other related concepts such as underemployment, unemployment and so on, as well as the increasing need to redefine these concepts in the ever-changing economy. Another issue in Vietnam worth mentioning is the role that higher education institutions play in graduate employability. As Tran (2013) points out, universities in the West have traditionally sought to "provide an institutional basis for research into all forms of knowledge", whereas

Vietnamese universities have focused more on the need "to meet the needs of industry" (p. 633). Perhaps that is why graduates have a tendency to blame the universities for graduate unemployment.

A comprehensive and reliable investigation that generates primary data about the question of graduate employability is not yet available. Aspects of the topic have, however, been investigated by different scholars, as mentioned previously. It has been estimated, for example, that 83% of higher education graduates in Vietnam have deficits in terms of their soft skills (Tran, 2012). As a result, 50% of graduates are unable to find jobs immediately (Vallely & Wilkinson, 2008). Statistics show that 50% of employees need to undergo on-the-job training because of deficiencies in their technical skills. In recent media debates in Vietnam, it is widely recognised that many employees need to undergo on-the-job training because of deficiencies in their technical skills. Duoc and Metzger (2007) identified 19 variables which represent graduate quality held by those with a business master's degree in Vietnam. Critical analysis, problem-solving skills and overall quality of work were said to be the most important indicators. The findings indicated a significant difference in perceptions of graduate quality between the three groups surveyed: deans, graduates and employers. Most recently, in a similar study conducted by Ly, Vickers, and Fernandez (2015), it was found that the MBA graduates' needs and expectations about offshore MBA programmes in Vietnam included business improvement and promotion in their workplace. Respondents in the study also recognised that the MBA curriculum needed updating to ensure that adequate opportunities existed for students in order for them to learn skills that would prepare them to deal with an uncertain future. Tran (2010) pointed out in a broader sense that all participants in the focus group interviews shared in their disappointment with what was provided by their universities in terms of enhanced graduate employability. They agreed that the curriculum was both too heavy theoretically and largely irrelevant to the needs of the employment market. Graduates expressed their disappointment with the knowledge gained while attending university, perceiving that university knowledge was outdated, impractical and irrelevant.

Recent findings

Bodewig and Badiani-Magnusson's (2014) recent report, entitled *Skilling up Vietnam: Preparing the Workforce for a Modern Market Economy*, was orchestrated using in-depth and semi-structured interviews, together with case studies. This report identified the kinds of skills new graduates need to acquire if they wish to succeed in Vietnam's changing labour market. The findings pointed out employers' perspectives on skills sets that they want to see in their employees. However, it seems that skills related to the broader concept of employability were not addressed. In another World Bank report entitled "*Putting Higher Education Into Work: Skills and Research for Growth in East Asia*" Di Gropello (2011) addresses key job-specific skill gaps in Vietnam and recorded the perceptions of university administrators, employers and graduates in regards to how higher education institutions in Vietnam have or have not been successful in preparing graduates for entry to the labour market.

The previous report was emphatic that skills development in Vietnam suffered from a disconnection between the higher education curriculum and the needs of the labour market. It also identified that one of the core reasons for graduate unemployment was the lack of labour market information available for prospective graduates, as well as for higher education providers. A feature found in the report provides evidence as to the limited contact that exists between higher education institutions and employers. For example, as shown in an employers' survey, the main reason why employers and universities contacted one another was in regards to issues of recruitment (83% of firms), and only a small proportion of employers had any contact with higher education institutions with the view to contribute to curriculum development (9% of firms) (Bodewig & Badiani-Magnusson, 2014, p. 119). This finding has significant implications for policy development, though it is not yet evident that such findings are being enacted into new policies. More importantly, the report contributes enormously to the development of a conceptual understanding in Vietnam relating to issues of employment. Notions of employment, unemployment, skill shortages, underemployment and even self-employment have yet to be properly articulated in a Vietnamese context, and so, as does other internationally based literature, the above World Bank publications make important contributions to policy analysis and discourse concerning graduate employment and employability in Vietnam.

Another recent report, produced in 2013 by Vietnam's Institute of Labour Science and Social Affairs (ILSSA), is of significant importance. The Institute addressed directly the extent of unemployment among university graduates, reporting that 30% of graduates were unemployed. It blamed this high level of graduate unemployment on three principal factors: the lack of useful market information; the overly optimistic expectations of graduates; and the imbalances between labour demand and supply. The study also pointed out that unemployed graduates saw the reasons for their unemployment to be related to the lack of practical training at university in the skills and qualities required for industrial work. Further detailed investigations into the links between graduate employability and the quality of the training curriculum in universities and colleges in Vietnam are not, however, widely evident in existing literature.

Since 2014, the Ministry of Labour, Invalids and Social Affairs (MOLISA) has worked in collaboration with the General Statistics Office (GSO) to produce and publish a quarterly report on the labour market. These reports are widely accessed and have routinely generated a great deal of public commentary in the media. The prevailing view is one that is critical of the higher education sector. For example, concerns have been expressed about university graduates returning to vocational schools with the hope of qualifying and obtaining a job as a low-skilled worker.[3] These concerns have prompted intense discussions among policy makers[4] and are putting enormous pressure on MOET to do something about improving the capacity in the higher education sector in meeting the needs of graduates seeking to enter the skilled labour market.

The policy response

In light of the growing public concern about the increased incidence of graduate unemployment, the National Assembly produced document *1498/UBVHTTN13* dated 27 March 2015, which requested that all ministries responsible for higher education institutions report on graduate employment. MOET subsequently produced a report, dated 24 April 2015, in which it documented a decrease over the period from 2011 to 2013 of 2.5% per year in the quota for enrolments in regular programmes in public higher education institutions. Because of the increased quotas in previous years, the number of graduates in this three-year period continued to grow from 318,400 in 2011 to 425,200 in 2013, and while employed graduates in 2014 increased 38% in 2010, the number of unemployed graduates doubled over the same period. The MOET report (based on self-reports by 100 of the 432 higher education institutions in Vietnam) stated that, on average, 60% of graduates were employed within three months of graduation.

More recently, MOET has responded to public concern that too many higher education institutions in Vietnam are producing underqualified graduates by tightening up on the licensing process for the establishment of new universities. The fact is that some private universities in Vietnam now have very low enrolment levels. A recent example is the Asia University of Industrial Art (ĐH Mỹ thuật Công nghiệp Á Châu), which had a total enrolment of only 135 students.[5] The government therefore announced in document *4015/VPCP-KGVX* dated 5 June 2014 that it would not accept any more applications for licences to establish new higher education institutions.[6] Some programmes, including economics, finance and so on no longer have the permission to be newly established in Ho Chi Minh City and Ha Noi. More recently, in *Decree 46/2017/NĐ-CP* dated 21 April 2017, MOET set the minimum investment requirement to VND1,000 billion (approximately USD45.5 million), excluding land value, for the establishment of a new private university.

MOET, in *Circular 05/2017/TT-BGDĐT on Regulations for University Admission 2018* dated 25 May 2017, makes it a requirement that higher education institutions report publicly on the percentage of their graduates in employment within 12 months of completing their training programme. Institutions failing to comply with this requirement will not be permitted to enrol new students. A flaw in this legislation, however, is that no guidance has been provided about how the data on graduate employment is to be collected. Furthermore, there are no provisions in the legislation to ensure institutional compliance.

MOET is also paying more attention to quality assurance. Since 2004, *Resolution 37-2004, Direction 25/2004/CT-BGDĐT* of the National Congress requested that all higher education institutions prepare for quality accreditation. Since then, much progress has been made in establishing a quality assurance system that has become increasingly more consistent with international quality assurance practices. Most recently, *Circular 12/2017/TT-BGDĐT* dated 19 May 2017 on Regulations on University Accreditation has identified 25 criteria and implementation procedures for quality assurance in the higher education sector. This effort is to respond to public criticism about the quality of higher education in Vietnam, which is currently seen as a major cause of graduate unemployment.

More specifically, MOET has issued document *6604/BGDĐT-CTHSSV* dated 18 November 2014, which requests that higher education institutions strengthen job placement(s), consulting provision(s) and skills training for students prior to commencement date. According to a report to the National Congress dated 24 April 2015, MOET claimed that most higher education institutions have been engaged with industries and alumni for better arrangement of student internships. Some have already invited industries and/or businesses to participate in curriculum revisions, development and assessment along with faculty members. This would align with the principles outlined by Cole and Tibby (2013) in the HEA employability framework mentioned previously.

Nevertheless, public concern about the quality of higher education in Vietnam remains, and the percentage of unemployed graduates continues to increase from one year to the next.[7] Commenting on the role by quality assurance in seeking to address this concern, one expert has claimed,

> To complete a self-assessment report, and have it screening in the accreditation process, it takes several months and is an enormous workload for both sides (the institution and the accreditation agency). If they see it as merely coping with criticism, rather than for the improvement of such institutions then the positive impacts could be limited.[8]

Discussions and implications

As set out in the first section of this chapter, government policies play a significantly important role in higher education in Vietnam, and graduate employability is an issue for all stakeholders in the higher education sector. Yet the role of the government and its policies have not to date been addressed in any relevant academic literature. Although some policy recommendations have recently been proposed, their influence(s) to curriculum development, teaching methodologies and learning outcome assessment remains unknown. More time is needed to assess their impact. Some of these initiatives could potentially have adverse unintended consequences; for example, a policy directed at limiting new entrants to higher education programs could discourage the competition between providers within the sector and the urgency for change.

Most importantly, all stakeholders in the higher education sector need to come together and focus on the problem of graduate employability as higher education institutions are unable to address the problems on their own. In Vietnam, the government has the authority required to stimulate the development of these networks. The government also has the authority to adopt such necessary policy frameworks, which provide incentives for industry participation, and to provide universities with more freedom to be proactive.

The need to build partnerships between university and industry has now been realised. However, most of institutions still struggle to seek win-win solutions in specific contexts of each school. At the institutional level, changes have been made in terms of curriculum thanks to greater autonomy granted in recent years.

The policy research community also has an important role to play. The research conducted by the International Labor Organization (ILO) and the General Statistics Office (GSO) in Vietnam over the period 2012 to 2015, as reported in the *School to Work Transition Survey* (2015), has demonstrated a strong correlation between the levels of educational attainment and a young person's labour market transition. Youths educated at university level needed an average of 7.3 months to complete the transition from school to a first stable or satisfactory job, while the equivalent figure for general secondary education was 17.8 months.[9] This finding supports claims about the effectiveness of higher education, including the claim that such education helps individuals transition better to the world of work, a point that is almost totally missed in the public criticisms of universities by the general public. More research-based evidence of this kind is needed to better inform policy makers. There is also a need for research-based evidence to be reported better to the public through the media.

Conclusion

This chapter has introduced various reports and policies that together form part of the response of the government of Vietnam in seeking to strengthen graduate employability. Many questions remain: Which research-based data provides a basis for the policies? What kinds of policies are required? How effective are the policies being implemented? What would be the impact of the policies on the training curriculum and the learning experiences of students? To what extent would new policies help to solve the problem? There are also further questions which need to be resolved concerning the gaps in the policies, especially concerning the link between universities and industry, the strength of motivation for quality improvements in these links and the quality of the infrastructure supporting links between such universities and the labour market. Institution-based case study reports regarding these matters would be especially helpful.

Several research reports have pointed to skills mismatch and the problems of graduate employability in Vietnam. The extent to which those sources have influenced policy making in Vietnam, and the effectiveness of the policies that have ensued, all remain as matters for conjecture. This review has drawn attention to relevant research-based reports on this matter. It has also pointed to some important evidence such as the better transition rate of higher education graduates from school to work. At the institutional level, the question presented asks where employability sits within individual schools? What infrastructure is already in place? And in taking into account the above findings, career services should also be considered as a part of a university program.

The response of the MOET to public concerns about graduate employability has included measures intended to restrict the establishment of new universities and to strengthen quality assurance and institutional accountability concerning graduate employability. These policies are a response to the public's criticism rather than to evidence-based research. Therefore, our findings suggest that theoretically, we need to create better links between the academics and the policy makers. Practically, the scholars also need to communicate better with the general public, especially in highly important matters and matters related to various stakeholders such as graduate employability. Without such links and communications, innovation in this matter would be restricted in the Vietnamese context.

Notes

1 Oxford Dictionary.
2 www.kent.ac.uk/careers/sk/skillsintro.htm
3 http://baovinhphuc.com.vn/giao-duc/17099/nghich-ly-chuyen-cu-nhan-%E2%80%9Choc-nguoc%E2%80%9D.html
4 http://vietnamnet.vn/vn/giao-duc/sau-4-nam-cu-nhan-that-nghiep-tang-gap-doi-234129.html
5 Pham Thi Huyen et al., Report on Non-Public Universities, MOET, 2017.
6 http://tuoitre.vn/tin/giao-duc/20150925/han-che-toi-da-thanh-lap-moi-truong-dh-cd/974695.html
7 www.molisa.gov.vn/vi/Pages/ThiTruongLaoDong.aspx
8 www.thesaigontimes.vn/157740/Ban-khoan-kie%CC%89m-di%CC%A3nh-cha%CC%81t-luo%CC%A3ng-gia%CC%81o-du%CC%A3c.html
9 www.ilo.org/wcmsp5/groups/public/---asia/---ro-bangkok/---ilo-hanoi/documents/publication/wcms_541516.pdf

References

Bodewig, C., & Badiani-Magnusson, R. (2014). *Skilling up Vietnam: Preparing the workforce for a modern market economy*. World Bank Publications.

Coffield, F. (Ed.). (1997). *A national strategy For LLL*. University of Newcastle: Department of Education.

Cole, D., & Tibby, M. (2013). *Defining and developing your approach to employability: A framework for higher education institutions*. Heslington: The Higher Education Academy.

Di Gropello, E. (2011). *Putting higher education to work: Skills and research for growth in East Asia*. World Bank Publications.

Do, H. M., & Do, Q. T. N. (2014). Higher and tertiary education in Vietnam. In *Higher education in Vietnam* (pp. 29–53). UK: Palgrave Macmillan.

Duoc, T. Q., & Metzger, C. (2007). Quality of business graduates in Vietnamese institutions: Multiple perspectives. *Journal of Management Development, 26*(7), 629–643.

Jones, E. (2013). Internationalization and employability: The role of intercultural experiences in the development of transferable skills. *Public Money & Management, 33*(2), 95–104.

Knight, P. T., & Yorke, M. (2003). Employability and good learning in higher education. *Teaching in Higher education, 8*(1), 3–16.

Lowden, K., Hall, S., Elliot, D., & Lewin, J. (2011). *Employers' perceptions of the employability skills of new graduates*. London: Edge Foundation.

Ly, C. T. M., Vickers, M. H., & Fernandez, S. (2015). Master of business administration (MBA) student outcomes in Vietnam: Graduate student insights from a qualitative study. *Education + Training, 57*(1), 88–107.

McQuaid, R. W., & Lindsay, C. (2005). The concept of employability. *Urban Studies, 42*(2), 197–219.

Nguyen, N. A., Nguyen, T. T., Nguyen, T. H., Trinh, T. T. N., & Nguyen, V. T. (2015). *Labour market transitions of young women and men in Viet Nam*, Work4Youth Publication Series No. 27. Geneva: ILO.

Tran, T. T. (2010, November). *Enhancing graduate employability: Challenges facing higher education*. In Australian Association for Research in Education (AARE) Conference, Melbourne.

Tran, T. T. (2012). Vietnamese higher education and the issue of enhancing graduate employability. *Journal of Teaching and Learning for Graduate Employability, 3*(1), 2–16.

Tran, T. T. (2013). Limitation on the development of skills in higher education in Vietnam. *Higher Education, 65*(5), 631–644.

Vallely, T. J., & Wilkinson, B. (2008). *Vietnamese higher education: Crisis and response.* Memorandum: Higher Education Task Force, Harvard Kennedy School.

World Bank (2013). *Vietnam: Achieving success as a middle-income country.* Retrieved from www.worldbank.org/en/results/2013/04/12/vietnam-achieving-success-as-a-middle-income-country

14

GRADUATE EMPLOYABILITY

Beyond the skills agenda

Thi Tuyet Tran

Introduction

Globalisation, knowledge economy, the changing needs of the post-industrial economy and the expansion of higher education (HE) have created considerable changes in the relationship between HE and society. On the one hand, mass HE reduces the rates of return to HE (i.e. students have to pay higher tuition fees and compete in a much more crowded and competitive skilled labour market after graduation). On the other hand, the rapid changes in the globalised labour market create uncertainties about the kinds of jobs awaiting graduates at the end of their studies; there are no more clear employment prospects for graduates in most disciplines (Clarke, 2008; Clarke & Patrickson, 2008; Tomlinson, 2012). The job security phenomenon is gradually fading out (Barnett, 2006; The Association of Graduate Recruiters, 2009). Graduate employability (GE) has now become one of the key drivers for higher education institutions (HEIs) regardless of their institutional bases.

Although employability is high on the university agenda worldwide, there is no common definition and no 'ingredients' for it. What employability is and what HEIs should do about it are still lively topics of debate in the literature. Nonetheless, the dominant discourse of enhancing GE in HEIs still focuses on the skills agenda. Researchers and universities have spent time investigating employers' needs and developing lists of attributes and skills desirable by employers. University curricula are adjusted to best address the development of these skills.

Although the skill-led agenda does have its own merit, it also reveals problems. This chapter aims to highlight the limitations of the skills agenda and argue that employability is a complex trajectory, where skills development for students is essential but not sufficient to ensure positive outcomes or positive career prospects. It will first discuss the notion of employability and the emerging of the skills agenda. Then the problems associated with the way employability is often measured will be reviewed before approaching some alternative frameworks to address the situated nature of learning and employability. The roles of HEIs and of students themselves in the process of enhancing GE will also be identified accordingly.

Employability and the emerging of the skills agenda

Although employability has become a familiar term in the HE context, the dominant approach to enhance GE in universities is mostly based on the assumption that employability is defined as having the skills and abilities to find and retain employment and to obtain new employment if required (Cox & King, 2006; Hillage & Pollard, 1998; Moreland, 2006; Tran, 2016; UK Commission for Employment and Skills, 2009; Yorke, 2006, 2010). For example, Yorke (2006, p. 8) suggests, "Employability is a set of achievements – skills, understandings and personal attributes – that makes graduates more likely to gain employment and be successful in their chosen occupations".

Employability is understood as fitness or suitability for graduate employment. It cannot assure employment outcome. Since gaining an appropriate employment highly depends on the context of the labour market (Clarke, 2007) and personal circumstances and attributes (McQuaid, 2006), employability may increase graduates' chances of obtaining graduate-level jobs but does not assure them (Cabellero & Walker, 2010; Clarke, 2007; Helyer, Lee, & Evans, 2011; Knight & Yorke, 2004; Leong & Kavanagh, 2013; Yorke, 2006).

Since employability is regarded as fitness or suitability for graduate employment, it is rather subjective, and thus, the primary responsibility for employability rests with individual students and graduates (Leong & Kavanagh, 2013; McQuaid & Lindsay, 2005; Tan & French-Arnold, 2012; Tomlinson, 2007, 2010). University students are expected to be proactive and to actively improve their knowledge and skills to meet the demand of the workplace in the changing context (Bridgstock, 2009). Then, when they finish university and start searching for jobs in the labour market, the responsibility is also on them as potential employees to "acquire knowledge, skills and abilities, and other characteristics valued by current and prospective employers" (Fugate, Kinicki, & Ashforth, 2004, p. 15).

Nonetheless, still dominant in the GE literature is the research with suggestions about what universities should do to enhance work-readiness for their students. Although it is claimed widely both in government policy papers and the general literature that, in changing labour markets with such characteristics as economic crisis and employment uncertainty, employability is individuals' responsibility, HEIs are now "cast in an utilitarian role: to equip students with the necessary skills" (Sin & Neave, 2016, pp. 1453–1454). This process is called "instrumentalising HE" (Sin & Neave, 2016, p. 1454) or the magic bullet model of employability (Harvey, 2001).

Despite suspicions and criticism, the skills agenda has emerged in the HE context worldwide over the last two decades. It has largely developed based on the assumption that there is a 'skills gap' between what students could acquire in universities and what is needed in the labour market, and thus, university curriculum and practices need to be adjusted in order to bridge "the disparity between industry needs and HE provision" (Jackson, 2013, p. 778). Accordingly, different projects have been designed to explore employers' needs, different lists of skills have been developed and university curriculum and practices have been adjusted to accommodate the needs of the industry. There seems to be a popular belief that the tasks in universities (the learning setting) should be created as similarly as possible to the tasks in the real workplace (the application setting), and that the closer the learning setting and the application setting are aligned, the better the development and transfer of such skills will be (Analoui, 1993).

The skills agenda or the shifting focus in HE on providing students with the knowledge, skills and competencies they need for their future career prospects has its own merits. First, it creates the basis for a highly trained labour force (Kalfa & Taksa, 2015), thus may help reduce the 'learning curve' for students in the transition from university to employment (Mason, William, & Cranmer, 2009). In other words, when the new employees are work-ready and highly adaptable, it not only saves employers' time and money for in-house training for these new staff members, but also promises higher productivity levels, contributing to the national economic growth and competitiveness in the global market (Harvey, 2000; Watson, 2003). Second, it provides rich information about the requirements of the knowledge economy and helps individuals to come up with informed decisions to enhance their knowledge and skills to not be excluded from the labour market or to re-enter employment (Pont & Werquin, 2001). Thus, it is unsurprising when the skills agenda informed by human capital theory, with a heavy emphasis on the acquisition of generic/core/transferable skills desired by employers (such as communication skills, problem solving, teamwork or interpersonal skills), has become one of the most significant developments in HE over the last few decades (Clarke, 2017; Kalfa & Taksa, 2015; Moore & Morton, 2017).

Nonetheless, the skills-led approach of employability does reveal problems. Indeed, many educational researchers have criticised the instrumental approach of this agenda, where skills are either embedded into degree programs or expected to be developed through internships, work placements and international mobility in different programs. This approach fails to take into account other critical factors. First, Gallagher (2001) questions the underlying assumption of this approach whether what to be taught is also open to negotiation with employers. Tight (1998) and Jarvis (2000) complain that the skills-led approach is informed by a naïve interpretation of employability when it is based on the assumption that all related stakeholders, employers and employees included share a common point of view about the necessary skills and skills performance. Many academics and researchers also express their worry over the vocational focus of the skills agenda which may lead to the devaluing of teaching and learning. They also criticise the simplistic view of employability popular in many universities which sees the skills agenda as "narrowly conceived, relatively mechanical, and inimical to the purposes of HE" (Yorke & Knight, 2006, p. 567), and support Hyslop-Margison and Sears's (2007, p. 14) claim that skills-led approaches aim to equip students with transferable employability skills, narrowing down teaching practices, and that this education policy "reduces learning to discursive ideological apparatus that encourages student conformity to the market economy".

Measuring of employability

Universities are now under pressure from governments and other external stakeholders to provide measurable outcomes of employability, and most often to meet the learning outcome standards required by different accrediting bodies (Jackson, 2012). In many countries, surveys collecting information on employment of recent graduates are conducted at four/six months or one year after graduation. Efforts have been made to increase the graduate employment indicators. Nonetheless, after decades of effort, these indicators do not show any significantly positive signals when both the number and the proportion of graduates unemployed or underemployed after four months, six months or a year after graduation are still on upward trend. This is also one of the findings in Mason et al.'s (2009) study of the effects of employability skills initiatives on graduate labour market outcomes at an institutional level. They could not see any evidence of the correspondent relationship between the focus on teaching, learning and assessment of employability skills and the labour market outcomes; that is, whether graduates had found jobs within six months of graduation or whether they had secured graduate-level jobs. Mason et al.'s research findings are supported by other studies in the area, which all point to a common conclusion that employment outcomes show that possessing employability skills does not guarantee employment, not to say graduate-level employment (Clarke, 2017; Piróg, 2016; Scurry & Blenkinsopp, 2011). Many employers keep the perception that academic achievement is an insufficient indicator of a graduate's employability as they often do not see "a tight fit between HE studies and specific employment niches" (Sin & Neave, 2016, p. 1457). It seems naïve to think that the skills developed in the learning setting will be directly transferred to the application setting.

Nonetheless, using labour market outcomes as a popular way to measure GE also seems to be problematic. First, these measurable outcomes, as Clarke (2017) pointed out, largely refer to institutional outcomes rather than graduate outcomes. Harvey (2001, p. 97) also criticised the tendency to see employability as an institutional achievement rather than "the propensity of the individual student to get employment". Since graduates are now required to be in charge of their own employability, these general labour market indicators do not seem to make much sense for them, and many still cannot see their responsibility in the process of enhancing and managing their own career prospects.

Second, and more profoundly, most graduate surveys measure current employment status, not employability – compared to the way employability is generally defined (Clarke, 2017; Harvey, 2001). Employability, as discussed earlier, refers to the graduates' potential to obtain a job, while employment is actual job acquisition; or in other words, employability does not assure employment (Yorke, 2006). Gaining employment does not only depend on graduate knowledge, skills or the level of suitability for employment; it also depends on many other personal attributes and external factors. The popular way of using graduate employment outcomes as an employability indicator challenges the normal way of defining employability. Should employability also include other factors apart from the knowledge and skills desired by employers? And if that is the case, how far can universities go to enhance their student employability, and how much can they claim the success of their graduates in the university-to-work transition is also their achievement? Further, the validity of the assumptions underpinning employability as individual responsibility is also questionable, as students may not possess the will and/or the capacity to manage their own careers in a labour market full of uncertainties (Sin & Neave, 2016).

The general outcomes of graduate surveys (which often indicate the proportion of graduates finding full-time jobs in a given time period) also negate the differences in employment opportunities and outcomes for different demographic groups. There is an established body of literature suggesting poorer employment opportunities and outcomes among low socio-economic status groups such as immigrants, minority ethnic groups, regional, indigenous people or children from working class families (Andrewartha & Harvey, 2017; Brooks, 2017; Pitman, Roberts, Bennett, & Richardson, 2017). There is no clear and reasonable explanation linking these demographic characteristics with the knowledge and skills graduates could develop during their university time, or in other words, "there are no reasonable grounds for assuming that such graduates systematically differ from others in their 'possession' of such purported skills" (Leonard Holmes, 2013, p. 546). Obviously, socio-economic and cultural status does have a certain impact on the employment outcome of graduates, and this seems to be out of the control of both individual students and their universities.

The indicator of the proportion of graduates finding full-time jobs in a given time period is also being criticised as it does not look at the quality aspect of the jobs graduates gain access to after graduation. Underemployment has become a popular situation among graduates in graduate-oversupply of labour markets. Being employed is not necessarily a true indicator of a successful university-to-work transition. Thus, being employed at an individual level and the number of graduates who are in employment at an institutional level should not be enough to be counted as a clear measure of graduate success (Blenkinsopp & Scurry, 2007; Scurry & Blenkinsopp, 2011).

Obviously, external labour market factors have impacted graduate employment outcomes. Thus, the employability approach, with a general focus on skills and the perception that graduates being employed is the outcome of the match between graduate possessed skills and employers' needs, downplays the important demand-side factors, such as the scarcity of jobs in the market, economic crisis, labour shortage or the distance from economically dynamic areas

(Lindsay & Pascual, 2009; McQuaid & Lindsay, 2005; Sin & Neave, 2016; Tomlinson, 2012). Unemployment is often explained as personal and institutional failure rather than the outcome of the lack of market opportunities (Lindsay & Pascual, 2009). This explanation fails to address the labour market problems or unfavourable economic conditions, which both individual students and their universities have no means to control or interfere with.

Rethinking GE and the subsequence role of HEIs

Many educational researchers have recognised the limitations of the skills-led agenda in HE and have proposed alternative frameworks to overcome such limitations. Kalfa and Taksa (2015) and Clarke (2013), for example, criticise the underlying assumption of the skills-led approach that skills can be transferred across contexts, which ignores the situated nature of learning; it decontextualises, generalises and isolates skills from the learner's world. Kalfa and Taksa (2015), then, based on Bourdieu's cultural theory, developed an alternative conceptual framework which consists of three main components: field and doxa, habitus and cultural capital. With this framework, employability is placed within each specific field of study (field) where not only skills or knowledge are important, but also the network or the way agents see themselves with others in the field also matters. Fields are differentiated from one another by the fundamental principles, beliefs and rules of behaviour (doxa). Doxa is not always explicit and is often taken for granted and viewed as inherently true by agents in the same field. Thus, challenges will arise when "one field is increasingly influenced by the doxa of other fields" (Kalfa & Taksa, 2015, p. 586). Employability also depends on the way people think, feel and act subconsciously rather than consciously and in an instrumental manner (habitus).

Cultural capital, the last component of the Kalfa and Taksa's (2015) framework, refers to widely shared, high status cultural signals (attitudes, preferences, formal knowledge, behaviours, goods and credentials). Thus, cultural capital is used for "social and cultural exclusion, the former referring to exclusion from jobs and the latter to exclusion from high status groups" (Lamont & Lareau, 1988, p. 156). Exclusion is a critical issue that is often overlooked when assessing employability. Nonetheless, investment in HE study is also considered a process of cultural accumulation, and it offers a route for students from disadvantaged backgrounds to develop cosmopolitan identities for social inclusion (Beck, 2004).

Clarke (2017) developed another employability framework where skills, competencies and work experience together are only one component of GE, called human capital. Human capital, social capital (network, social class and university ranking), individual behaviours and attributes are four main components forming perceived employability. The perceived employability is the employee's own perception of their chance of success in the labour market and how they approach a job search. Nonetheless, perceived employability is also affected by labour market factors, especially in mass HE when graduates are often over-supplied.

Hinchliffe and Jolly (2011), on the other hand, accept the neoliberal pressure for HE to provide work-ready graduates and the need to understand and to 'take in' employers' requirements. Nonetheless, they criticise the skills approach since it is based on the assumption that skills performance must be measurable and observable, thus ignoring the complexity of graduateness and the fact that even employers also "think beyond conventional skill discourse and attempt to probe a broader range of graduate experience in order to assess their potential" (Hinchliffe & Jolly, 2011, p. 575). They, then, based on Holmes's (2001) argument emphasising the need to examine the condition of performance and the employer perceptions of graduates in respect of their employability, developed the concept of graduate identity, and claim that it is a way to deepen the understanding of GE. Their four-stranded concept of identity includes values (personal ethics, social values and contextual, organisational values, including the value of entrepreneurship), intellect (graduate's ability to think critically, analyse and communicate information, reflect on all aspects of their work and bring challenge and ideas to an organisation), performance (the ability to learn quickly and effectively and to develop skills appropriate to the role) and engagement (a willingness to meet personal, employment and social challenges and to be 'outward looking'). They claim that performance – one of the four elements in their concept – is most closely aligned to the employability skills matrix popular in current employability literature. When assessing the potential of graduates, performance is only part of the criteria that employers take into account; instead, the four elements of identity interpenetrate, and different employers often emphasise different facets of this identity.

Although supporting the 'graduate identity' perspective on GE, Holmes's (2013) argument does not share common ground with Hinchliffe and Jolly's (2011) argument. Holmes (2013) argues that graduate identity is socially negotiated and constructed and names it as "processual perspective on graduate employability"; he compares this perspective with the other two perspectives, namely, possessive (the skills agenda) and positioning perspectives (considering cultural capitals, personal capitals and habitus are those decide societal positioning of graduates) on GE, and points out the limitations of the two latter perspectives. Similar to other researchers, he criticises the possessive approach and names numerous limitations associated with the names of different skills, how to measure and assess such skills, how different parties make sense of the lists of skills and, most importantly, he claims, the focus on skills and attributes as requirements for employability fails to explain employment outcomes which are generally different among different demographic groups.

The above-discussed employability frameworks vary; however, they were all developed with the aim to overcome the limitations of the instrumental, simplistic skills-led employability approach popularly deployed in the contemporary HE context. Their conceptualising frameworks also point out clearly that HE is only one factor alongside many others that make for employability, and thus, at best, HE can play only an enabling role (Yorke, 2006). Universities need to develop a better understanding of the broad contexts in which their graduates are likely to be engaged in the future, then develop plans to assist their students in building not only human capital (relevant knowledge, skills and attributes), but also social and cultural capital.

Universities should also help students understand the importance of career self-management and personal responsibility in managing, maintaining and enhancing GE. This is especially important in a market with over-supply of graduates. Students need to be clear that their future prospects depend much on their individual attributes (flexibility, adaptability, openness to challenges and new experience), and that the university-to-work transition is most often not straightforward and often depends on students' decisions and acts or the extent to which they enhance their perceived employability and persuade employers that they are graduates worthy of being employed.

Conclusion

This chapter has highlighted the limitations of the skills agenda currently dominating the HE context worldwide. By problematising the concept of employability, the instrumental approach of developing skills for students and the convenient but simplistic way of using labour market outcomes to measure employability, this chapter has pointed to the importance of contextual, social, institutional and individual factors that all have great impacts on GE and the labour market outcomes of graduates. Several alternative conceptual frameworks have also been introduced to pull up the complexity of the factors involved, where the input from HE matters are important but not sufficient. In other words, employability depends only in part on what universities provide.

Since GE is multi-faceted and involves different stakeholders, in order to ease the transition to employment for recent university graduates and increase the productivity of these young people – not only universities, but other stakeholders, that is, government – employers and students themselves need to rethink their roles in the process of developing GE. There is always room for different stakeholders to negotiate their roles and responsibilities in this process. It is time for a more meaningful dialogue between universities and employers on what is work-readiness and what each party can do for the employability trajectories of the future skilled labour force. Governments should, based on the current labour market contexts, adjust the way employability is measured. They should also engage in a dialogue with universities and employers to discuss issues, such as the demand versus supply in certain disciplines and working areas, and the characteristics and quality of jobs recent graduates often enter, and develop a feasible plan to regulate and direct the market (e.g. to manage the number of students enrolling in the disciplines already reaching market saturation, or to create the means to help underemployed graduates to map their way to better employment).

Employability is a journey, and universities or the first employment after graduation are just the beginning of that journey. It is up to graduates to enhance their knowledge and skills, expand their networks, understand challenges and opportunities in the market and come up with their own decisions and actions to lead their journey. More than anybody else, they should understand that in the mass HE era, the over-supply of graduates is unavoidable, and if they do not want to be unemployed or underemployed, they need to stand out in the crowd and develop their identity in a way to persuade employers that they are worth being selected.

References

Analoui, F. (1993). *Training and transfer of learning*. Aldershot: Avebury.

Andrewartha, L., & Harvey, A. (2017). Employability and student equity in higher education: The role of university careers services. *Australian Journal of Career Development, 26*(2), 71–80.

The Association of Graduate Recruiters (2009). *Skills for graduates in the 21st century*. Retrieved from www.funkygrad.com/ratedserious/displayarticle.php?artID=202&subcat=career

Barnett, R. (2006). Graduate attributes in an age of uncertainty. In P. Hager & S. Holland (Eds.), *Graduate attributes, learning and employability*. Dordrecht, The Netherlands: Springer.

Beck, U. (2004). Cosmopolitical realism: On the distinction between cosmopolitanism in philosophy and the social sciences. *Global Networks, 4*(2), 131–156.

Blenkinsopp, J., & Scurry, T. (2007). "Hey GRINGO!": The HR challenge of graduates in non-graduate occupations. *Personnel Review, 36*(4), 623–637.

Bridgstock, R. (2009). The graduate attributes we've overlooked: Enhancing graduate employability through career management skills. *Higher Education Research & Development, 28*(1), 31–44.

Brooks, R. (2017). *"Who wants a job anyway?": Student approaches to graduate employability*. The benefits of modifying social enterprise with higher education's social sciences curriculum. West Yorkshire, England: University of Huddersfield.

Cabellero, C. L., & Walker, A. (2010). Work readiness in graduate recruitment and selection: A review of current assessment methods. *Journal of Teaching and Learning for Graduate Employability, 1*(1), 13–25.

Clarke, M. (2007). Understanding and managing employability in changing career contexts. *Journal of European Industrial, 32*(4), 258–284.

Clarke, M. (2008). Plodders, pragmatists, visionaries and opportunists: Career patterns and employability. *Career Development International, 14*(1), 8–28.

Clarke, M. (2017). Rethinking graduate employability: The role of capital, individual attributes and context. *Studies in Higher Education*, 1–15.

Clarke, M., & Patrickson, M. (2008). The new covenant of employability. *Employee Relations, 30*(2), 121–141.

Cox, S., & King, D. (2006). Skill sets: An approach to embed employability in course design. *Education and Training, 48*(4), 262–274.

Fugate, M., Kinicki, A. J., & Ashforth, B. E. (2004). Employability: A psycho-social construct, its dimensions, and applications. *Journal of Vocational Behaviour, 65*, 14–38.

Gallagher, M. (2001). A review of government support for new forms of working. *AI & Society, 15*(1–2), 149–159.

Harvey, L. (2000). New realities: The relationship between higher education and employment. *Tertiary Education and Management, 6*(1), 3–17.

Harvey, L. (2001). Defining and measuring employability. *Quality in Higher Education, 7*(2), 97–109.

Helyer, R., Lee, D., & Evans, A. (2011). Hybrid HE: Knowledge, skills and innovation. *Work Based Learning e-Journal, 1*(2), 18–34.

Hillage, J., & Pollard, E. (1998). *Employability: Developing a framework for policy analysis.* London: Department for Education and Employment.

Hinchliffe, G. W., & Jolly, A. (2011). Graduate identity and employability. *British Educational Research Journal, 37*(4), 563–584.

Holmes, L. (2001). Reconsidering Graduate Employability: the 'graduate identity' approach. *Quality in Higher Education, 7*(2), 111–119.

Holmes, L. (2013). Competing perspectives on graduate employability: Possession, position or process? *Studies in Higher Education, 38*(4), 538–554.

Hyslop-Margison, E. J., & Sears, A. M. (2007). *Neo-liberalism, globalization and human capital learning: Reclaiming education for democratic citizenship.* Dordrecht: Springer.

Jackson, D. (2012). Business undergraduates' perceptions of their capabilities in employability skills: Implications for industry and higher education. *Industry and Higher Education, 26*(5), 345–356.

Jackson, D. (2013). Business graduate employability: Where are we going wrong? *Higher Education Research & Development, 32*(5), 776–790.

Jarvis, P. (2000). The changing university: Meeting a need and needing to change. *Higher Education Quarterly, 54*(1), 43–67.

Kalfa, S., & Taksa, L. (2015). Cultural capital in business higher education: Reconsidering the graduate attributes movement and the focus on employability. *Studies in Higher Education, 40*(4), 580–595.

Knight, P., & Yorke, M. (2004). *Learning, curriculum and employability in higher education.* London: Routledge Falmer.

Lamont, M., & Lareau, A. (1988). Cultural capital: Allusions, gaps and glissandos in recent theoretical developments. *Sociological Theory, 6*, 153–168.

Leong, R., & Kavanagh, M. (2013). A work-integrated learning (WIL) framework to develop graduate skills and attributes in an Australian university's accounting program. *Asia-Pacific Journal of Cooperative Education, 14*(1), 1–14.

Lindsay, C., & Pascual, A. S. (2009). New perspectives on employability and labour market policy: Reflecting on key issues. *Environmental and Planning C: Government and Policy, 27*(6), 951–957.

Mason, G., William, G., & Cranmer, S. (2009). Employability skills initiatives in higher education: What effects do they have on graduate labour market outcomes? *Education Economics, 17*(1), 1–30.

McQuaid, R. W. (2006). Job search success and employability in local labor markets. *The Annals of Regional Science, 40*, 407–421.

McQuaid, R. W., & Lindsay, C. (2005). The concept of employability. *Urban Studies, 42*(2), 197–219.

Moore, T., & Morton, J. (2017). The myth of job readiness? Written communication, employability, and the 'skills gap' in higher education. *Studies in Higher Education, 42*(3), 591–609.

Moreland, N. (2006). *Entrepreneurship and higher education: An employability perspective.* Heslington, York: Enhancing Student Employability Co-ordination Team, ESECT.

Piróg, D. (2016). The impact of degree programme educational capital on the transition of graduates to the labour market. *Studies in Higher Education, 41*(1), 95–109.

Pitman, T., Roberts, L., Bennett, D., & Richardson, S. (2017). An Australian study of graduate outcomes for disadvantaged students. *Journal of Further and Higher Education, 1*–13. doi:10.1080/0309877X.2017.1349895

Pont, B., & Werquin, P. (2001). Competencies for the knowledge economy. In OECD (Ed.), *Education Policy Analysis* (pp. 99–118). Paris: OECD.

Scurry, T., & Blenkinsopp, J. (2011). Under-employment among recent graduates: A review of the literature. *Personnel Review, 40*(5), 643–659.

Sin, C., & Neave, G. (2016). Employability deconstructed: Perceptions of Bologna stakeholders. *Studies in Higher Education, 41*(8), 1447–1462.

Tan, L. C., & French-Arnold, E. (2012). Employability of graduates in Asia: An overview of case studies. In UNESCO (Ed.), *Graduate employability in Asia* (pp. 1–4). Bangkok: UNESCO Bangkok, Asia and Pacific Regional Bureau for Education.

Tight, M. (1998). Lifelong learning: Opportunity or compulsion? *British Journal of Educational Studies, 46*, 251–263

Tomlinson, M. (2007). Graduate employability and student attitudes and orientations to the labour market. *Journal of Education and Work, 20*(4), 285–304.

Tomlinson, M. (2010). Investing in the self: Structure, agency and identity in graduates' employability. *Education, Knowledge & Economy, 4*(2), 73–88.

Tomlinson, M. (2012). Graduate employability: A review of conceptual and empirical themes. *Higher Education Policy, 25*(4), 407–431.

Tran, T. T. (2016). Enhancing graduate employability and the need for university-enterprise collaboration. *Journal of Teaching and Learning for Graduate Employability, 7*(1), 58–71.

UK Commission for Employment and Skills. (2009). *Employee demand for skills: A review of evidence & policy – Executive summary*. London: WM Enterprise and Employment Research Institute, Edinburgh Napier University.

Watson, L. (2003). *Lifelong learning in Australia*. Canberra: Department of Education, Science & Training.

Yorke, M. (2006). *Employability in higher education: What it is – What it is not* (Vol. 1). York: The Higher Education Academy.

Yorke, M. (2010). Employability: Aligning the message, the medium and academic values. *Journal of Teaching and Learning for Graduate Employability, 1*(1), 2–12.

INDEX